DOMINIC MATTEO

IN MY DEFENCE

THE AUTOBIOGRAPHY

WRITTEN WITH

RICHARD SUTCLIFFE

GREAT NORTHERN

For Luisa

For Luisa and Elin

Great Northern Books
PO Box 213, Ilkley, LS29 9WS
www.greatnorthernbooks.co.uk

ISBN: 978-1905080-90-8

Design and layout: David Burrill

Printed in Great Britain

CIP Data
A catalogue for this book is available from the British Library

CONTENTS

…

Foreword by

Lucas Radebe

I knew from the first time I met Dominic Matteo that he was going to be the sort of lad who would fit in well at Leeds United. When Dom signed for the club ahead of the 2000-01 season, I already knew all about his playing ability from the times he had played against us for Liverpool in the Premier League. But it was only after David O'Leary paid £4.25m to sign Dom that I first got the chance to chat to him and that was when I knew we'd got ourselves a decent man as well as a very good footballer. My first impressions were correct, too, with Dom going on to be one of the most important characters at Elland Road for the next four years.

We quickly discovered that Dom was a typical Scouser, in that he was always up for fun. I lost count of the number of times he pulled a prank on one of the lads or a member of staff at Thorp Arch. On one occasion he was responsible for strapping one of the physios to the treatment table and then carrying him outside. The lads laughed about it for days.

In my opinion, Dom was under-rated as a player. I know the Leeds fans sing his name today but I still don't believe his contribution to the team that reached the Champions League semi-finals under David O'Leary is truly appreciated. for me, he was one of the very best buys that Leeds United made during a period when we signed a lot of players. Not only could Dom play in the centre of defence, but he was also very effective in midfield – either in the centre or when filling in on the left side as he did in the first few months after joining Leeds from Liverpool. It was when playing on the wing, in fact, that Dom scored 'that' goal against AC Milan – the one that is the subject of the song that the Leeds fans still belt out at games. As someone who was hardly renowned for scoring during my time at Leeds, I know exactly how special finding the net can be. I was fortunate to get a couple of important goals in Europe, including a late winner against Spartak Moscow in the UEFA Cup the season before Dom joined us. So, when I look at footage of

Dom's face as he celebrates scoring in the San Siro, I know exactly how he feels. It is a moment he is unlikely to ever forget – as he proves by bringing the subject up every time all the Leeds lads get together! Only joking, Dom....

One of the great things about Leeds United fans is that you don't have to be goalscorer or striker to win their adulation. Leeds fans have always respected someone who they can see cares passionately about the club and that was definitely the case with him. They appreciate defensive players who give everything. That was the case with Dom, and he became a firm favourite at Elland Road. The great thing about Dom is he was a real team player. Personal glory never interested him, just Leeds United getting the right result. The club's progress was all that mattered and I like to think that is why the Leeds fans remember him so fondly. That was apparent to me during the slide that took us from challenging for the Premier League title to being relegated to the Championship in what felt like the blink of an eye. Relegation hurt Dom every bit as much as it did any Leeds fan and I know it was a sad day when he had to leave for Blackburn Rovers during the summer of 2004.

As good a footballer as Dom was and no matter how important he was to Leeds United, what I think of first is his tremendous loyalty. He is a good friend to everyone he meets, and is someone who you can rely on during difficult times. I know this from the time when my wife Feziwe passed away and Dom flew out to Johannesburg to attend the funeral. He had also been at the wedding and the support of friends such as Dom helped me through what was a very difficult time. And that is why I will always consider Dominic Matteo to be one of life's good guys. Enjoy reading his story.

Lucas Radebe

Introduction

Being a professional footballer really is the perfect job. Well, I say 'job'. It isn't really, is it? To be paid a fortune, as even many Championship players are today, for doing something you love is, to me, the best thing imaginable. That is why the life of a footballer is probably the most popular and sought-after in the world. I know I have been fortunate that an ability to kick a ball around to a decent standard has allowed me not only to see the world but also look after my family. In that respect, I feel incredibly privileged. But I will never allow anyone to tell me that life as a footballer is a free ride that comes without a price. Not after the last 12 months that I have been through.

Injuries are, as even a Sunday League player will be able to testify, part and parcel of being a footballer. But what I have faced over the past year goes way beyond that. Basically, my back problems came very close to ruining my life. At one stage, I was facing the very real possibility of permanent spinal damage if an operation to try and cure a problem that dated back to my playing days had failed. Thankfully, the surgeon did a magnificent job and I am now well down the road to recovery. So much so that I am now able to scoop my two beautiful daughters up in my arms and say how much I love them. I can also do a bit of jogging, while I am hoping to build my fitness up further in the months to come with more regular visits to the gym. But, for a time, my outlook was not so bright. For months, I couldn't sleep. I also wasn't able to lift anything that was remotely heavy and I looked like the Hunchback of Notre Dame, so acute was the pain that I felt whenever trying to stand up straight. It was horrible and the thought of not being able to pick up my kids, Luisa and Elin, would often move me to tears.

Tony Pulis had already said he wanted me to move into coaching at Stoke City rather than playing on in the Premier League. I was 34 and still felt able to do a job for the club. But when I broke down during what should have been a leisurely jog, a short tour of back specialists soon saw the message being drummed into me that the best – in fact, the only – option was to call it a day. Those were horrible words to hear. Every footballer knows age will catch up with him one day. But we expect the end to be on our terms, when we feel good and ready. For me, that choice was taken away. After stressing I needed to give up, the surgeon said that if I wanted to do any sport in the future then it was going to have to be of the low-impact variety. More encouragingly, though, he did say that rest and a bit of rehabilitation might help me get better. Unfortunately, that didn't prove to be the case. Instead, once the pain had become too much to bear and I was struggling to pick up even the TV remote, I went back to see the specialist and was sent for a scan. It showed that my back had deteriorated quite a lot since the day I had hung up my boots for good in 2008.

Basically, and without being too technical, there are six discs at the bottom of my back which, in a scan, should show up white. Instead, they were black. Clearly, I couldn't go on and I went in for the operation shortly before Christmas, 2010. The doctors ended up taking out the two lowest discs and replacing them with metal ones. The other four were damaged, but it was decided to try and realign them rather than take the drastic action of replacing them.

Looking back, my problems started very early in my career at Liverpool. I'd supported the club since moving to Southport from Scotland at the age of four and, once old enough, been a regular on the Kop. So, signing for Liverpool had been a dream come true – especially as my hero Kenny Dalglish was manager when I first joined as a YTS apprentice. That sense of excitement never went, either. Wearing the famous red shirt of 'my' team made me burst with pride, so much so that I put my body through the pain barrier to make sure I was available to play. Pain-killing injections became the norm for me, particularly once I had started to hold down a regular place in the side. Sitting out a couple of games could have led to months on the sidelines, particularly if the team was winning. So, I had the injections to numb the pain and played on. That continued when I was at Leeds United and Stoke City, Blackburn Rovers being the only club where I didn't need loads of injections to get me through games. Knowing what I know today, I can't believe how naïve I was in allowing myself to have so many of those injections. I should have realised the long-term implications.

No-one forced me, of course. It was always my own decision. But my overwhelming desire to play regardless of injury almost cost me dear in terms of my long-term health. That is why if I ever speak to kids now about being a footballer, the one thing I drum into them is the need to stay away from any kind of injections. All they do is store up problems for the future, as I know to my cost. So, I tell the kids, "For the sake of missing one or two games, please think of your health". Mind, I am not sure the message really hits home and, deep down, I can't blame the youngsters for that. If I was about to embark on a career in football, I would probably go on to repeat my own mistakes. Put it this way, if I was still at Elland Road and Leeds United were about to play Valencia in the Champions League semi-final, the chances of me asking to sit the game out through injury would be nil. It would take a broken leg to do that, and even then I'd probably be begging the physio staff for help in patching me up! I can't think of many who I played alongside in my career being any different.

The warning signs about the damage being done by the injections were, looking back, flashing for some time. At Stoke City, for example, we played at Cardiff City on the opening day of what turned out to be my final season and I asked the home doctor to administer two injections in my foot. I had broken two bones but, as captain, was desperate to play. I will never forget the look on his face as he did so. I could tell he thought I should pack the game in, there and then. He was probably right, too. But I wouldn't listen to any advice, even from my horrified team-mates who would recoil from the sight of my swollen, bruised foot in the dressing room after a game. My foot looked like it belonged to the Elephant Man and yet, still, I thought the sacrifice was worth it. Clearly, I was wrong – a point that finally hit home last year when the doctors said I had to undergo the operation on my back that could have had such serious ramifications.

Happily, the Doomsday scenario outlined by the surgeon beforehand didn't happen. It was, though, the worst pain I have ever felt in my life. For ten days after the operation, I felt like someone had given me a good kicking – and that is from someone who previously felt he had a high pain threshold.

Eventually, however, the pain started to ease and today I feel the best I have felt for a long time. I can't thank the doctors enough. Now, I can get on with my life and look to the future, with the intention being to finish my coaching badges and then get back involved in a game that has been my life for so long.

Dominic Matteo, October 2011

Chapter 1

King Kenny Comes Calling

As starts to a budding football career go, mine must take some beating. No less a legend than Kenny Dalglish, then still a player at Liverpool, was the man who set me on my way at the age of just ten-years-old after spotting me playing for a boys' team called Birkdale United. Kenny's son Paul, who was a bit younger than me, played for the same club and his dad would often come down to watch. We all knew Kenny had arrived each week as this big white Mercedes would pull up in the car park and no-one else in Southport had a car like that. It was amazing how, even at such a young age, every one of the lads would up their game the moment Kenny's Merc was spotted in the car park, thinking this was their chance to shine and be spotted by one of Liverpool's greatest players. In truth, we were all trying so hard to impress that it is a wonder Kenny spotted any of us.

What possibly helped my case was that I asked for his autograph every single week. Or, at least, that's what it felt like as I must have got him to sign on bits of paper, programmes and the like at least 50 times. I don't think I ever let Kenny come down to Birkdale United without pestering him. I don't know why I wanted his autograph so many times, it is not as if ebay was around at the time and I could have made a few quid. Maybe I just wanted to say 'hello' to my hero. The great thing is he never once complained, even though every time I approached Kenny he must have thought, 'Not you again!' What I particularly remember from those Sunday mornings was that every time Kenny signed an autograph, he always looked me in the eye – not like some so-called big stars who would look into the distance as they scribbled down their autograph. The way Kenny did it made each of us think he was genuinely interested in us, which, as I found out later, is the sort of bloke he is. Later, when I became a footballer I made sure I did exactly the same every time I was asked for my own autograph.

Through Kenny's involvement, Birkdale established a link with the Liverpool FC Centre of Excellence and five or six of our players would go down for trials from time to time. After seeing me play a few times, Kenny had a word with the Birkdale manager, a guy called George Lowe, and made sure I was one of them. That was how I went on to spend the next 16 years of my life representing the club I supported. And not, as Robbie Fowler once claimed in his autobiography, because I was spotted by Kenny's greengrocer – as great a sounding story as that is!

Just being invited for a trial by Liverpool was a thrill. Everton had been sniffing around a year or so earlier but I hadn't paid much attention because I'd been a Red ever since our family had moved to Southport when I was four-and-a-half. Before then, we had lived in Dumfries, Scotland. I had been born there, which may come as a surprise to all those critics who lined up later in my career to question why I was being allowed to play for Scotland. The Matteo family home was in Badminton Gardens, which was not too far away from Queen of the South's home ground, Palmerston Park. That was where I first watched a live game of football. It was a few months before we moved to England and my Dad, Albert, took me in at three-quarters time for free. He wanted to give me a feel for what it was like watching a proper game. The visiting team were Celtic, who my Dad has always supported. I was so young that I can't remember too much about the game or the atmosphere but I do remember thinking, 'This is exciting'. I'd loved football from the very start and am told by the family that I was kicking a ball about from the moment I could walk. I had also insisted on wearing my Scotland kit all the time. After watching my first live game, I was totally hooked. Soon after, my Mum and Dad bought me a Queen of the South kit. My first pair of boots followed a few weeks later and, from then on, all I ever wanted for Christmas and birthdays was either a new kit or a new pair of boots. I was never interested in any other toys, just football. My Dad, who had been a decent amateur player and got to semi-pro level, made sure they were good football boots as well. He took a real pride and joy in them, probably more than me to be fair. Dad was always the one who would clean them for me. That continued right up until I signed for Liverpool as an apprentice. Whenever I came home, I would put my boots outside the back door and then nip upstairs. Then, by the time I came back down, Dad would be cleaning them for me. His advice that I should look after my boots was something I took on board and I made sure I took good care of them throughout my career.

The decision to move to England must have been a tough one for

Mum and Dad. From what I remember, we had a good life in Scotland. Dad had a successful business in Dumfries, where he ran a fish and chip shop with a restaurant above it. He also had a stake in a cake shop and a sweet shop so clearly had a lot going on. But he decided it wasn't for him and that there would be more opportunities for us all in England. The schools, for one, were better. So, he put his own needs and wishes second and the Matteo clan moved to Ainsdale, which is a suburb of Southport. I have no idea why Mum and Dad picked there but it proved to be a good choice. Southport is a really nice area. At first, we couldn't find a house so Mum, Dad, me and my elder brother Victor all lived in Pontin's. That was great for me and Victor, who is three years older. We were only there a short space of time but we loved it. What was not to love? We had our own swimming pool and our own arcade machines. Basically, everything a young boy wants was on site. When it came to moving out and into a tiny flat, we were both absolutely gutted.

My brother Victor is very much the opposite of me. He wasn't into sport, for a start. He did do a bit of swimming when we were both kids but soon realised it wasn't for him. Instead, he wanted to hang around with his mates. Later and once he was old enough, he would go down and watch Everton quite a bit, but I wouldn't say he was a big fan. Basically, Victor went because his mates went. They all enjoyed a few beers and the craic, particularly the big games like Everton v Chelsea and Everton v Millwall. When it came to school, he wanted to leave as soon as he could and get a proper job, which was the exact opposite of what I wanted to do. I always say it must have been quite difficult for my brother because I got my fair share of the attention due to the football. It can't have been easy to see your little brother getting a bit of the limelight with little mentions in the local paper and so on. From an early age, I was winning trophies and my parents were running me to training or a game. We also only had one car and that meant maybe the football took over a little bit. Victor never complained or anything like that but, now I am older, I realise that could have been difficult for him.

As brothers usually do, we fought a fair bit as we were growing up. He was fairly handy so would put me in my place from time to time and I had a fair few slaps off him, certainly more than I was able to give him back. That is how it goes with brothers. We also weren't the sort of brothers who did the same things. As he would be getting home from school or work and going up to his room to listen to Paul Weller, I would be going out training. Or he would be out chasing a woman, while I annoyed the neighbours by kicking the ball against the wall. He must have found me very boring – and annoying when I used to sneak into his room and draw over all his Weller posters to wind him up. We love each other but have totally different interests in life, even to this day. As a result of not really having a common ground, we have led very separate lives. Victor has still backed me up, though, whenever I have needed it. This was particularly the case at school, where a few of the other pupils were jealous that I was with the Liverpool Centre of Excellence and would call me all sorts of names. They didn't like it that I was at Liverpool and they weren't. Thankfully, it didn't cause me too many problems and I have always put that down to my older brother still being at school for a lot of the time and ready to back me up if ever I needed it.

In terms of football, Dad getting a job on the buses helped steer me towards the club where I was spotted by Kenny Dalglish. I was about nine when Dad started working there and he became friends with a guy called Sam Benbow. One day, Dad was talking about how much I loved football so Sam said, 'Do you want Dominic to come and play for Birkdale United?' Sam had formed the club a few years earlier and they had quickly developed a really good reputation. Dad asked me if I fancied going along. I said 'yes' straight away, went down the following week and really enjoyed it. So, I decided to stay. The only problem was that there was a big rivalry between Birkdale and Ainsdale, where I lived and attended St John Stone Primary School after leaving the Sacred Heart Infant School. Me playing for Birkdale, therefore, didn't go down too well with a few at school. I always felt that made things a bit harder when we played Ainsdale as the lads I went to school with wanted to boot me. But, in a funny way, in terms of the career I followed I don't think that was too much of a bad thing as it gave me a grounding in what to expect. It toughened me up.

Dad also helped in that respect. He was from a big Italian family but had been a huge Celtic fan all his life. He even took my Mum to the 1967 European Cup final when Celtic beat Inter Milan, the romantic so and so! Dad was also a big fan of European football and Real Madrid, in particular. He would love to tell me all about great players such as Alfredo De Stefano and Ferenc Puskas. Whether he realised it or not, Dad was passing on his love of good football by talking about what set these legendary players apart. He also once taped me the '101 Great Sporting Moments' show about the famous European Cup final between Real Madrid and Eintracht Frankfurt at Hampden Park. Real won 7-3 and Dad had gone to the game. Hampden was so full that night he had to watch from the aisle as he couldn't get anywhere near his seat. In the end, I watched that tape so many times that it eventually wore out. I just loved watching the quality of the football, even though I was probably only about six or seven when Dad first showed me it. The great thing about my Dad was that he passed on his love of football but never once put any pressure on me. It was always a case of, 'If you're happy then keep doing it'. It should be about enjoyment at that age and nothing else.

Dad did, though, want to make sure I stood up for myself. My old fella wasn't a competitive Dad but he is a strong man. There were quite a few times when he would teach me the Queensbury rules. I don't mean we would fight or anything like that. But he did make sure I knew how to look after myself. Dad wanted to pass on the basics of life, not just football. He had every job under the sun – from being a businessman to a bus driver and on to selling gas canisters. He did whatever he had to do to support the family. That is how he has always been and I feel very privileged to have him as my Dad. I feel the same about my Mum, Marie. She is a wonderful woman who has done so much for all the family and always been there for all of us. I love seeing how happy my parents are after more than 50 years of marriage as I know just how fortunate me and Victor are to have been part of such a loving and supportive family.

Being toughened up by both my Dad and coping with the Birkdale-Ainsdale rivalry at Primary School proved invaluable when I became a teenager and was picked to play for Sefton Boys team. I had a couple of years with Sefton, playing every Saturday against sides from other districts. By now, I'd moved to Christ The King High School in Birkdale and was starting to take my football more seriously. Playing for the district side turned out to be a huge learning curve. For a start, the football was much more competitive than I had been used to. When playing for the school team, any player who is decent will shine and the best player can usually run through the opposition and score. I've seen it countless times. But once you step up to play district football, there are countless players every bit as good as you and probably better so that can make it difficult to adapt. I certainly found that to be the case once picked for Sefton Boys. There was one early game in Kirkby that proved to be a real eye-opener as I was up against a lot of big lads, who all seemed to know how to handle themselves. That was the moment when I realised I had a lot still to do if I wanted to realise my ambition of being a footballer. Between the ages of 13 and 15, it became really hard. When you live in Southport and travel to some of the places in Liverpool and Manchester, it is a big culture shock. The kids were big, physical lads who would try to intimidate the opposition. All the parents would be there on the sidelines as well and they were a lot more aggressive than ours. There were even a couple of times when a parent of an opposition player wanted to have a go at one of us for kicking his son. It got quite scary at times. There was one game when we had won in Liverpool and in the dressing room afterwards our manager said, 'Get your gear lads quickly as they are all waiting for us outside'.

School football was similar. When playing for Christ The King, Mr Mulhearn, the teacher in charge of the team, brought a baseball bat with him to one match that he thought might be a bit lively. We'd had a set-to with this particular school when beating them a week earlier so the second leg had the potential to be nasty. He got the bat out in the dressing room before the game and said, 'We'll be all right lads'. He was a Liverpool guy and knew the script a bit better than us. We still beat them, even though the pitch was surrounded by all these big lads shouting all sorts of abuse at us. Luckily, he didn't have to use the baseball but at the final whistle I ran off that pitch as quickly as I could and thought, 'Get me home'. I would have given anything to be anywhere else during games like that but, looking back, those experiences made me that bit tougher. Possibly a bit too tough, in fact. I was still really small when with Sefton Boys but played in midfield, meaning I had to at least make out I was tough. If anything, though, I went too far and was continually being told to calm down by friends, families and schoolteachers. I was someone who didn't really care about the consequences of what I did on the pitch. It wasn't my temper or anything like that, more that when I went into a tackle I wanted to win the ball so badly that I didn't hold back. Looking back, I think I was actually tougher as a kid than a professional. I had to be or I would not have survived.

While at Christ The King, I also really got into athletics. I had always been good at running from a very early age, probably because of the times I had to run away from my brother when he wanted to chin me.

But it was only after stepping up to senior school that I started to compete in cross country races and discovered that I was quite good. In those first few races, I started to finish further and further in front of the field. Once, I finished ten or so minutes before everyone else, which was unheard of at the time, and then in a 1,500 metre race I knocked 19 seconds off the school record. I also once beat the track record at Kirkby Stadium, which had been set by Great Britain international runner Ade Mafe. Later, after winning an AAA event, I did wonder if this was the way I was going to go rather than play football. That was, however, until I stepped up a level to compete in a race for all the best kids in the north of England and ended up losing the race before it had even begun. It was a 1500-metre event at a school in Liverpool and, basically, there were a lot of attempts at psyching each other out before the race with all sort of things being said. I had never lost over that distance but the digs started and I couldn't handle it. No-one had ever come up to me before a race and said, 'I'm going to run you into the ground today'. I was 14 but realised after finishing second or third that competitive running just wasn't for me. I had already realised athletics is a lonely sport and that I didn't enjoy the training. I have always been someone who enjoys being part of a team and being around people. I didn't get the same buzz from training on my own. So, when I was well beaten that day in Liverpool over 1500 metres I decided athletics wasn't for me. It was a big decision because I had enjoyed the races. I don't know how far I could have gone. Maybe a long way, maybe not. But, bearing in mind how my career panned out in football, I definitely made the right choice.

As with all the decisions in my life, it was one Mum and Dad were happy for me to make. I have always appreciated that approach as it helped breed responsibility. Over the years, I have seen a lot of parents shouting at their kids from the touchline. It is great to be enthusiastic but there is a fine line between that and putting too much pressure on. Okay, if a kid is doing something out of order on the pitch then they need telling off. Or if they score a goal or make a good pass, then tell them they have done well. But I have seen parents actually giving their kid a load of abuse during a game and I found it awful. My Dad has always felt the same. Often, he would stand with the opposition fans on the touchline when I was playing for either Sefton or Christ The King and listen to what they were saying about me. But he never got involved.

Even when it got nasty like the baseball bat incident, he would not interfere. He wanted me to be able to look after myself on a football field. Dad knew I had to be able to stand on my own two feet. He understood that if a player can't look after himself then he gets hurt. I learned that lesson from him and it stayed with me. Even towards the end of my career with Blackburn and Stoke City, the words 'look after yourselves boys' were the last thing I said before leaving the dressing room.

Along with playing for my district side, I was also attending Liverpool's Centre of Excellence. It was run by a Scottish guy called Malcolm Cook, who was very, very strict. He would tell us straight and swear at us if we stepped out of line. Nowadays, that wouldn't be acceptable but it was Malcolm's way of trying to toughen us up. It was his way of saying, 'Come on, you're at Liverpool now so don't waste this chance'. As soon as I started attending the Centre of Excellence, the coaches began working on the basics – passing, control and so on. Malcolm was very big on that. We did play a few friendlies against other Centres of Excellence and I really enjoyed those as it was my chance to represent Liverpool in the famous red kit. But we didn't have too many as Malcolm was keener for us to work on our technique.

My Mum and Dad tried to get to the games as often as possible, but work often got in the way. Dad was a bus driver and Mum a home-help, meaning it wasn't always easy to get time off. Luckily for me, there were a few kids from Southport attending the Centre of Excellence so I would often get a lift off one of my Dad's friends.

The way youth football was set-up back then was that I signed schoolboy forms every two years in the hope that it would lead to a place as one of the apprentices at 16. Then, from the age of 14, training went up to two nights a week on Tuesdays and Thursdays. That was great, the only problem for me being that I was still doing athletics and playing for my school team so it meant I never got a night off. Eventually, such a gruelling schedule took its toll, which is another reason why I am glad I ditched the athletics.

Once young players reach their early teenage years, it can be that little bit of luck that makes all the difference. Every single lad at a Centre of Excellence has a bit of something, otherwise they wouldn't be there. So, you have to ask yourself, 'How can I become one of the better ones in the group?' It meant I always worked at my game and I think my Dad making me think about how football should be played at a very young age probably helped. Once you get to somewhere like Liverpool, if you really want to improve then you can. Half the battle is the mental side. The ones who have a chance are those who learn quickly. I have seen loads of talented players fall by the wayside. There were so many at Liverpool who had a little trick or the ability to create a bit of magic to score a goal. But when it came to a simple pass or a crucial tackle, they wouldn't make it. One of the things I had in my locker was an ability to pass the simple ball. I didn't think I had to beat a man. Others who maybe had more technical skill didn't do that, and it worked against them.

I used to practice, practice, practice. Our next door neighbour must have hated me because I would be knocking the ball against the door of our semi-detached house all day long. I lost count of the times she came out to tell me off. But it was my way of working on my weaknesses. I would also mentally pick a spot on the wall and make sure I could hit it every time, while I would also play the ball off the kerb so that I would then have to react quickly.

As helpful as all that practice will have been, however, I think my real lucky break came when Steve Heighway, who had been such a great player for Liverpool in the 1970s, returned to Anfield as youth development officer. I couldn't have had a better person to teach me how to be a human being and a footballer. To me, Steve is second to none in terms of influences on my career.

From the moment Malcolm left and Steve came in, I noticed a big change. The whole set-up was transformed, almost overnight. Steve got all the lads in various age groups together and said to us, 'I am not only going to make you better footballers but better people as well'. That was his philosophy. Malcolm had been quite abrupt and loud. But Steve got his message across in a much calmer fashion, even if, as I found out later, he could shout just as much as Malcolm when he wanted. Steve changed everything – from how we trained through to how we spoke to each other and what we ate. Manners were very important to Steve. If someone stepped out of line, Steve would pull him to one side and explain, 'You don't speak to people like that'. He wouldn't make a big fuss but, if it happened again, there was a chance the lad in question wouldn't be there the following week. Kids need that strictness.

He also had a great team behind him, particularly Under-18s coach

Hugh McAuley and physio Dave Galley. They all worked so well together. Steve is a very intelligent guy and had a knack of knowing how to deal with people and get the best out of them. He made us feel good about ourselves but when something needed to be said then he said it. Steve's communication skills were second to none, particularly in getting his point across to young lads – which can be difficult. I can't thank him enough. A lot of people did a lot for my career but Steve was the biggest influence by far. I am in no doubt about that. He took me to the next level. I still see Steve from time to time today and I always make a point of telling him how important he was to my career. I know the other lads who came through under him feel the same. A few of us were at Steve's leaving do at the Academy a couple of years ago and it was quite emotional. They were all there – Robbie Fowler, Steve McManaman, Jamie Carragher, Stevie Gerrard, Jamie Redknapp, Michael Owen – to say thanks to Steve.

Before returning to Anfield, Steve had been working in America and seen a different side to how football could be coached. Him coming back was the best thing that happened to Liverpool. A lot of lads owe him a lot. Steve didn't just focus on football, he made sure he became very involved with the lads' backgrounds, whether they came from good areas or bad areas. He wanted to make sure we could all get into training, for instance. A lot of kids had to get a couple of buses or travel quite a distance. I saw a lot of kids fall by the wayside that could have made it with, maybe, better parental support. Some just couldn't afford to get them to Liverpool's training ground at Melwood. As a result, Steve always tried his best to ensure that, between himself and his staff, there were plenty of full cars.

Mind, even with Steve doing all he could for me, as I approached my 16th birthday I still wasn't 100 per cent sure I would make it at Liverpool. Seven or eight of us had been at the club since we were 10 or 11 but I still wasn't confident about my chances. My problem was I was still playing in a lot of positions and that wasn't helping my development. The only position I didn't play was in goal and I got the impression that even the coaches at Liverpool weren't sure where I should play. Mind, to be fair, I don't think even when I was playing my last game for Stoke City that anyone really knew what my best position was.

I was finally put out of my misery on the night when I played for the

North of England Boys against the South. Steve drove me down as I was the only Liverpool player involved along with a lad from Manchester United called Ryan Giggs, while the South had lads like Nick Barmby and Sol Campbell in their side. I would love to get a programme from that game. There was a real rivalry, I think they called us 'Northern Monkeys' but we put it right by booting them off the pitch, as we always seemed to do with the South. I played well so was really pleased as we drove back to Liverpool. That, though, was nothing compared to the feeling of elation I had during the journey when Steve told me I was being offered a contract. At first, I wasn't sure if I had heard him right. I was sitting in the car smiling, but thinking 'I need to ask him to check I understood him right – Liverpool really are going to sign me?' Once I realised I had got it right, my emotions were a mixture of elation and relief. We had got to the stage where we were a month away from being told and I had been so desperate to know that I'd got more and more nervous with every passing week. It was all I wanted in the world, so much so I hadn't been able to concentrate at school. In a way, that is something I regret about my schooldays – football was too important to me. I didn't take an interest in anything else. As a result, I wasn't any good at any subjects and never even took my GCSEs. There didn't seem to be much point. School just didn't interest me. In lessons, all I could do was think about dinner-break and being able to play football. I know now it was stupid but back then it seemed natural. I dread to think what I would have done if Liverpool had not offered me a YTS contract.

The one thing Steve made me promise on that journey back from the North v South game was that I would not tell anyone apart from my Mum and Dad. The rest of the kids hadn't been told about their future and Steve didn't want them finding out about me before he'd spoken to them. I'd like to say I obeyed Steve's orders but I couldn't stop telling people. I was just so excited at the prospect of signing YTS forms with Liverpool.

Chapter 2

The Apprentice

In common with a lot of families in the area back then, ours was split between Red and Blue when it came to football. Well, I say split, it was more me as a Liverpool fan against my Dad and brother. Poor Mum had to stay neutral. I don't know why, after moving to England, that they went for Everton and me Liverpool but we did. It meant there was plenty of banter in our house on Thirlmere Drive at a time when Everton and Liverpool were the two top teams in the country, and possibly even Europe. Once I reached the age of 10 or 11, I started to go to Anfield with my mates. We would get the train from Ainsdale to Bank Hall Station and walk for half-an-hour to the ground. Then, we would queue up and pay to go on the Kop. In those days, you could go on your own to the match as no-one bought tickets in advance and the admission price was not too steep. Lads could do a paper round or whatever and be able to afford to go to the match. Today, that just wouldn't be possible.

The Kop was amazing. There were so many people on there for some games that we had no control where we would end up standing. Often, I would start behind the goal but, by the final whistle, somehow end up in the left hand corner or down the front. It was a thrilling experience to be part of that crowd. I was also really privileged as a Liverpool fan to be able to watch such a great team. My hero was Kenny Dalglish, and not just because he signed so many autographs for me! He was such a special player and I loved to watch him. Around about the time I started to go with my mates, he was also appointed player-manager. It wasn't just Kenny, though, that made Liverpool such a great team. There were so many talented players with Ian Rush, Ronnie Whelan, Mark Lawrenson and Bruce Grobbelaar all among my heroes, though the one I tried to style my own game on was Alan Hansen. He played centre-half but never seemed to be in trouble. He also always looked for the pass out, whereas other centre halves would just lump it forward. Bruce would throw it out to Alan and he would start every attack for Liverpool, or at least that's what it seemed like to me.

Living where I did, I was also fortunate to catch a glimpse of these superstars from time to time because most of them lived round our way. A few would have a big sponsored car with their name written on it. We would catch a glimpse of an Escort driving past with 'Ronnie Whelan' down the side and we would all say to each other, 'I'd love one of them one day'. Later, when I moved up to the Liverpool first-team, a few of these great players were still at the club and that was surreal. I just couldn't get my head round the fact that I was sharing a dressing room with Rushy, Ronnie Whelan and Bruce Grobbelaar.

So many games stand out in my mind, with probably the worst being the night Arsenal won the title at Anfield in 1989 when Michael Thomas got the winner in stoppage time. I remember crying my eyes out after that one. It was devastating but the funny thing is I ended up playing with Michael as my career got going and we have stayed in touch. He was in my bar in Leeds not so long ago, after we had played in a charity game at Elland Road.

I joined Liverpool as a YTS trainee in 1990 at the age of 16. The club had just won the league title, finishing nine points clear of Aston Villa in second place, so were flying high. What I – nor anyone else, for that matter – could have imagined was that Liverpool would still be waiting for their next title more than two decades later. I'll never forget my first day, mainly because I was so nervous. Seven of us had been taken on and Kenny, who was manager, welcomed us all to the club. Me and a friend of mine called Stephen Walsh were both from Southport, and we started to travel in with a couple of lads from the year above called Andy Howard and Alex Russell. Alex went on to play for a few clubs. Having those three lads to travel in with helped me settle a bit, as it gave us a bit of camaraderie. The first team squad were also encouraging, even if they did enjoy a wind-up at the expense of us young lads from time to time. We were subjected to the usual piss-takes, such as sending us out to the local hardware shop to ask for a 'long weight'. The people at the shop would be in on the joke and, after keeping us hanging around for half an hour, they would ask, 'Was that wait long enough for you?' Then, there would be the days when I was sent to buy some stripy paint and elbow grease. I fell for them all. The thing is when you have someone like Stevie Nicol or Ronnie Whelan making the request, you don't question what they are saying. You just want to do whatever these star players are asking. A few times, I would come back and say, 'Sorry, they haven't got any' and the first-team lads would fall about laughing. But I didn't care being the butt of the jokes, I just enjoyed being part of the club I supported. Anyway, it was all meant in good humour and was what Liverpool Football Club was all about when I started out. There was a real spirit to the place and I believe a lot of the success Liverpool enjoyed down the years came out of that camaraderie. I can't think of anyone who wasn't pleasant to us younger lads. Don't get me wrong, the first-team players could be tough on us. There were a lot of rules and regulations and anyone who didn't follow them would soon find out about it. But, on the whole, they were great and very encouraging. The senior lads did, though, have a way of testing the YTS lads out, asking for them to get a new top from time to time or to bring their boots in. It was a way of sniffing out if any of us had an attitude problem. It was very subtle and was their way of seeing if the new young lads would fit in to the club.

We saw quite a bit of the first-team because of the way the club was set up. Now, Liverpool have a state-of-the-art training ground where the first-team, the reserves and the juniors have their own space. But, back when I first joined as a YTS, everyone used to change at Anfield and then travel together to the training ground at Melwood on this proper old banger of a bus. Once on board, there was a definite pecking order with players having their own specific seats. The rule was not to sit in anyone's seat or you were in trouble. Basically, the lower you were down the pecking order then the closer you were to the front of this bus. All the top dogs were at the back. Jan Molby, Rushy and Ronnie Whelan would usually be on the back seat, with Barry Venison and Bruce also there. Those two were real jokers and would slaughter the coach driver, who insisted on playing the same Roy 'Chubby' Brown tape every day, all the way to Melwood and all the way back. The only person who didn't travel on the bus was the manager, who would drive to training in his Merc. No-one blamed Kenny, either, as there was no competition between travelling in style in a nice clean Merc or on a sweaty old bus while listening to the same jokes from Chubby Brown.

That first day as a YTS kid was weird, right from the very moment I arrived at Anfield and was directed to the away team dressing room, which is where the reserves and youngsters would change before making the half-hour trip to Melwood. The first-team had the home dressing room and I remember looking at them as they got on the bus that first morning. I was 16 and really shy and yet, here I was, rubbing shoulders with some of the best players in the world. Once training was over, we all came back to Anfield on the bus and it was then that it was explained to the new lads what was expected of us.

There were all sorts of jobs that needed to be done around the place and they were all organised on a rota. So, one day I could be in charge of keeping the home dressing room tidy and the next cleaning the bathrooms. We then might have to do the staff room or the famous Boot Room. Or, if it was a Monday or midweek and a game had been played the night before, even sweep the Kop. One of the more bizarre jobs was having to clean Kenny's Jacuzzi. Whatever duties we were assigned, they would usually last two or three hours and then we would be free to go home. Kids don't have to do those kind of menial jobs at football clubs these days and maybe that is a mistake as it would, in my experience, make them that little bit more grounded. Later in my career, I saw some kids come through thinking they were 'it'. Not so much at Liverpool, more at my other clubs. I always thought they should have been given these jobs to keep their feet on the ground.

Personally, I actually enjoyed doing all the menial jobs. I'll admit that, at first, I found going in the home dressing room to clear up intimidating. I was only 16 and here were all these great players with seven or eight league titles apiece sitting around, swapping banter and having a cup of tea with their feet up. I went in hoping no-one would spot me at first but, eventually, I felt more comfortable. In a way, it helped me get over my initial awkwardness around the senior players, which is another reason why the young lads of today would probably benefit from having to do a few jobs. Okay, there were times when I was still there at 5pm sweeping the corridors or whatever and I just wanted to be at home. But, on the whole, I don't think being asked to clean a Jacuzzi or sweep the terraces was too much of a hardship. One aspect I didn't enjoy at all, though, was the bollockings I would get from Phil Thompson. He was reserve team manager at the time and always seemed to enjoy telling me in no uncertain terms if there was a problem with any of my work. But, on the whole, I just enjoyed being in and around Liverpool Football Club. I was only on £27.50 a week but I didn't care. The togetherness of all the young lads was brilliant. They were two of the hardest years in my life but also two of the best.

After a few months at the club, I finally started to feel settled. I still found a few things weird, most notably the Monday afternoon ritual that would see Kenny and his staff challenge a few of the younger lads to a game. It was bizarre to see Ronnie Moran at full-back, Roy Evans in midfield and Kenny up front – all taking us on. The games were very competitive, too, and I lost count of the number of times the staff were losing with 60 seconds to play but end up winning with a couple of dodgy penalties. Those challenge matches aside, though, I had managed to get my mind round the fact I was at Liverpool and, as a result, I felt that bit more confident around Anfield. I think being on that bus with the first-team players helped, as did cleaning the boots of a couple of them. If you got the right player, it could be quite lucrative. At first, I cleaned Gary Ablett's boots. Later, it was Peter Beardsley and Glenn Hysen. Peter was great, every single morning he would come into our dressing room and say, 'Hello'. All three of them weren't bad at tipping, either, which when you are on £27.50 a week is quite important. When I was a player, the going rate to tip the lad who cleaned your boots at Christmas was about £200. That's what I gave Steven Gerrard one year and he was made up. Back when I did it, you were lucky to get £20 but Peter gave me £60, Hyson about £50 and I think big Gary was the same. I was quite fortunate as that was the equivalent of two weeks' wages. Robbie Fowler did even better as he did Rushy's. He really looked after Robbie, though you have to remember Rushy and Barnesy were earning three or four times what anyone else at the club was on because they were the superstars of the team. The worst tipper was, without doubt, Ronnie Rosenthal. I can't remember who did his boots but he gave them a fiver. A couple of the older lads had to explain to Ronnie about the going rate but, even then, he only handed over another tenner. How tight is that?

Another way the YTS lads used to boost our earnings during a season was to get ten footballs signed or maybe a few shirts for the first-team lads. We would have to blow the balls up, go round the whole squad and then hand them back to the player who wanted them – often on the same day. On top of all the other jobs we were doing it was a bit much but, if we wanted an extra fiver or whatever, that is what we had to do. Sometimes, we just wouldn't have time or a few of the first-team would have gone before we'd got to them. That gave us a real problem. If things became really desperate, we eventually resorted to doing a few of the signatures ourselves as well. I became quite good in the end! The alternative was going back to the player who had asked you to get the balls signed and that wasn't an option as it would be seen as disrespectful. There have even been a couple of occasions where I have seen an old signed Liverpool shirt on someone's wall and thought, 'I did that one!'

Football-wise, I also felt I had started to find my feet after a few months at the club. So, when the FA Youth Cup, which is still the big competition for all the young lads today, came round, I couldn't wait – even after we had been given a really tough draw against Middlesbrough. They had been beaten in the previous season's final by Tottenham Hotspur so were likely to be tough opponents. Or so we thought. I played at left-back as we walloped them 3-0 at Anfield on a freezing cold Saturday to set up a third round tie against Walsall, which we also won after a replay. I scored our first goal that night in a 4-1 victory that earned us the tie we all wanted in the next round, against Manchester United. Any game between two such bitter rivals is big news and we had a small taste of the limelight during the build-up. Unfortunately, we lost the game with Giggsy getting a couple for United but it was still a good experience. After pushing such a good team so close and with many of us still involved, I fancied us to have a real chance of winning the Youth Cup the following season. Sadly, I couldn't have been more mistaken with Tranmere Rovers knocking us out in the first round. It was a total nightmare. To be fair, Tranmere played really well on the night. Most of their lads had not made it with either Liverpool or Everton so clearly had a point to prove, which is just what they did with a 2-1 win at Anfield. Everyone was gutted. Liverpool were a club where it was expected that we won things and the Youth Cup was no different. So, it did not go down too well that we had lost to our neighbours. There had been a few thousand at the game, too, and we let them all down. We were gutted, as was Steve Heighway. Not only had we lost but it also meant we were unlikely to be playing at Anfield again in front of a decent crowd any time soon. Tranmere went on to have a decent run before being knocked out in the fifth round by Manchester United but that did little to ease the disappointment we all felt at our failure in a competition regarded as 'the FA Cup for kids'.

As disappointing as that defeat to Tranmere had been, however, I still felt my game was developing. By now, I was in the second year of my YTS and my mind was starting to think more and more about whether

Liverpool would want to keep me on. There had been a change of manager during February of my first year at the club when Kenny Dalglish had quit for health reasons. It came as a big shock. As someone who had met Kenny at an early age, I was gutted. Kenny was the King, it was as simple as that. The entire club looked up to him. He had this knack of making everyone smile, from the superstars in the first team to the dinner ladies in the canteen. You would never guess by how he was with people around Anfield just how famous and recognisable he was. As I was 16 and still 15 months or so away from finding out if Liverpool would want me to turn professional, Kenny leaving was unlikely to make much difference to my career. But I was still gutted due to him being such a big part of the club. Back home in Southport, everyone wanted to know why he had gone but all I could say was I knew as much as them. As I later found out, the Hillsborough disaster had taken a lot out of Kenny and he had to step down as his health was suffering. Anyone who was in the city at the time of the disaster that claimed 96 lives will know just what an awful period it was. Everyone in Liverpool seemed to know someone who had been affected. One of the lads I knew from school, Philip Steele, died at Hillsborough. Philip was in the year above me while his brother was in the year below. They both went to the game together and Philip, who was only 15 at the time, never came home. It was so, so sad. By the time I got to school on the Monday, people had found out and it was very difficult to comprehend what had happened. The one major thing I remember about that time was that I went to a few of the Mass services held in Southport, and Liverpool made sure they had a representative at every one. There was also at least one player at every funeral, which was important. The players really, really did care about what had happened to the families of the city.

I had tried to get a ticket for the semi-final at Hillsborough but had no luck. That was always the case with semi-finals or finals, even for those of us who were on the books. I was gutted not to be able to go at the time, especially as back then the games were not shown live on television. Now, though, I am glad I didn't as it would have put my Mum and Dad through a lot of upset. They had enough to worry about anyway due to my brother Victor having gone to the other semi-final at Villa Park between Everton and Norwich City. When the news first broke about problems at the semi-final, my Mum and Dad initially had a bit of a panic. This was in the days before mobile phones or 24-hour news channels so, for a short time, they didn't know if the problems were at Villa Park or Hillsborough and were going mad with worry. Eventually, it became clear the problems were in Sheffield and not Birmingham. Similar scenes will, no doubt, have been played out across Southport as there are a lot of Liverpool fans in the area. The families of all those who went to the game must have gone through hell waiting next to the 'phone for news.

April 15 is my brother's birthday so it is a date I would always remember anyway. But every time it comes round each year, all those old feelings come back. I always make a point of nipping into the local church where I live on the day and saying a prayer. That is my way of not forgetting. The Hillsborough disaster is something that I have thought about as I got older, in terms of what actually happened. When you are younger, you don't really take things in as much. But I have watched some of the television programmes on the disaster in recent years and it is upsetting to see how it unfolded and how it could have been avoided. I think being a father also makes it more upsetting. Even so, I can't imagine what the families have gone through since that awful day. Or, for that matter, just what impact the disaster must have had on Kenny, who attended more than half of the funerals and took so much on his shoulders.

Kenny stepping down as manager led to the club appointing Graeme Souness, who had been such a tremendous player at Anfield before heading up to Scotland to be a big success as the manager of Rangers. Graeme, like Kenny, had a huge presence around the club. The moment he walked in a room, everyone stopped. He had a real swagger about him as well. I quickly found out Graeme was the sort of manager who would come in the dressing room after a reserve game and say a few things. Once, after I had played sweeper for the reserves against Sheffield Wednesday, Graeme came straight up to me and said: "You didn't give the ball away tonight, well done." I was so happy but didn't know whether to say 'yes', 'thank you' or nothing at all. I didn't want to come across as cocky so just mumbled something that I doubt he even heard. It was probably the only game of my life where everything went right, which is typical as there were about 200 people there on a cold night at Anfield. But Graeme coming over and saying a few words of congratulation made it probably the highlight of my early career. It gave me a lot of self-belief, just when I needed it the most.

By that time, I was quite a way into my second year as a YTS apprentice and got the impression the staff were still not sure about me. There were quite a few lads playing ahead of me, even though I had been getting more games for the reserves. The problem was that I was still being played in several positions, meaning it was difficult to get into a rhythm. Against the better teams, I'd be played at centre-half but I also slotted in at left-back, left-midfield and in the centre. What reserve-team football was doing for me, though, was making me think quicker. I wanted the senior players to trust me and that meant making sure I thought more like them when on the ball. Trust is vital. There were a few times in my career when I opted not to pass to a team-mate in space because I thought he might give it away. That was probably a hangover from my time at Liverpool, where earning someone's trust was a major thing. It was only when that trust had been earned that you truly felt part of the club.

Playing in the reserves was something I'd enjoyed right from the start. My first game had been against Manchester United at Old Trafford and I scored. Thommo had picked me on the left side of midfield and I went on a run before hitting a cross-cum-shot that ended up going in. The rivalry between the two clubs is there even at that level, so it was a great feeling. Having Graeme Souness in the stand also made playing for the reserves that bit more special. It served as a big motivation, not just to me but also the other lads. I know from later in my career that playing in the reserves can be hard for experienced players. I used to hate it, for instance. Subconsciously, I would often perform below-par because I just didn't want to be there. That is why a team of youngsters can often beat an opposing side featuring several senior players in reserve-team football. Bearing in mind how I felt later in my career, I have always admired the attitude the senior Liverpool lads showed when I was starting out. Jan Molby was one, in particular, who was great to play alongside. He would always be wanting the ball and pushing us on. The other senior lads were the same. No-one was allowed to toss it off, basically because if either Kenny or Graeme weren't there then Roy Evans and Ronnie Moran were. The information was always going back to the manager. At a lot of clubs, I don't think players realise that. It probably helped at Liverpool, too, that Phil Thompson was in charge of the reserves. Thommo was someone who was never afraid of telling the older players the facts of life if he felt something needed to be said. A lot of them fell out with him as a result but he was often right.

After Steve Heighway, I would say Thommo did the most for my development at Liverpool. I'll be honest and say there were times when I hated him. He probably couldn't get away now with some of the stuff he said but I thought he was a good reserve team manager. Thommo was someone who cared deeply about the club and so badly wanted them to do well, no matter what the level. He just wanted us to live up to the Liverpool name. I know him and Robbie Fowler didn't get on but that is something that built-up over a lot of years. The thing with Thommo is that he had been there, seen it and done it during his own career. So, if he saw a cocky young kid come along then he would not hold back. He was maybe sometimes too honest and I know a few of the lads thought he was a bit of a tosser at times. But, on the whole, I got on fine with Thommo and realise what he did for my career. I probably needed a lot of the straight talking that he directed my way. He toughened me up, no question. He had been a defender so knew what I had to improve in my game.

Eventually, our second year as YTS lads was drawing to an end and that meant a decision was due about our futures. There were seven or eight of us and it was nerve-wracking waiting for news. It was all any of us could talk about for weeks. I was desperate to stay, not least because I had no other interests outside football at the age of 18. The arcades in Southport were probably the only other thing I did, or go down the fair. So, if I was not wanted by Liverpool, I really had no idea what I would do next.

Anyway, D-day finally arrived and we were summoned to the ground. We all had to go in one by one. By the time it was my turn, a couple of the lads had been in and been told they were being released. I could tell from their faces and was gutted for them. We had been together for years so it was hard, and I can honestly say I never thought, 'If they are leaving, it might give me a better chance'. I can't remember ever being as nervous as I was when walking into the office to hear my fate off Steve Heighway. He could probably sense my nerves as he wasted no time in telling me Liverpool wanted to offer me a one-year contract. As with two years earlier when Steve had broken the news of me being offered YTS terms, my reaction was a mixture of ecstasy and relief. I just couldn't wait to get home and tell Mum and Dad. It must be like people are when they get their GCSEs, wanting to rush home with the results. For my parents, it was also like the end of a road and the start of another. They'd supported me all the way and now, here I was, a professional footballer with Liverpool.

Amid my own joy, I did feel really sorry for the other lads. Only me and Stuart Gelling of our age group were taken on, in the end. Someone who I felt really sorry for was Stephen Walsh, who I'd travelled in with every day from Southport. He was a really good player but had a couple of hernia operations that went wrong and never really recovered. It was a real shame because he could have done well in the game. It shows how cruel football can be.

Later, Steve Heighway told me that he and Graeme had ummed and ahhed about whether to take me on. It wasn't a straight-forward decision, by any means. But, eventually, they decided I had a chance as I was starting to develop as a player. I always remember the words Graeme said to me soon after I'd been offered my first pro contract. "Don't think you have made it," was his advice and I never forgot those words. He said them before the 1992 FA Cup final against Sunderland. We had all travelled down to London by bus and I loved it. Steve McManaman, who had come through the youth team a couple of years earlier, was the man of the match as Michael Thomas and Ian Rush scored the goals in a 2-0 win. Seeing Macca do so well just made the day. I left Wembley that day dreaming of one day doing the same.

Chapter 3

Friends with 'God'

I'll never forget the first time I met Robbie Fowler. We'd both just signed for Liverpool, which at the age of 10 and nine respectively meant we had to go down to the Centre of Excellence to train one night a week. As I arrived for that first session, I was a bit nervous and wondering who else would be there and how good they would be. Living in Southport, I hadn't played for Liverpool Boys or anyone like that so didn't know who was who. The first person I noticed was the striker destined to be dubbed 'God' by the Kop later in life. In fact, it was impossible to miss Robbie as he had turned up wearing an Everton kit! I thought I was seeing things at first. I mean, who in their right mind would turn up at Liverpool's Centre of Excellence wearing the shirt of their city rivals? But that was Robbie, who was a mad keen Evertonian as a boy. It showed the confidence he had, even at that age. I quickly realised that confidence was justified, as he had the most natural ability I have ever seen. He just scored, scored, scored....everyone could see he was the one the Liverpool staff thought would make it because of the way they looked after him.

This little lad in the Everton kit clearly had a gift and I'll admit seeing someone as talented as Robbie did put doubts in my own mind as to whether I would make it or not. Little did I know, however, as the coaches split our group of 30 into two teams of 15 that we would go on to be great friends. So much so, if I am ever asked, 'Who is your oldest mate in football?' then I always reply 'Robbie Fowler'. We joined Liverpool at the same time, came through the youth set-up together after Robbie had stepped up a year at an early age and even signed our first professional contracts on the same day. Later, our Premier League debuts would come within a few weeks of each other. Robbie's came against Chelsea in a 1-0 defeat at Stamford Bridge when he hit the crossbar, while mine was at Maine Road in a 1-1 draw with Manchester City. By then, we were thick as thieves and I had become almost a fixture at the Fowler family home.

What did change after we'd both signed those first pro deals for £100 per week was the rate that our respective careers progressed. My Dad always used to say to me that life was a ladder and you have to climb it. I did go on to climb it one step at a time, nice and slowly. But Robbie went from the bottom to the top in one stride. The goals started to flow almost as soon as he got in the first-team at Anfield and his career never looked back. I had always thought it was just a case of when he played for the first-team, not if. And I got the impression Robbie felt the same. He hadn't signed anything with Liverpool until he was 16, so confident was he about his future prospects. I'd gratefully signed whatever Liverpool had put in front of me every two years, meaning I was not allowed to train with anyone else. Robbie refused, even though it would have given him some form of security. To me, it showed the total belief he had in his own ability. As confident as he was, though, even Robbie must have been surprised by how quickly things took off. Sky Sports had just been launched and they were on the lookout for new heroes to drive their coverage forward. Robbie fitted the bill perfectly and his profile shot through the roof. We had a great bond back then and did everything together. Being such close mates, I got an insight into how Robbie's life was changing and it was weird to watch. Where before, we would finish training and go into town to do a bit of shopping and no-one would bat an eyelid, now, all these people were recognising Robbie. He must have felt like a goldfish in a bowl at times, with everyone pointing at him or just staring. There was no doubt he was becoming a big household name and, before long, it started to cause problems on a night out. I'd go out with Robbie and his big mate Stephen Calvey in Liverpool and we'd behave like any other 19 or 20-year-olds. We liked a girl, we liked a few beers and a few laughs. But, as Robbie's profile grew and he became more famous, things got that little bit more tricky. Life was still easy for me as no-one knew me from Adam but Robbie had to watch his step and that showed us both the downside that could come with fame.

The best thing about Robbie, though, was that success on the pitch didn't change him off it in the slightest. He was still the same lad he had always been, very humble and incredibly loyal to his family. One of the first things he did after getting his first big contract was buy his Mum a house. It was in Woolton, which is in south-east Liverpool, and Robbie's way of saying 'thanks' to his Mum. I ended up staying there most of the week as it saved travelling time to Anfield from my parents' house in Ainsdale. Mind, Robbie's offer of hospitality didn't extend too far as, while he had the biggest room with the en-suite bathroom, I would be top-and-tail in the pantry! Sleeping arrangements aside, though, he was very loyal to his mates as well. As footballers, a sort of unwritten rule is that if you go ahead of your mate in terms of money, getting a better car or whatever, then you look out for the other. I was always aware of Robbie looking out for me. He made sure I was okay on a night out, for example. Back then, he was getting paid cash for newspaper interviews. Everyone wanted a piece of Robbie so he had a lot of interest. It meant that he had a stash of these £50 notes on top of his wardrobe. Then, when we were on our way out for the night, he would take a couple off the top and spend them on us both. That was Robbie, he looked after people. That generosity and loyalty were two of the reasons why I was so happy for Robbie when his career took off. I didn't feel any rivalry, that's for sure. I knew I didn't have his ability and that goalscoring wasn't my thing anyway, so it was not as if we were rivals. It was just great to see my mate doing so well.

We share a very similar sense of humour as well and would crucify each other all day long. I remember after we'd signed those first professional contracts, which had basically quadrupled our weekly wage, we felt like we had won the lottery. Despite that, the only extravagant buy I made was a dodgy suit jacket because I thought I might need one on a matchday because the senior players had to wear a suit. It was maroon. I still don't know what I was thinking and it didn't last long, mainly because Robbie took the piss almost from the moment I'd bought it.

Our shared sense of humour meant we had countless great holidays together. Once, we arrived in Magaluf without anywhere to stay. So, we did what any sensible person would do, and headed straight to the first bar! It was while sinking our third or fourth pint that we got chatting to a couple of Liverpool fans and they invited us back to crash at their place. They even offered to give up their beds for us, which I felt was taking things a bit far. Robbie, though, just said, 'Sod that – let's have a good night's kip'. The only thing these fans asked was for Robbie to wake up their little lad in the morning. He was a mad keen Liverpool fan, so you can imagine what his face was like. It was an absolute picture. I think the poor lad still thought he was dreaming, which I suppose you would if Robbie Fowler was waking you up. Eventually, we got ourselves sorted with a big villa and went on to have a great holiday. Magaluf is a mental place. The following year, we opted for another quiet destination – Falaraki! Again, we weren't shy when it came to drinking and we eventually came up with a great idea. We should either get a tattoo each or have our hair dyed blond. The toss of a coin would decide which it was and, thankfully, it came down in favour of dying our hair. What a lucky escape, as I don't think I'd have enjoyed having to walk round for the past 16 or so years with a tattoo saying 'Falaraki '95' on my arm? At least with the blond hair, it was only temporary – even if, once we got back to Liverpool, we went and had it re-done before pre-season training got under way.

I had such a good time in Falaraki with Robbie that I went back a year later with Jamie Carragher, who had just made the breakthrough into the first-team. Being four years older than Carra, I, of course, made sure I didn't lead him astray. Some hope! One of the first things we did was go bungee-jumping. I'd done the same with Robbie the year before but this time Roy Evans, who by then had become the manager of Liverpool, was on the island as well. He was visiting his son, who worked in Falaraki at the time. Let's just say he wasn't overly impressed to find two of his players bungee-jumping. Mind, Roy couldn't have too much of a go, as one night I'd found him sleeping off a drink and had to help the gaffer back to his room.

That summer turned into a mental one for me. I decided to stay for a month, whereas Carra'd had enough after two days and wanted to go home. Kids, eh! I stayed on and ended up drinking so much Heineken that I had to have my stomach pumped. I think it's fair to say I lost the plot a bit that summer.

At Liverpool, we had quite a few good holidays. At the end of one season, we went to Marbella. All the boys were there, including John Barnes and Ian Rush. Robbie Williams also tagged along. He was a mate of Phil Babb and turned out to be a great lad. He was just like a footballer, even going as far as joining in with the practical jokes such as shaving one of my eyebrows off or stripes in my legs. Robbie was into drinking back then, and determined to have a good time after having just left Take That. Mind, he wanted a game of football next to the pool every morning. The lads were all saying, 'We've spent the last ten months playing football, we don't want to'. But Robbie would insist. I really enjoyed those trips. They were a good way of forging a bond between the lads, who all enjoyed getting away together after a tough season.

That was understandable, especially during my first few years at Liverpool as we went through plenty of tough times. The club was in transition with a lot of the experienced players having grown old together and not been replaced by a similar standard of player. We had young lads like me and Robbie coming through but Graeme Souness realised it was going to take a couple of years to get the team where he wanted it to be. Initially, it took me some time to make the breakthrough. I didn't play at all in my first year as a professional at Anfield, for instance. I still enjoyed it, though. Now considered to be a member of the senior squad, the big change for me was I could ask the YTS lads to do jobs for me and be cleaned up after – even though I was still in the dressing room set aside for the reserves and juniors. It was now my turn to send someone else for elbow grease or a 'long weight'. Well, that was the theory. In reality, that wasn't what I was about so I still did everything for myself, including cleaning my own boots. My thinking was also coloured by knowing I had done precisely nothing in the game other than be awarded my first one-year contract. That was a proud achievement for me but, in terms of Liverpool Football Club, it meant little. I knew as I came back for pre-season in 1992 it was going to be a year where I had to prove myself. To me, that included showing the staff of the famous Boot Room I didn't think I had made it.

The Anfield Boot Room has become part of football folklore, mainly because of the aura that built up around it during Liverpool's most successful days in the 1970s and 1980s. Originally what the title suggests, a place for the players' boots to be stored, Bill Shankly turned it into a meeting room for his coaching staff. As a Liverpool fan, I had grown up hearing all the stories about this famous inner sanctum of the club. So, when I first joined Liverpool, I was in awe of the place. Along with the first-team dressing room, it was where I was most nervous before knocking to see if I could enter. I would always wonder to myself about the conversations that could have taken place. Was it where they decided to sign Kenny Dalglish? Or maybe Keegan? Was this where all those European Cup triumphs were plotted? I loved just being in there. Cleaning the boots in the freezing cold may not sound the most enjoyable of tasks but I enjoyed every minute. It was a sad day when the Boot Room was done away with as part of the training ground development that saw the playing staff move to Melwood, though at least I can say I was at Liverpool when it was still an important part of the club.

So many great coaches and managers came through the Boot Room over the years. Shankly, Bob Paisley and Joe Fagan are just three of those who made it such a special place along with Ronnie Moran and Roy Evans. When I signed, there was also a guy called John Benson, who took the reserves with Phil Thompson. Steve Heighway was another member of the Boot Room along with Hugh McAuley and Dave Shannon, while there was also a great old character called Tom Saunders, who sadly died a couple of years ago. He would come in and just walk round the training pitch but was a great old guy.

The Boot Room didn't change for years. Before and after training, the coaches would be in there having a cup of tea and just chatting about football. There was no other topic discussed in there, I know that from eavesdropping when cleaning the boots in the facility next door where the vice, wire brushes and so on could be found. There was just a wall dividing the two in what was, basically, the same room. We weren't supposed to listen but it was hard not to. The coaches would discuss everything, from deciding on the first-team training routines through to who from the reserves should step up. Team selection was also decided in there, though only after making sure there was no-one cleaning the boots next door who could overhear the discussions. The manager was a big part of the Boot Room, even though he had his own office. After being players at Liverpool, it must have been strange for Kenny and Graeme at first to feel part of the Boot Room. But, as you would expect from two such big characters, they quickly adapted. However, if I had to pick one person who embodied what the Boot Room was all about, it would be Ronnie Moran. Ronnie was, quite simply, a Liverpool institution. In all, he spent 46 years at Anfield as a player, coach and, on a couple of occasions, caretaker manager. To me, he was always the one I looked to for guidance as to whether I was doing the right things or not. When I signed, Ronnie had been there longer than anyone and you could tell by his body language what he was thinking. He also used to join in with training at times and definitely still had the ability that had made him a regular at Anfield for more than ten years. Ronnie is, without doubt, an unsung hero at Anfield and, to me, doesn't get the credit he deserves for all the trophies that were won during his time at the club. Ronnie was definitely a big influence on me, even though he probably didn't realise it at the time. I am sure if you asked Robbie Fowler and Steve McManaman about Ronnie then they would say more or less the same. He was a tough guy and old school. But in being like that, it meant you were never told any lies and I always preferred that sort of approach. I had many a telling-off from Ronnie, sometimes for not marking tightly at a corner or on other occasions he felt I hadn't played out from the back like Liverpool had always done. But it was done because he loved Liverpool Football Club and badly wanted the club to do better. Back then, I was very skinny and Ronnie wanted me to be a bit tougher. I had been tough as a kid but had calmed myself down a bit as I got older, mainly to stop myself getting into trouble in matches. Ronnie wanted it back in my game and would constantly offer me advice. I really appreciated his help and feel he helped turn me into a better player.

Ronnie was someone who watched every game of football that was on television. Then, the next day he would ask you about it. At times, it felt like I was being tested but I don't think I was. Ronnie was just obsessed with football. In a lot of ways, Ronnie reminded me of Bobby Robson. I was only lucky enough to meet Bobby a couple of times, after games up at Newcastle. But I was massively impressed by him. Like Ronnie, he didn't want to speak about anything but football. I love people like that and it is sad that football doesn't seem to make characters like those two any more.

He had a very important role at Anfield, too, in that no-one got in the first-team unless the coaching staff trusted you. And it was Ronnie who seemed to know when a player was ready to be trusted. In my first year as a pro, he clearly didn't think I was ready – hence all those chats we had about me needing to be tougher and so on. To be fair, I hadn't been expecting to get in the first team during those first 12 months with the reserves instead being my priority. Back then, there were only two substitutes allowed in the Premier League so a lot of very good players got a game in the reserves. That meant I was playing against men who would give you a smack from time to time. My game had to become better and I think it did. The Boot Room obviously agreed as I was offered another contract at the end of 1992-93, this time for two years at £225 per week. Now I really was in the money, though this time I did manage to resist the temptation to buy myself a new maroon jacket!

The following season started really well for the first-team with four wins from the opening five games. After finishing sixth in the first Premier League campaign, the hope was that we could push on and challenge for the title. Unfortunately, a run of four straight defeats – the last of which was Robbie Fowler's debut at Stamford Bridge – served to dampen down any enthusiasm. A 0-0 draw at home to Arsenal was then followed by Robbie scoring his first league goal in a 2-1 win at home to Oldham Athletic. I was delighted for my mate, while secretly hoping I would soon be joining him in the first-team. I was certainly getting closer. A few days before that win over the Latics, I had played at Anfield in Steve Nicol's testimonial. Unfortunately, I'd not been in the Liverpool team but a Great Britain XI who went on to win 2-1. It was great to be involved, though being on the opposing side was a bit of a letdown as it meant I still didn't feel part of the first-team set-up. All that, however, was about to change with my big chance coming on the Tuesday after Robbie had scored his first Premier League goal. I was named in the squad for a trip to Dublin, where we were due to play a League of Ireland XI. The club used to play in Ireland at the same time every year, with the game basically being used as bonding trip for the lads. It may have been a friendly but I saw this as my big chance to impress.

Liverpool are huge in Ireland, as I soon found out when we landed. There were so many fans waiting at our hotel that we couldn't get in the place. It was a real eye-opener as to how the club was seen outside Merseyside. The game was played at Lansdowne Road and we won 2-1, with me getting the man of the match award. I had to go up on stage in the clubhouse afterwards with all my team-mates jeering and taking the piss to collect my prize, a green Alessi watch. I didn't mind, though, as the girl presenting the watch was an absolute stunner. I remember thinking, 'This is what it's all about'.

After that, we all went out on a bender round Dublin. It turned out to be my first introduction to the team's drinking and a real eye-opener. As the youngest, I was given the kitty to look after by Rushy – which meant I had to get the round in wherever we went. I'd never seen so much money in my whole life. At the time, I didn't drink a lot but I got into the spirit and was still out with the rest of the lads when we headed for Leeson Street, which was the only place you could get served in the early hours. The problem was all they sold was wine so I downed loads of that. No matter how much I drank, though, I still didn't feel drunk. The senior lads were really impressed by my staying power and even gave me the nickname 'Hollow Legs'. We were due to leave the hotel at 9am and I think I only went back to my room to get showered and collect my bag. It was a crazy 24 hours. Little did I know, though, that life was about to get even more hectic. Just two days later, I made my Premier League debut in front of more than 30,000 fans at Manchester City.

Once again, I was on the left wing due to John Barnes having injured his Achilles. It wasn't my best position but I was not going to complain. I was making my Premier League debut for Liverpool. Unfortunately, Mum and Dad couldn't get there because the team was only named on the lunchtime of the game. So, they had to listen to it on the radio. But they told me afterwards how proud they had been. I just about had enough energy to tell them what a great atmosphere it had been and how big the giant Kippax terrace that ran down one side of Maine Road had looked from the pitch. I lasted 80 minutes, which bearing in mind the preparation I'd had in Ireland wasn't too bad. I also felt I'd done okay, while to top the day off Ian Rush, one of the most legendary players in the club's history, scored for us in a 1-1 draw.

I went on to stay in the side for quite a few games. The following week saw us beat Southampton 4-2 on my home debut with Rushy again getting on the scoresheet and Robbie getting a hat-trick. The crowd was 32,818 but I swear it felt more like 60,000. The hairs on the back of my neck were standing up when the Kop started to sing 'You'll Never Walk Alone' before kick-off. I then got a bit carried away and found myself singing along to the words. It took me a few seconds to snap out of thinking like a fan and get my mind on the game. Thankfully, I was never someone who got nervous in my career before a game so playing against Southampton was fine – once I'd stopped thinking like a fan and staring at the Kop. A week later, the crowd had swelled by around 10,000 for the visit of West Ham United. Once again, we won but this time I scored my first goal. Or, at least, I thought I had. We were already 1-0 up and attacking the Kop when the ball came to me in the penalty area and I shot towards goal. Now, I am the first to admit that it took a deflection off Alvin Martin on its way into the net. But the ball was on target. Nowadays, the Premier League's dodgy-goals panel would award me it but they weren't around back then and the Sunday 'papers instead gave it as an own goal. The lads gave me almighty stick in the dressing room afterwards, saying 'you can't claim that'. But I really wanted it. I came out of the dressing room and got hold of the old Saturday night sports paper that the *Liverpool Echo* printed. It said the goal was mine and I did show the 'paper to the reporters from the nationals who wanted to interview me afterwards, which was again something new to me. But, despite my attempts, they all wrote that our second goal had been down to Alvin Martin and that was that. I wish I'd known then just what a terrible scoring record I'd have for Liverpool as I would have made more of a fuss.

Even without my 'goal', I stayed in the side for a good few weeks but then the senior lads started to return from injury and I dropped out. I was fine about that as, by then, I did feel part of the first-team set-up and knew other chances would come in the future. Part of that thinking was down to the new contract I'd just signed. After making my debut, the club had been straight in touch to offer a new deal. It meant I went from £225 a week to £3,000 in one go. I remember thinking, 'Here we go! What am I going to do with all this?' Roy Evans was in the office with Graeme as I signed and he caught sight of the look in my eye. Straight away, Roy said, 'You better behave yourself'. After the Dublin trip and a few weeks in the first-team, I had started to get the reputation of someone who enjoyed a beer with the boys. I was pretty easily led so Roy was just letting me know not to get carried away.

To be fair, Roy had a point. Being easily led is just something that is in my nature. Right through my career, I liked a beer with the lads. In fact, I can honestly say that I never missed a social night out with the team once in my career. Even if I felt like I was on my deathbed, I would struggle in. There were a couple of times when I might be running late but no-one ever thought I wouldn't be there. That was just how I was, a social lad. Sometimes, that would make me a bit of a loose cannon and, as I'll come to later in this book, the drinking probably prevented me realising my true potential. In that respect, I wish I had listened a lot more to what Roy had to say when I was signing that first big contract.

Chapter 4

Souness And Sunderland

I owe a debt of gratitude to a lot of people at Liverpool for all the help and advice they gave me as I was starting out. Steve Heighway, Kenny Dalglish, Ronnie Moran, Graeme Souness, Phil Thompson and Roy Evans are all near the top of a list that, literally, includes dozens and dozens of names. All played their part, whether big or small, in helping me become a professional footballer and I am grateful to every single one of them. One man who also deserves to be included in that list is John Barnes, who when I signed YTS forms as a 16-year-old, was already an Anfield legend. I didn't have a lot of contact with him in those first couple of years on the staff. But, once I'd made my debut, Barnesy was one of those who helped me settle. I got the impression he saw me as a bit easily led. As one of the senior pros at the club, he liked to look out for the young lads. He knew the money that was starting to flood into football had quickly led to player wages shooting up. And that meant footballers were, suddenly, very attractive propositions for those looking to make a quick buck. Let's face it, we are not always the brightest bunch in the world and need help when it comes to financial matters. I am sure the same can be said about most people. The difference with footballers is they have all this money, so are naturally a target for those who might not have their best interests at heart. I didn't have an agent at the time but plenty were interested. I didn't know which way to turn, to be honest, and needed advice. John realised that and took me to one side to outline the potential dangers. He also recommended the same company who acted for him, Park Associates. I appreciated John's advice and agreed to meet one of their representatives, Struan Marshall. Jon Holmes had set up Park Associates and Stru worked with him. A meeting was set up at the Est, Est, Est restaurant in Manchester, which Barnesy came along to. That was a nice touch on his part as he didn't have to take time out to see I was all right. I appreciated the gesture. Committing to an agent was a big thing, as I was 20 by now and starting to earn serious money. I needed advice and Barnesy did me a big favour that day as Stru has been brilliant. I am still with him now, even though I don't really need an agent these days. Agents may not have the best of press and I have heard some real horror stories over the years of players being ripped off. But Stru has been great and more like a best mate to me. We still spend a bit of time together, even though he is now one of the most successful agents in the world. I've always appreciated the work he has done on my part and I think he feels the same about me, especially as I later introduced him to Steven Gerrard and Jamie Carragher. As a nice touch, Stru recently treated me to a trip to Barcelona to watch the Champions League semi-final with Real Madrid in the Nou Camp.

Through Stru, I met a financial adviser called Andy Sterling. Again, Andy is someone who is still with me today. His advice has been invaluable. He goes for safe investments and is not one to take big risks. He is also very clever at picking the right investment. For example, a few years ago, he got me involved with a film project that was basically a way of helping me save tax. To be honest, I'd forgotten all about it until a few months ago when some correspondence arrived saying my investment had paid off and that I was due a decent payout. Andy had only gone and invested my money in the company that made the James Cameron film Avatar, which went on to become one of the most successful films of all time following its release in 2009. The investment group I had joined wasn't just footballers, it was all manner of people. But it was typical of the sort of project that Andy picks out. I have invested in all sorts of things down the years, but the main thing Andy preached at the start was to get my houses paid off as soon as possible. Then, he sorted me out a nice pension for life. If it had been left to me, I'd have put the money in a bank and probably been given a load of bad advice. But thanks to Stru and Andy coming as a pair, I have been fortunate. And I owe that good fortune to Barnesy for taking time to steer me in the right direction.

The great thing about Stru and Andy is that, underneath everything, they are concerned about my welfare. Stru was, of course, concerned about me financially during my career. But he also wanted to make sure I got the right move and got the right wages. He wasn't pushy, which I appreciated. Some agents push their client to a certain club because it brings them more money. I hear stories all the time about this player or that player demanding a pay rise because their team-mate is on £100,000 a week. And if they don't get it, they threaten to leave. That is one change in football that I don't like. My thinking was always, 'If I am playing all right then the club will come to me'. There is only so much money one person can spend anyway. If you are sensible with your money as a footballer then you are set up for life. Stru was never that kind of agent, anyway. You only have to look at the career of another of his clients, Steven Gerrard, to see that. How many offers must Stevie have had down the years to leave Liverpool? I imagine every team in Europe must have been in for him at some time in his career. Yet, he is still at Anfield. That says a lot to me.

With my career in safe hands, I started the 1994-95 season hopeful of building on the previous year. I'd made 11 Premier League starts and, in my own mind if not the record books, scored one goal. One major change that had taken place was Roy Evans taking over as manager after Graeme Souness had quit the previous January. I felt sorry for Graeme. He was someone I respected and I liked him as a person, mainly because he never lied and always told you straight what he thought. If I had a good game, he would say so. And if I didn't, he would make that clear too. Players appreciate that sort of honesty in a manager, even if they might not agree in the heat of the moment. Graeme was what I would describe as a 'real man' and I was sad to see him leave. The end had come after First Division Bristol City had knocked us out of the FA Cup at Anfield in a third round replay. I had been part of the squad at Ashton Gate but not featured. I also wasn't involved in the replay as Brian Tinnion scored the winner. It was a bad, bad night for Liverpool and showed the transition the club was going through. The fans didn't like it, understandably, and made their feelings known. We had also been struggling in the Premier League and were in mid-table. But being knocked out of the FA Cup at home by a team from a lower division proved the final straw for many fans and Graeme was gone within a couple of days.

With hindsight, I believe Graeme was unlucky. He could see the way English football was heading and tried to change things to be more in line with how he had lived as a player with Sampdoria in Italy. Graeme was a pioneer in that he wanted us to do all the right things, such as stretching properly before training and cutting certain things off the menu before games. Back then, training was basically a jog around the pitch and then straight into a game. Graeme had seen a different way of doing things in Italy and wanted to implement his ideas at Anfield. But the older players wouldn't buy into it. They'd had mega careers and won everything, so thought, 'Why should we change?' They couldn't see the point of stretching for 20 minutes before training. It didn't help Graeme that a couple of the lads got injured after he had started to make changes, which meant the rest refused to trust the new ideas. It was almost as if they convinced themselves it wasn't the right way and picked up strains or injuries as a result. I got the impression a couple of the older coaches also didn't see the need for change. But Graeme firmly believed it was the way football was heading and he was right. Now, everyone watches their diet and looks after their body better. The game has got so much faster since even I first made my debut, and that means players have to live their lives better or risk falling by the wayside. Graeme was unlucky in that people just weren't ready to accept his ideas. It is a shame the older players couldn't see that and be more receptive.

Graeme's attitude to drinking was another that did not go down well with the squad. He wanted to stop it but couldn't. The culture was just too ingrained in English football at the time and it took the emergence of the next generation after me, the Gerrards and the Carraghers of this world, for things to change. Because of how attitudes within the game have changed since, I firmly believe Graeme could have brought success to Liverpool if he had been appointed a few years later. He also won a trophy, the 1992 FA Cup, and that is not something all the managers of the club have been able to say during the past 20 years.

Maybe he just tried to change things too quickly, I don't know. What was true, though, was that some of his signings didn't work. He got a lot of stick when the Julian Dicks transfer flopped but what many chose to forget was that the fans loved the signing at the time because Julian had been such a big success at West Ham. Maybe Anfield just wasn't the right place for Julian? But Graeme was not to know that when he signed. Nigel Clough was another of Graeme's signings that everyone thought would be a big hit because he had been a great player at Nottingham Forest. Neil 'Razor' Ruddock, who went on to do really well at Anfield, was also bought by Graeme, who helped develop Robbie Fowler and Macca. That is why I believe Graeme got a rough deal at Liverpool. One big mistake he did make, though, was selling the story about his heart problems to *The Sun*. I am sure Graeme would admit that today. I still can't understand why he went to them with the story in the first place. Since Hillsborough, the reputation of *The Sun* on Merseyside had been rock bottom because of their disgraceful coverage of the disaster. In fact, it has never managed to recover sales lost in the aftermath of the tragedy. Graeme simply chose the wrong newspaper and the decision turned a lot of fans against him. After the Cup defeat to Bristol City, the fans wanted a scapegoat and he was it.

Graeme's exit meant Roy stepped up to become manager. As sad as I was to see Graeme leave, I thought Roy would be a good appointment. He had been a coach and physio when I first signed. It is hard to believe today but in the mid-1990s even clubs as big as Liverpool didn't really have much medical care. A doctor would come in once a week to see the injured lads but for the rest of the time the coaches would look after us. Ronnie Moran and Roy would, basically, put the injury in ice and tell us to rest. There was no full-time physio and no treatment. And if you were a first-year pro, you were at the bottom of the queue behind the first team and reserves. Sometimes, you could sit there for two or three hours waiting to see Ronnie or Roy. The ice would then come out and we would have to wait for the doctor to come in on a Friday for a proper diagnosis. Usually, he would then just tell you to put more ice on it! Looking back, it is no wonder that injuries took so long to heal. Back then, a hernia injury meant being out for three to four months whereas now it can often be a week. Once I got to Leeds, I was back inside seven days after a knee operation.

As old fashioned as the approach to player care was, the treatment room was one of my favourite places at Anfield. I am not saying I ever wanted to be injured or anything like that. But the craic that went on in there every day had to be heard to be believed. There were so many characters in there such as Rushy or Jan Molby, who made sure it was one of the funniest places I've ever been. Ronnie Whelan was another who was always in there for a massage. Wayne Harrison, a lad who had once come in for quite a bit of money from Oldham but suffered horrendous luck with injuries, was a bit of a nightmare because he loved a practical joke. Deep heat in your undies or cutting the toes out of your socks, Wayne did them all. Because I enjoyed the banter, I started to make a point of wandering into the treatment room whenever I could. After a while, Ronnie spotted this and, without any fuss, pulled me to one side. Ronnie, who was a very astute and clever guy, said: "If you're not injured, stay away from the treatment room or you will get injured."

He was right, as a player can get in the habit of imagining an injury when around people who are injured. It might be a little thing like coming in from training, heading to the treatment room to have a laugh with the lads but then thinking, 'My ankle is a bit sore, I'll put a bit of ice on it'. It can become a psychological thing. It was part of Ronnie's attempts to toughen up my character and I heeded his advice.

Roy's first season as manager went well for Liverpool. We finished fourth in the Premier League, up four places from 12 months earlier. We also reached the FA Cup quarter-finals and beat Bolton Wanderers at Wembley to lift the League Cup. Roy had established a decent blend of youth and experience, with Macca and Robbie doing well alongside Barnesy, Rushy and Mark Wright. Roy's signings also worked out with both Phil Babb and John Scales missing only a handful of games between them. For me, however, that season turned out to be a nightmare. I just couldn't get into the team and started just two games – against Nottingham Forest in February and West Ham United during the final week of the campaign. The team were playing well, so I understood the reasons why. But that didn't make it any easier to handle. After thinking I had made something of a breakthrough the previous year, I felt like I was back to square one. Roy could see I was not happy and suggested I go out on loan to get some games under my belt. I was desperate to play football so, when Sunderland came in with an offer, I jumped at the chance of moving to Roker Park. Mick Buxton was the manager and they were fighting relegation near the bottom of Division One. Dropping down a division didn't bother me, I just fancied the challenge. So, on transfer deadline day, I joined Sunderland on loan for the rest of the season. Brett Angel also came in on a permanent deal for £600,000 from Everton and we were both interviewed by the *Sunderland Echo*. The piece appeared under the headline 'Scouse Swoop Boosts Roker' along with a photo of me playing for Liverpool. Underneath, the caption read: 'Dominic Matteo will play for Sunderland at Barnsley tomorrow night.' So, it looked like I was starting! Sure enough, I was in the line-up at Oakwell but, unfortunately, we lost 2-0. The game was a bit of a farce due to a strong wind, which at one stage saw the goalkeeper boot the ball forward only to then see it blow back and over the crossbar. I have never seen that before or since in a professional game. I played left-midfield that night in what was a rough and ready Sunderland team packed full of characters. Richard Ord, Dave Bennett, Steve Agnew and

Craig Russell all started and they were good players. I might not have played too well but I was still looking forward to playing my part in helping to keep Sunderland up. Those hopes were dashed, however, just a couple of days later when it emerged that I had not been signed in time to beat the transfer deadline and was, therefore, not technically a Sunderland player. Worst of all, it meant I'd been ineligible to play at Barnsley – and the Football League were threatening to punish the club with a points deduction, which could have been a disaster for Sunderland and their fight for survival. I was distraught, even though none of it was my fault. An almighty cock-up had taken place and someone at Roker Park had failed to register my loan. I was later told the confusion was caused by Mick Buxton being sacked around about the same time as I got there, which meant there was all kinds going on at the club and that is why the paperwork was not submitted in time. I had been sitting around at the club for ages waiting for the deal to be finalised but, unbeknown to me, it never was. As far as I was concerned, I had signed the contract and then played at Barnsley. End of story. Peter Reid was then appointed and one of the first things he said to me was, 'I'm sorry but you can't play'. The following day the newspapers were full of how my playing at Barnsley could lead to Sunderland having points deducted. Apparently, there were a couple of precedents: Halifax Town had been deducted a point a few years earlier for fielding an unregistered player, while Mansfield Town, Aldershot, Newport County and Preston North End had all suffered a similar fate.

With Reidy saying I wasn't allowed to play until the League made a decision, I was left in limbo. Roy Evans had spoken to the Football Association and told me I could come back and train at Liverpool but not play. A few days later, a Football League Commission met in York and decided to fine Sunderland £2,500 but, most importantly, the club would not be deducted any points. It was a big relief for everyone at the club, who went on to stay up by finishing 20th. The sting in the tail for me, though, was that my registration could not be back-dated, meaning I could not play again for Sunderland that season. I was still in limbo. I asked Reidy what I should do and he just said, 'Stay up here with us and we can have a good look at you in training'. So, I opted to stay. It was a bad decision. I lived in the Royal County Hotel in Durham and it turned into a few weeks where I boozed seriously. I didn't know anyone, there was nothing to do and I ended up getting very low, which probably explains why I did so much boozing. Probably the worst part was that most of my boozing was on my own. That is not me. I am a social person and only really enjoy a drink when out with my mates. I knew drinking on my own was a bad sign but still kept doing it. I didn't cause anyone at Sunderland any trouble or anything like that but I must have been a picture of misery around the club. I wasn't much happier when I returned to Liverpool. While I had been away in the North East, Liverpool had invited me down to the League Cup final against Bolton. But, because I didn't feel part of it and was probably feeling a bit sorry for myself over how things had panned out at Sunderland, I decided not to go. I did go to the party back at Anfield later that night after the lads had won 2-1 thanks to two goals from Steve McManaman. But, again, I just felt like a spare part. A lot of my mates were in the team such as Macca, Jamie Redknapp, Robbie and Razor, and I was delighted for them all. I was also pleased Liverpool had won a trophy in Roy's first full season. But it was still difficult to celebrate with them while feeling so down about my own career. Eventually, I went back to Liverpool and came off the bench a few times, as well as starting against West Ham. But it failed to raise my spirits. During my career, I had never been the sort of player who made a big impact off the bench. It wasn't as if I was a striker, who could score a couple of goals to rescue a point. I was just a hard-working player who gave his all, not the type that managers usually turn to when in trouble during a game. It is probably why I must hold some sort of record for being an unused substitute during my days at Liverpool. I did come on as a substitute on the final day at home to Blackburn when they clinched the Premier League title thanks to Manchester United only drawing at West Ham. Kenny Dalglish had returned to football and was Blackburn manager, so I was really pleased for him. It had also been nice to get a bit of playing time, especially as we had won the game 2-1. But, even so, as I made my way on holiday a few days later I couldn't help but think it had been a wasted year for me. I'd become a bit-part player at Anfield and the loan move to Sunderland that was supposed to have kick-started my year had back-fired spectacularly through no fault of my own. The worst thing of all was that I had not seen it coming, mainly because of how good the previous season had been. It was awful and I let things get on top of me. And because I didn't have the maturity or experience to cope with such a major setback, I increasingly turned to drink.

Chapter 5

The Demon Drink

Looking back, I had started to get sucked into football's drinking culture almost from the moment I stepped up to the first-team. That first trip to Dublin in 1993 had been a real eye-opener and left me believing drinking was a big part of being a footballer. I had been out with some of the most seasoned boozers in football - lads like Steve Nicol, Jan Molby and Rushy – but managed to match them drink for drink, hence the nickname 'Hollow Legs' that I had been christened with on the trip. From then on, I just saw football and drinking as a natural pair. Certainly, that was the case at Anfield. Maybe it was because the season when I made my debut turned out to be such a disappointing one with results being poor and Graeme Souness leaving. It was a difficult year for everyone at the club, not least because we finished in our lowest league position for 30 years. I think the staff at Anfield had recognised it was going to be a long season even before a ball had been kicked. The team had aged and while there may have been a few young lads coming through, it was going to take time. The situation was probably made that bit harder by some of the older lads not wanting to pack in, even though their best years were behind them. Results were then poor so we got a bit of stick off the fans, mainly because they weren't used to it. For years, Liverpool had been challenging for every trophy. But now, it was no longer the case and we had become also-rans. It was difficult for the fans to adapt to and we were booed off regularly that season. That, in turn, brought even more pressure on to the team's shoulders and maybe that was why everyone went out so often. It would explain why even those who weren't big drinkers such as John Barnes would still come out with the lads to enjoy the social side.

Whatever the reason for the huge number of days and nights out, I was more than willing to join in with the socialising. There were not many days of the week when at least a few of us didn't go out in Liverpool, often ending up at the Continental Hotel. Even if there wasn't a big night out planned, I would still end up having a few pints with someone. Often, it was Ronnie Whelan. If I wasn't staying at Robbie Fowler's house, I would get a lift back to my Mum and Dad's with Ronnie, who lived nearby in Birkdale. He owned three pubs near Anfield so, after training had finished at 1pm, we would call in and have a game of pool so Ronnie could see how they were doing. Nearer home, we would then often stop for a game of snooker and I would have another couple of drinks. Before I knew it, I'd had half a dozen pints and was getting home to my Mum's and trying to eat my tea while half-cut. In my head, I saw the drinking as part of being a footballer. I realise now I shouldn't have thought like that but I did.

As much as we enjoyed going out any night of the week but Friday, Wednesday was always the big session for the lads. If we played that night, we'd go out straight after the game – win, lose or draw. But if we had no midweek game, we would start the boozing during the day and then end up at the Paradox, a nightclub near Aintree. It was a massive place and their busiest night was Wednesday, which suited us just fine. We took no prisoners and really went for it. Then, after getting in at 3am or even later, we would all be back in training at Melwood on Thursday morning. I look back now at those times and shudder. The modern-day footballer uses his day off very differently, mainly to rest and recuperate. But, to us, a day off was just an excuse to go out drinking and I would imagine most clubs were the same around that time.

As much as the couple of days we spent in Dublin had opened my eyes to the culture that existed at Liverpool, I think what really cemented the belief that football and drinking went together was our trip to South Africa at the end of my first season in the team. At the time, the only place I had been outside either Southport or Liverpool was to Italy on a few family holidays. My Dad's family were from a tiny village called Venafro and I'd really enjoyed our visits. But the prospect of going to South Africa was something else entirely. It was a really big deal, especially to the younger lads who made the trip such as me, Robbie, Ashley Neal – Phil's son - and a couple of others. The drinking began from the moment we got to the airport in England and never really stopped. In fact, during the ten days we spent in South Africa, I don't think either Steve Nicol or Razor were seen without a pint in their hands.

We stayed in Sun City and were told in no uncertain terms on arrival that we were not allowed to head out of the hotel without security, no matter where we were going. The main security guy was an old boxer and he followed us everywhere in this car that had a red light on top, as though he was someone from the Dukes of Hazard. He also carried a gun, which surprised a few of the boys. Thankfully, he didn't need it – even though we did end up being quite rowdy wherever we went. Steve Harkness was the only one who got in any real bother after diving into a fountain one night. The police were called but, thankfully, they let him off with a warning. In between the drinking, a few of us had some success with the ladies on that trip, too. By chance, loads of air hostesses were staying out there so, as you can imagine, there were a few fireworks.

The trip turned out to be one of the best for team-bonding that I ever went on and I loved every minute. The football wasn't bad, either. We might not have been the most sensible team in the world by going out drinking the night before a game that was due to be played in 100 degrees of heat. But we did okay. I scored in a 2-1 win over Aston Villa, while we also beat Cape Town Spurs 3-0 and drew 0-0 with the Kaizer Chiefs. Bizarrely, Lucas Radebe played in goal for Kaizer Chiefs that day. When I joined Leeds a few years later, I had to check I hadn't dreamt it – especially as by then he had become one of the best centre-halves in the Premier League. Sure enough, The Chief confirmed what I remembered and told me he had also been a centre-forward before moving to defence. Knowing Lucas as I do, I am sure he'll have been brilliant up front as well.

Mind, the sight of my future team-mate throwing himself around the goalmouth is not what I most remember from that trip to South Africa. Instead, it is the couple of meetings I was fortunate enough to have with Nelson Mandela. The first time I was introduced, I went to shake his hand and found myself stepping backwards. The aura that surrounds him had, somehow, knocked me off my stride. I am not religious or spiritual but I was in total awe of the man. There was just something about him. Mr Mandela was also very friendly and seemed to know his football. He told a few of us that he had played quite a bit when in prison on Robben Island. Later in the trip, we all met Mandela again when he came into our dressing room and thanked us for coming to South Africa. The security around him was phenomenal but he seemed like a normal guy.

Bruce Grobbelaar was on that trip to South Africa and, as you can no doubt imagine, he was in his element. He loved telling us about his days in Africa and all the things he had got up to. With most people, you'd have put some of his claims down to exaggeration. But not Bruce. We all believed he had done everything he said. Bruce was someone I enjoyed being around and that is why I found the match-fixing allegations that surfaced later about him so unbelievable. People ask me about the games he was supposed to have thrown because I was in the same dressing room at the time. One was at Newcastle in November, 1993, when we lost 3-0, just a couple of weeks after I'd made my debut. Another was a 3-3 draw with Manchester United at Anfield that had seen us come from three goals down to snatch a point through a diving header by Razor. Personally, I think it is almost impossible to fix a game. And knowing Bruce as I do, I just don't think he is the sort of character to get involved in something like that. I appreciate footage emerged at the time of the allegations, showing him saying certain things. But I just can't believe it happened. You only have to look at the games that the allegations were centred around to realise it just isn't possible. Newcastle hammered us at St James' Park and could, with steadier finishing, have scored five. And of the three goals they did score, no goalkeeper in the world could have stopped them. As good as Newcastle were, we could also have grabbed a couple of goals on the break. So, the score could easily have been 5-2 rather than 3-0. That is why I don't believe there is any way that a game can be fixed unless every single player on both teams is in on it. And no-one was, I can tell you that for sure. The same goes for the Manchester United game. I was on the bench that night and didn't get on. But even from the dugout, I could see that a night as dramatic as that could not be scripted. It would be impossible. Nigel Clough, who had received quite a bit of stick in the weeks before the United game because his move from Forest hadn't quite worked out, started the fightback with two goals before half-time. I roomed with Nigel for a time so I was delighted for him. Then, near the end, my good mate Razor bravely threw himself at a cross to equalise - and got clattered for his trouble. He was really groggy and asking, 'Who am I?' One of the lads said, 'Tell him he's Pele and see what he does next!'

When the accusations about Bruce were first published, the boys just turned it into a big joke. So did Bruce. We used to play three-card brag on the team coach and when Bruce lost, he would pay out in £50 notes. It was his way of having a bit of banter with us all. Bruce loved Liverpool Football Club. He had been there for a long time and was idolised by the fans. So to me, he just wouldn't have got involved in any match-fixing. I can't remember anyone asking him, certainly not in front of the squad at least. Mind, it would have been a brave man to confront Bruce about something like that. He was a tough, tough guy who had been in the Rhodesian Army for many years. Bruce was someone you didn't want to get on the wrong side of, on or off the pitch. I had a few bollockings off Bruce, some deserved and some not. But what I also recognised was just how important a big character like Bruce was to the spirit within our dressing room. He was certainly larger than life.

In those days, there were no speciality goalkeeping coaches at even the big clubs. So, Bruce would just train with the rest of us as an outfield player, which is probably why he was so good on the ball whenever he came dribbling out of the penalty area. He would tell us all, 'Give the ball to the Hound Dog,' which was his nickname for himself. He also had this bizarre ritual before every game, where he would boot the ball at the light switch to try and turn it off. Until he turned it off, we couldn't go out. Eventually, some of the lads would be saying things like, 'Come on Bruce, today would be nice'. But he was such a relaxed guy, he just kept going until the light was off. He was a crazy guy but a great one to have around the club.

By the time we'd got back from South Africa, I firmly believed that drinking was a perfectly normal part of life as a footballer and something to embrace rather than be frowned upon. From then on, pre-season became the biggest drink of the year for me. I would have gone away with my mates in the summer to the beach and always got stuck into the booze. But the drinking on those holidays was nothing compared to what happened when the Liverpool boys got back together. We would be drunk every night, all the way through pre-season. It sounds crazy, bearing in mind what football is like now. But, to us, that was just how it was. I was probably part of the last generation who thought boozing was acceptable in football. Certainly, those that came along a few years later were much more professional than anyone of my age group or above when it came to looking after their bodies.

One thing the excessive drinking that went on at Liverpool did ensure was that our Christmas parties were destined to go down in history. I can't imagine any other club threw a party like we did. They were complete free-for-alls. The boys looked forward to them so much that, once December had arrived, we started to tick the days off in the dressing room, almost like an Advent calendar. In my first few years, the parties were always fancy dress. Some took it very seriously. Robbie Fowler, for instance, would spend months choosing his costume, while Razor came one year in two outfits. The first was as a famous King, whose name escapes me. Then, underneath, he had a Manchester United shirt with 'Cuntona' written on the back of it and a number '7'. We enjoyed that one, though I am not sure Eric would have done had news of Razor's costume leaked out. It would have certainly added extra spice to the next Liverpool v Manchester United game, that's for sure! Thankfully, there were no camera phones or anything like that around in the mid-1990s so, apart from those of us at the party, no-one was ever any the wiser. A few of the other lads' fancy dress efforts stood out with Don Hutchison coming one year as a really impressive Scouser, complete with curly wig and 'tache. As for me, I played it safe – going as low-key as possible. I was there for the drinking and the girls, not to dress up. One year, I even went as one of the Three Musketeers, which meant I definitely blended in to the crowd.

For the parties, a venue would have been hired months in advance and then, once the night came round, the guests would be queuing all the way down the street to get in. Well, I say 'guests'. We had a very simple door policy, no blokes and plenty of birds. It meant the club would be packed full of 500 women and 30 professional footballers, which was just how we liked it! Most of the boys were single as well, which really helped get the party started. Restricting entry to just the girls meant nothing ever turned nasty inside, or at least that's what we told ourselves to justify it. As part of the entertainment, the first year professionals would all have to sing a song on stage. When it was my turn, I chose 'There she was, just a walking down the street' – mainly because I knew it was so catchy that everyone would not be able to resist joining in, in the process drowning out my less than tuneful efforts. That is exactly what happened – though it didn't stop me getting swilled in beer by the senior lads at the end. No-one was safe from a good swilling, either. One year, I smuggled in a couple of my mates and, for months afterwards, they would be saying to me, 'I can't believe I swilled John Barnes in lager on that night out with you'. It was mad.

Some years, one of the young lads would have to service one of the strippers. Razor used to try and orchestrate it, picking out the poor young lad. I am glad to say I never got picked and I'm not saying who did each year but, over time, it became almost a tradition. Some were keener than others. I'll never forget looking up on stage one year, for example, and seeing one of the young lads banging the stripper with another of the players having stuck his finger up his arse. This poor young lad thought it was another bird and was loving it. Again, no names. But you know who you are! Another tradition that developed down the years was an 'Egg of the Year' award for the thickest person at the club. I think Rob Jones and Jason McAteer shared that every year.

The amount of booze we stuck away at the parties was enough to sink a battleship, even though usually the boys would have been out all day beforehand. A typical Christmas Party day would start for me and Razor at about 10am with a full English breakfast, complete with champagne, at our local, The Grapes in Formby. We would then get a taxi into town, have a few drinks and then head to the venue. The night would then only end about 4-5am. One year, the manager arranged a training session for the following morning – meaning a couple of the lads turned up still wearing their fancy dress costumes from the night before. So, we all knew what they had been up to!

Towards the end of my time at Liverpool, the parties had started to be toned down. Part of the reason was that a couple of the lads got 'done' one year when a camera was sneaked in by a girl, who had been paid by one of the tabloids. The photos duly appeared a couple of days later, though because everyone was in fancy dress there was no way the 'paper in question could be certain of who was who. Instead, the caption to the photos would read something like 'Ronald McDonald seen here with a blonde' and 'The Hunchback of Notre Dame kisses a brunette'. We had a good laugh about that in the dressing room, especially those lads who had managed to keep their identity secret courtesy of being in fancy dress. It did make the boys a lot warier, though. I suppose we should have learned from what had happened to Don Hutchison a couple of years earlier. He was a good player and a decent lad. But he ended up getting bombed out of Liverpool after over-stepping the mark once too often. We'd all been out for the day but Hutch, unfortunately, took it to the next level by a dropping his trousers in front of some students and putting a Budwesier label over his knob. One of the girls took a photo and, a couple of days later, it appeared in the newspapers. Roy Evans went ballistic and the next thing we knew, Hutch was on his way.

Footballers had became like pop stars when the money started to go up, so the 'papers wanted scandal. It meant the days of the old-style

Liverpool Christmas party were coming to an end. What finally killed them off was Gerard Houllier being appointed manager in 1998. He wasn't keen at all, probably because he didn't like parties. One year, he stopped Stevie Gerrard from going – which I didn't agree with. It was one day a year when the whole squad got together and Stevie was part of the squad.

You can't have the parties nowadays as there is too much chance of it getting in the 'papers. I remember one players' night out at Christmas after I had moved to Leeds when Robbie Fowler was photographed asleep in the front of a taxi and it made the front pages. I was in the same taxi and we had stopped at a petrol station, where this photographer jumped out and started taking a few shots. We'd got dressed up in fancy dress but there had been no bother or anything like that. But Robbie sitting in a car asleep still became big news. It made me think just what would have happened had any of those Liverpool parties found their way into the headlines.

Times have changed and if Liverpool held one now that was attended by 30 or 40 international players, how many of the girls outside would be being paid by *The Sun* or one of the other tabloids for snippets of information? There would be no way of knowing and that is why a party these days would just be too dangerous, as Manchester United found out a couple of years ago when they were splashed all over the front pages after their own 'do'. Plus, the whole culture surrounding football has changed – and for the better. I certainly can't imagine any footballer hitting the booze as badly as I did during those first few years at Liverpool. I particularly cringe when I think about how I was in the summer of 1995 as I moped around wondering what was going to happen to my career after such a disappointing season. My experience at Sunderland had left me crushed and I spent most of my time getting leathered. My career felt to be stalling and I didn't know which way it was going. I didn't know if Liverpool still wanted me or whether I would have to move on. I was just about to move out of my parents in Ainsdale as well. I'd lived there since I was four so it was a big thing to leave and it proved to be a big mistake. Robbie had moved house a couple of years earlier but, crucially, his family had gone with him. So he still had them around, whereas I was suddenly in this big house on my own. I have no idea why I chose to move out on my own, it was probably something I felt I had to do. But it didn't help my situation and I felt totally lost during that summer, hence why I drank so much I suppose. That may sound like I was failing to realise how fortunate I was to be able to afford a big house. But, a big house is no fun when it is completely empty. In the end, I was going out for going out's sake.

Once the 1995-96 season started, I did hope I could turn myself around. However, after starting the first two games, I developed problems with my ankle and was out for so long that I only made five appearances – the first two games and three near the end. And back then, being injured basically meant you had a licence to drink. All the injured lads drank more because they didn't have to play at the weekend, we weren't savvy enough to realise the damage that the drinking was doing. It slows down the healing process. Knowing what I do today, I can't believe I was so reckless. It is cringe worthy. In fact, I look back on the drinking I did during my entire career with a sense of regret. Don't get me wrong, I enjoyed every minute of those nights out and trips away with the lads. But I'll also never really know whether I fulfilled my potential or not. Sure, I had a good career and got to play for some great clubs. But, could I have achieved more with the talent I had? It is a question I often ask myself and one I'll never truly be able to answer because of how much time I used to spend with a drink in my hand.

Chapter 6

Three Lions

Considering the amount of socialising I did during my career, it is perhaps not a surprise to anyone that drink featured prominently throughout my involvement with England. The Toulon Tournament in 1994 turned out to be pretty typical of my time with the Three Lions set-up, coming as it did straight after the boozy end-of-season trip Liverpool had just had to South Africa. Robbie Fowler was also in the Under-21s squad so we flew together straight to the south of France, still feeling hungover from the effects of ten days' drinking with the Liverpool lads. So, what did we do to try and feel better? Yes, that's right, we hit the booze! By the time the plane landed in France, we were both steaming. Again, crazy behaviour and, by the standards of today, totally unprofessional. But that was how it was.

I had been named in the squad for Toulon by Dave Sexton towards the end of the domestic season. It was my first call-up at that level, though I had been involved with the England Youth set-up. I'd been part of several training squads and been on the bench when the Under-19s played Turkey at Wycombe Wanderers a couple of years earlier. But a call-up for the Toulon Tournament, which England had won three times in the previous four years, was something else – even to a Scot like myself! I was actually qualified to play for three countries: Scotland through my place of birth, England because of where my Mum was born and Italy due to Dad's family. That isn't to say I had the chance to play for all three. Far from it, in fact. For a start, I doubt anyone in Italy had ever heard of me, never mind seen me play. Also, Scotland never once got in touch with either me or Liverpool to ask whether I would be interested in representing them. That was something I couldn't understand, particularly when I broke through into the first-team at Anfield. All the yearbooks correctly stated I was born in Dumfries and there were more than a few times when I wondered what I had done wrong. My first kit as a kid had been a Scotland one and, even though my family had moved south when I was four, I still considered myself

Scottish. And yet they weren't interested in me. I did try to find out via the staff at Liverpool if Scotland had ever asked after me and the answer came back 'no'. So, when England came in there really wasn't a decision to make – a point I tried to get across when I first joined up with the Scotland squad in 2000 and some members of the Press were making me out to be some sort of turncoat.

Anyway, back to England and the Under-21s tournament in Toulon. I had a ball, on and off the pitch, and consider those few weeks in France to be among the best in my life. After touching down feeling the worse for wear, me and Robbie headed to the team hotel to meet up with the rest of the lads. What a great bunch of characters they were. Jamie Redknapp had also been selected from Liverpool. From London, there was Sol Campbell, Ray Parlour, Trevor Sinclair and Bruce Dyer, every one of them great lads. Chris Makin of Oldham Athletic and later Sunderland was also in the squad along with a great guy called Alan Nicholls, who tragically died in a motorbike accident the following year. We became really tight as a group and had a great laugh, with booze playing a big part in our fun. In fact, I would go as far as to say we had an absolute ball. What can be better than playing for international football in the south of France with the sun blazing down and all your mates around?

We were drawn in a group with France, Russia and the United States so knew it was going to be tough, especially against the hosts who were building a bit of a reputation at that age group. Our first game was against Russia and we won 2-0 thanks to a goal from Trevor Sinclair and a Chris Bart-Williams penalty. I wasn't involved other than being on the bench but I did come on for Crystal Palace's Dean Gordon during the second game against France, worse luck! Bixente Lizarazu and Lilian Thuram, who between them would go on to win almost 250 senior caps plus the World Cup and European Championships, were in the French side as we were given the total run-around in a 3-0 defeat. I felt pretty deflated afterwards because, as international debuts go, it couldn't have gone much worse. As a result, I didn't fancy my chances of being involved in the final group game against and the U.S. Sure enough, Dave Sexton stuck with pretty much the same starting XI and the lads rewarded his faith with a 3-0 win thanks to goals from Robbie, Jamie and Bruce Dyer. It meant we were through to the semi-finals, where we were paired with Belgium as France played Portugal. Again, I wasn't overly confident of playing but this time Dave decided to put me in the team. I was in midfield with Jamie and Ray Parlour, while Trevor Sinclair was to push forward to join an attack of Bruce Dyer and Chris Bart-Williams, who had come in for Robbie. Bruce was our main striker, which may sound strange considering the comparative careers him and Robbie went on to have, but he really did have a good tournament that year in France. He scored again in the semi-final as we beat Belgium 2-1, Sol getting the other on a day when our bus broke down in the middle of nowhere on the way to the game. The wind also whipped up a bit of a sandstorm that left the pitch covered so the conditions weren't ideal. But, such was the strong spirit in the team that we just laughed at our bad luck and produced a really professional display. I was pleased with my own contribution, especially as I'd been involved in the move that led to our first goal on five minutes when Sol converted my cross. Beating the Belgians meant I was also through to the first – and, as it turned out, only – final of my career. I was desperate to retain my place. So, what did I do to ensure I was in peak condition for what at the time was the biggest game of my career? Yes, that's right. I went on an almighty bender with the rest of the lads on the day before the final!

It had started after Dave Sexton had sent us down to the beach to chill-out during the afternoon. He didn't want us hanging around the hotel and getting nervous, so thought a bit of relaxation couldn't do any harm. We arrived fully intending to do just that. Unfortunately, after choosing a table where we could watch the world go by, we then spotted a group of lads enjoying a few cold beers. Ray Parlour was the first to break. "Anyone fancy a beer?" Straight away, everyone said 'yes' and that was the start of an amazing session. The usual suspects were present – me, Robbie, Ray, Jamie, Alan Nicholls, Chris Makin – and we spent the rest of the afternoon enjoying a proper session in the sunshine. Eventually, as the sun started to go down, we decided it would be best to head back to the hotel. We did have a big game on! The problem was no-one wanted to stop drinking so, as we arrived at the hotel, I suggested everyone come back to me and Robbie's room to carry on the party. Once again, no-one needed asking twice. We ordered three cases of Heineken and off we went. Before long, what felt like the entire squad were in my room drinking and smoking, and having a great time. I don't know if we were particularly loud or what but word soon got back to the coaching staff. Suddenly, Ray Wilkins, who was Dave Sexton's assistant, walked in to what by then was a scene of total devastation. I had a fag in my mouth, Alan Nicholls had about five on the go and people were strewn around the room in various states. I was one of the first to spot Ray and immediately thought, 'Shit, this is me out of the final'. I was expecting the mother and father of all bollockings but, instead, Ray just calmly sat down and cracked open a beer. He then said, 'Right lads, you've clearly all had a good day. But if you pack it in now, I won't tell the gaffer'. With that, we all sobered up on the spot. Everyone put down their drink and left. It was brilliant man-management from Ray and the perfect way to deal with the situation. If he had come in and had a go, maybe things wouldn't have ended so well. Instead, everyone headed back to their rooms and, as far as I know, the manager was none the wiser. It also meant the same team was named for the final, so I was in. Even better, Portugal had somehow beaten France in the other semi-final - which came as a big relief to us all after the pummelling we'd been given in the group stage.

We went on to annihilate the Portuguese with Trevor opening the scoring almost straight after half-time and Bruce adding a second five minutes later. I was again in a three-man midfield and we bossed the game. There was no way they could complain about the 2-0 scoreline as being unjust. The only disappointment for me was that Robbie hadn't played in the final. We'd been in such control that the manager didn't make any substitutions, meaning Robbie remained on the bench. It felt a bit weird, to be honest, for me to be in the team and Robbie not, especially as ever since the age of ten he had been the one who was clearly destined to make it. Robbie being Robbie, though, he never complained. He knew Bruce, who scored five goals in that tournament, was on fire and had to start. Robbie may have been disappointed not to get on in the final but that didn't stop him joining in the celebrations. It turned into a mad night with Ray Parlour even surfing on the roof of a car at one stage as it travelled down the road. We also thought it would be a good idea to jump on to these big, posh boats in the harbour – though it nearly back-fired badly as, on one of them, a guard dog leapt up to chase us off. Nowadays, that sort of behaviour would be all over the newspapers and the players involved would get into big trouble back at their clubs. But it was just a case of young lads letting off a bit of steam. Plus, if you look at that squad, I bet there won't be many who didn't go on to have good careers so it can't have done us all that much harm in the long-run.

Winning a tournament like Toulon was a big thing back then, particularly as it was more or less a mini-European Championship with so many good teams taking part. Our victory over Portugal meant it was a very proud squad that flew back to England the following day. On a personal level, I'd been pleased with my contribution. My debut against France had not been the best introduction but I'd started both the semi-final and the final so hoped it was the start of a long career in international football. I also presumed the door had finally been closed on Scotland through me playing for England in Toulon. That was a shame, though not something that was my fault as I'd waited and waited for Scotland to come calling but they never had. What I didn't realise was that Toulon is not an official UEFA tournament, meaning the games are not technically competitive ones. And, as I found out later, it is only a competitive match that ties a player to one country – which is why six years later I was able to realise my ambition of playing for Scotland.

What I also didn't realise as I left France with the Under-21s was that my next involvement in the England set-up would be two years away. There were a couple of reasons for that, namely I injured my ankle in the first few months of the 1994-95 season and then, once fit, I couldn't get back in the Liverpool team. And without playing first-team football, there was no way England Under-21s were going to select me. That continued to be the case throughout most of the following season, so much so I only made five appearances in the Premier League. The upshot of all that time on the sidelines was that, by the time Euro '96 came round, I was nowhere near the England set-up. Robbie, Macca and Jamie were in the senior squad, though, so as they drank spirits in dentist's chairs in Hong Kong and wrecked Cathay Pacific planes (only joking lads!), I headed to Rhodes with a few mates from Southport. A good friend of ours was living in Falaraki and it seemed as good a place as any to watch Euro '96. We ended up having a ball out there and even dressed up as footballers, complete with shinpads, to watch a couple of England games. The atmosphere was brilliant with 'Three Lions' by Baddiel and Skinner being sung in every bar. There was a real holiday vibe and a couple of the lads even had dodgy Three Lions tattoos done. I'm glad I didn't join in. Can you imagine the stick I would have got four years later getting changed in the Scotland dressing room with an England tattoo on my chest? I wouldn't have got out alive and the

Scottish Press really would have had some ammunition to hit me with. I enjoyed watching the games. Not having had a sniff of being involved with the Under-21s since two years earlier meant I wasn't sitting there thinking, 'That should be me'. There were no regrets about not being involved, more a wish that my injury problems would clear up and allow me an extended run in the Liverpool first-team. So, with International football not on my radar, I just enjoyed watching Euro '96 as a fan. The only game where I felt a bit strange was Scotland v England at Wembley. The best way to describe my feelings watching on television in Falaraki is 'confused'. I had played for England but, deep down, felt Scottish and I still couldn't understand why they had never been in touch. I also copped for a lot of banter before, during and after the game from my mates. I was being called 'turncoat' for being born in Scotland and playing for England. Just to add to the confusion, I'd supported Scotland (sorry Robbie!) so was gutted when Gary McAllister missed the penalty and Gazza went up the other end to score 'that' goal. Defeat meant the Scots were as good as out so I then cheered for England for the rest of the tournament. England did brilliantly and deserved to win Euro '96. I thought they would as well so when the Germans won on penalties in the semi-final I was as distraught as everyone else. What I could never have imagined watching Gareth Southgate miss the crucial spotkick is that just three months later, I would be in the full England squad.

Glenn Hoddle's appointment was the reason for that. Glenn had replaced Terry Venables and, as all managers want to do, he was keen to stamp his own mark on the squad. I didn't know at the time but Glenn had tried to sign me on loan a few years earlier. I was 18 and still in the reserves at Anfield. Glenn was manager of Swindon Town and, unbeknown to me, came to watch me with his assistant John Gorman. Roy Evans later told *The Kop*, the Liverpool club newspaper, that Glenn's interest was one of 30 loan enquiries he'd had for me along with a £1m bid from Leeds United which had been made in 1995. After succeeding Glenn, John made another bid to take me to Swindon but was again turned down. So, it meant I was highly thought of by the two men now in charge of the England senior side. I didn't realise this until Glenn first got in touch after taking over from Terry. He said: "I want you involved." I'd started playing sweeper at Liverpool by then and Glenn wanted England to play a similar formation with three centre-halves. He wanted someone to get on the ball in the middle and start attacks from the back, just as he had done in the final years of his career. And he thought I could do it. I'll admit I was stunned at what I was hearing. I'd only been back in the Liverpool side a few weeks and yet here was the England manager saying I was an important part of his plans. To say I was chuffed is a massive understatement.

Even so, I still couldn't believe it was true and that I was wanted by the England manager. Even when Harry Harris wrote in the *Daily Mirror* about how pleased John Gorman had been with my performance in a 2-1 win against West Ham, I still refused to believe I was going to be called up. Harris had written: "A perfectly crafted move that lasted almost two minutes and involved 15 passes ended in Michael Thomas scoring the winning goal that keeps Liverpool on top of the Premiership. But for the watching England No 2 John Gorman, the most pleasing performance came from the emerging talent of central defender Dominic Matteo. Glenn Hoddle witnessed the player who has been dubbed 'Anfield's Alan Hansen of the 90s' destroy Chelsea 5-1 and yesterday he sent his right-hand man to Upton Park for a progress report before the England squad get together for the World Cup qualifier against Poland at Wembley. Matteo may not be as spectacular as Patrik Berger, and he may not have been given as much room by West Ham as he was at Chelsea, but he's certainly the jewel in Liverpool's crown at the moment. Even without Mark Wright, who is recovering from a fractured cheekbone, Matteo has given Liverpool a new dimension at the back that Hoddle believes will be a central part of England's future." Glowing stuff! Even so, I still wasn't really expecting to be in the squad to face Poland at Wembley as England's home qualifying campaign for the 1998 World Cup got under way. But, sure enough, when the 23 names were announced a few days before the October 9 fixture, mine was one of them. I was the only new call-up, though David James was still waiting for his senior debut and David Beckham had just one cap to his name. There was no doubt whose selection had caused the biggest stir, though, and it was Paul Merson. Less than two years earlier, Merse had tearfully admitted to the problems he'd been having with alcohol, gambling and drugs. So, the recall of a now clean Merse was big news and all the newspapers wanted to write about him. That suited me fine as I was able to slip under the radar. I did speak to a few of the Press lads and mumbled a few replies nervously but I clearly didn't say anything interesting as none of it appeared on the following morning's back pages.

I may have avoided the spotlight in terms of the media but, unfortunately, my late arrival at the team hotel with the other Liverpool lads didn't pass unnoticed by the manager. Me, Robbie, David James, Macca and Jamie had all been picked up in Liverpool and then driven down to where the squad were staying at Burnham Beeches. The only problem was that the lads had become used to having a few drinks on the way down so persuaded the two drivers to stop off on the way. I didn't know any better and just went along with it. By the time we got to the hotel, we were quite drunk. We also arrived late, which didn't go down too well. To make matters worse, once we got to the hotel the first thing we did was head straight for the bar to join the rest of the lads. I realise now I should have been stronger, particularly on the journey south from Liverpool, though in my defence drinking had become such an established part of being a footballer that I didn't see what I was doing wrong. Glenn did, though, and he pulled me before training the following day and said, 'What are you playing at? Top international players do not behave like this – learn that fast'. I felt bad and couldn't believe I'd been so stupid. The other Liverpool lads were all established internationals but I was the new boy and supposed to be creating a good impression. Instead, I had done the exact opposite. I had let myself down. Maybe, it was another case of me being easily led. I was in a car with a few of the lads and just went along with them. Don't get me wrong, I enjoyed myself and had my usual great time out with the boys. But it was pretty daft to stop off at four or five pubs and have a drink on my way to meeting up with the England senior squad for the first time. With hindsight, I should have stuck to Coca-Cola or another soft drink. But I didn't and that is a regret. I had got myself on the wrong side of Glenn, who was a modern-thinking manager, who it soon became clear, wanted to move the England squad forward without a drink culture. Glenn had played abroad so knew how much more professional English footballers could be. I think he realised all the Liverpool lads liked a drink and maybe that was why we didn't get too many games under Glenn. Certainly, the Manchester United lads weren't involved in the drinking culture and they played a hell of a lot more games than us. I might be wrong but I have always thought that could have been a factor.

One thing I did notice from that first England get-together was how all the United lads stuck together. They would eat on the same table, hang around in their own group and even walk on to the training pitch together. They were probably so close at Old Trafford that it seemed natural. But I still found it a bit strange how aloof they could be, especially as all the lads from the other clubs mixed in really well. The staff tried to make us mingle more as a group but it never really happened, maybe because the Manchester United and Liverpool lads didn't really get on. In the end, the staff realised they were fighting a losing battle and left it as it was.

My first meeting with Glenn as a member of the senior squad may have been a bit of a disaster but I did enjoy working with him. I loved the training, which was very technical. I particularly enjoyed Glenn wanting us to bring the ball out of defence, which is how we had increasingly started to play at Anfield.

The first thing I detected was how the standard was a step-up from club level. I was nervous at the start because the eyes are always on someone new. It means the pressure is on a little, which is something I'd not felt at Liverpool since I had first broken into the team. I was also playing with some of the best players in the world and that was a bit daunting, especially at first. What probably helped me settle, though, was how welcoming all the players were. Gazza, in particular, was great to me. I can't say we hung around loads as he had people he knocked about within the squad. But we did play quite a bit of three-card brag, which helped pass the time. All the down-time we had was the big negative I quickly noticed about international football. We would train in the morning and then have all this free time on our hands. Some would go off golfing, but I am not a golfer. Gazza and David Seaman would go off fishing but, again, that wasn't for me. So, what I ended up doing was going for a few pints in the local town with a couple of the lads. Again, I don't know what I was thinking but I can't imagine Glenn having been amused if he had found out. I look back now and wish I'd got into golf as I think my career would have been a lot more successful.

In that respect, I look at someone like David Beckham and have full admiration for how he has conducted himself. That Poland game was only the second senior squad David had been involved in but he was already doing everything right off the pitch. He would come on the odd night out but nothing like as many as the rest of us. David just loved his football and was determined to give himself the best chance possible by acting professionally. As a result, he went on to have a fantastic career. When I speak to young kids today, I always point out how David

Beckham and Paul Scholes looked after themselves. They may have had a few nights out as young lads but had quickly learned their lesson. I didn't and it hampered my career, especially in terms of recovering from injuries. My basic rule of thumb until the very end of my career was that if I was free, I'd go out for a beer - whereas the really good professionals would rest up at home.

Another thing I noticed from the very first moment I joined up with England was how good the team spirit was. This was probably to be expected after how well England had done in Euro '96 and Glenn's first game against Moldova having ended in a 3-0 victory. It meant confidence was high ahead of the Poles' visit to Wembley. I wasn't expecting to play and wasn't even named among the substitutes. But I still got a real thrill from sitting at Wembley as a member of the England squad. I remember looking around as the game kicked off in front of a full house and thinking, 'I must be doing something right to be here'. England went on to win 2-1 and go top of the early Group Two table. As we went our separate ways afterwards, I thought the manager might say a few things or wish us all the best individually. But he didn't say a word to me, which I was a bit worried about on my way back to Liverpool. I knew, deep down, I had let myself down when arriving late after a few beers and hoped that hadn't spelt the end for me with England. Thankfully, it didn't and I was named in the squad for the next home qualifier against Italy in February. I'd missed the trip to Georgia that had resulted in a 2-0 win three months earlier through injury so it came as a big relief to hear I had been called up again. This time, I vowed to be more professional and knuckle down. I wasn't expecting to be involved but I wanted to create a much better impression. England went on to lose 1-0 as I watched from the old Royal Box at Wembley on a night that would, due to Scotland manager Craig Brown being at the game, lead eventually to me switching allegiances. But, as I headed back to Liverpool after the defeat, I did so believing my first England cap might not be too far away. Glenn had been very encouraging in training and I got the impression he might be prepared to give me a chance in the following month's friendly with Mexico. Sure enough, a week or so before the game, Glenn rang and said, 'Dom, you are definitely playing'. He explained how I would be starting in a three-man defence to see how I got on and that was my opportunity to stake a claim. The match couldn't come round quick enough. All I had to do was get through

Liverpool's home game against Coventry City unscathed and I would be ready to make my international debut at Wembley. It was the stuff dreams are made of. This being me, though, nothing runs smoothly and, through no fault of my own, I got injured against Coventry when I caught the bottom of Dion Dublin's boot. There was nothing malicious in the challenge, I just caught the bottom of his blades. But I knew I was in trouble straight away. I played on and did finish the game, though I needed patching up at half-time. The problem was that the blades had opened up my leg and this huge gash was bleeding like mad. I kept touching the bottom of my sock during the game and it was soaked with blood. Afterwards, it started bleeding again and I had to have 18 stitches in the wound. As he did the repair job, the doctor said I couldn't play for at least a week – meaning I was out of the England game. I had to ring the England staff straight away and tell them the bad news. I was absolutely gutted because this was supposed to be my big chance and now it was gone.

Looking back, missing that friendly against Mexico was probably the turning point for me and England. I was still selected for another half a dozen squads but I always seemed to arrive at the team hotel carrying some form of injury. My knee was the main problem and Liverpool wanted me to rest during the international breaks. Roy Evans never told me not to join up with England but he would say things like, 'Come back okay, Dom, as I need you a week on Saturday'. Liverpool were paying my wages and I didn't want to let them down. I also realised that if I came back from England duty injured, chances are I would be out of the team at Anfield because the competition for places was so fierce. I didn't want to risk that. I'd experienced enough of being on the sidelines with Liverpool to last me a lifetime so was desperate to avoid going back to that kind of existence. I had been in and out of the team so much that I knew how soul-destroying it could be.

To be fair to Glenn, though, he continued to encourage me. I think he took it as a big positive that I kept turning up for England duty even when I was injured. It showed I was keen and Glenn seemed to like that. Glenn would keep telling me that he still saw me as the middle man in a back three and that I had a chance of making the 1998 World Cup in France. That really gave me a lift. Unfortunately, every time I thought I was getting closer to playing, I would suffer an injury. They were never serious ones, just the annoying niggling variety that were enough to keep a player out for a couple of weeks – which in my case always seemed to be when England were playing. In fact, I don't think I turned up for one squad feeling 100 per cent fit and that just about sums up my luck.

In the end, the friendly with Mexico towards the end of the 1996-97 season turned out to be the closest I came to playing for England. I wasn't involved in the squad for the game in Rome when a brilliant team display earned a goalless draw and a place in the World Cup. But, early in 1998, Glenn again opened the door for me by ensuring I was named in the England B side to face Chile at The Hawthorns. It was the first time the B team had played in four years and was Glenn's way of seeing if any of us were ready for the step-up. Peter Taylor, the Under-21s manager, was in charge and he named me in defence. Paul Merson, Emile Heskey, Ray Parlour and Keiron Dyer were also in the starting line-up but, although we had plenty of possession, we never really clicked and lost 2-1. Even so, Glenn persevered and the following month I was named as an over-age player in the Under-21s side to face Switzerland. Again, I was in a back three – this time with Jamie Redknapp and John Curtis of Manchester United – as we lost 2-0. I felt I'd done okay, a view that Glenn must have shared as I was immediately called up to the senior side for the following night's game. I'd played 71 minutes for the Under-21s but readily agreed, hoping that with the World Cup less than three months away that this would be when I finally made the breakthrough. I was named on the bench but, unfortunately, again didn't get on and it was then that I thought time was running out. A few weeks later, though, I was named in a provisional 34-man squad to face Portugal at the end of April. I was one of three uncapped players in the squad, Ray Parlour and Sheffield Wednesday goalkeeper Kevin Pressman being the others, and thought my chances of getting a run-out were slim. So it proved with Glenn later naming a 28-man squad to take to La Manga in Spain for a final training camp before whittling the numbers down to a final 23. Dion Dublin, Andy Hinchliffe, Phil Neville, Ian Walker and, most famously of all, Paul Gascoigne were the ones dumped in Spain, which must have been awful for all five of them. I hadn't made the cut for La Manga and that was disappointing enough. But to spend an extra few weeks training with the rest of the lads before hearing you wouldn't be going to the World Cup, which is the pinnacle of any professional's career, must have been hard to bear. In my case, I hadn't been surprised not to make the La Manga trip. Glenn had done his best and waited as long as he could. But injuries and bad luck on my part meant I hadn't done anywhere near enough to be included. So, I watched the World Cup on television as my Liverpool team-mate Michael Owen became an overnight sensation with 'that' goal against Argentina. I was delighted for Michael as he had proved himself to be a smashing lad at Anfield. But, on a personal level, watching the games on television was hard. All I could think was, 'I should be there'. Scotland, the country of my birth who I had been desperate to get in touch, had qualified and were also in my thoughts. I wanted so badly to be in France as part of the World Cup but, instead, I was in a pub in England with my mates. The feeling compared to watching Euro '96 was totally different. Two years earlier, I'd been nowhere near the England set-up under Terry Venables. But now I'd had a taste and not been able to make it happen for me. As a result, I didn't enjoy watching the games at all and was glad when the 1998 World Cup was over.

After that, I dropped off England's radar completely and never received another call-up. To be fair, I'd probably given up on England by then anyway. I just felt it wasn't going to happen. Glenn's sacking in 1999 merely confirmed that to be right. As a manager, he's shown tremendous belief in me – far more, I think, than anyone else would have. So, with Glenn gone, that was that as far as England were concerned. I felt sorry for Glenn when the end came because he was sacked for non-footballing reasons. The Press seemed to have it in for him and, eventually, got their way. He shouldn't have said what he did about the disabled, the offence that got him the sack. But the Press also made out Glenn to be this weird character and that just wasn't the case. Employing Eileen Drewery, the faith-healer, may have been unusual and I know a lot of the lads treated it as a bit of a joke, particularly Ray Parlour who, after she put her hands on his head, asked for a short back and sides. Thankfully, I was never put in that position – probably because Glenn had given up on me by the time Eileen had become a fixture in the England set-up. But that's all it was, a bit of a joke. Glenn was still respected as the manager and he'd shown his ability by leading England to the World Cup in first place from a group including Italy. Unfortunately, the Football Association lost sight of that and insisted Glenn had to go. And with him, went any hopes I had of playing for England.

Chapter 7

Spice Boys

When the history of the FA Cup final comes to be written, all manner of epic games, heroic deeds and dramatic games will feature. Plus, one infamous set of white suits. Never has so much damage been done to a team's reputation than by what we chose to wear for the 1996 FA Cup final against Manchester United at Wembley. David James was the culprit, having modelled for Armani a few months earlier, he assured us all he had a contact who could sort us out with some smart suits. The designer came up with white, which was about as far removed from a traditional Cup final suit as was possible. Seemingly, this bloke had been told that it was often a sunny day for the final so opted for a colour that would be appropriate. In that respect, he was right as it was a really hot day. Unfortunately, what this designer got very, very wrong was with his choice of white as the colour. At first, when the suits arrived, the lads thought Jamo was joking. To me, they looked a bit naff. Not only that, but I knew getting a pair of shoes to match was going to be a nightmare. But, along with the rest of the lads, I treated the choice as a bit of a laugh – once the shock had worn off, at least. Unfortunately, after we had lost at Wembley to a late Eric Cantona goal, no-one else saw the funny side and we got absolutely slaughtered. The Press, in particular, had a field day and laid into us. It hadn't helped that we were sponsored by Ray-Ban at the time, so had all turned up in shades and these ridiculous suits. We really should have seen it coming as all we had done was give the critics ammunition if we lost, which of course we did. All sorts were said about us, from being too big for our boots to a team that was more concerned with swanning round like playboys than playing football. None of it was true, as anyone who had been in our dressing room at Wembley would have known. The scene was one of total devastation. But, in terms of Liverpool's reputation, the damage was done. The Spice Boys had been born.

Now, I have no idea what a 'Spice Boy' is. None whatsoever. But, whatever it is, after the Cup final we had all suddenly become one. And it was all down to those suits. I still have mine at home, though I can honestly say it has never been out of the wardrobe since Wembley – and not just because it would probably be bit tight around my backside these days. No, I don't like that suit because it set in motion a way of thinking that still surrounds that Liverpool team today. Fans still come up to me and say we lost the Cup final because of it, which is plainly nonsense. Do people really believe that we didn't perform in our biggest game of the season because of what we wore on the bus to Wembley? I do concede, though, that they were a big mistake. We made a rod for our own backs by turning up wearing white and the fans soon followed the Press' lead by starting to believe all this nonsense about the 'Spice Boys'. They seemed to think we spent all our time at film premieres in Leicester Square or clubbing in the West End. In truth, there were a handful of the lads who did go down to London after a game when we had the weekend off. Jamie Redknapp, Jason McAteer, John Scales and Phil Babb were the ones who spent their time driving round London in limos every weekend and that's fair enough. But there is no way people like me and Razor were up for any of that. We just didn't fancy nights out in London. Nor did Robbie Fowler, who preferred to stay in Liverpool. Steve McManaman was the same. The trendy wine bars just weren't for us and neither were the poncey clubs. I went a couple of times but didn't really enjoy it, even though Jamie knew everyone in London so could get us all into whatever club we wanted. There were also plenty of women flying around and those four never went short. All of them thought they were God's gift to women back then, which they probably were. They were all good-looking lads – well, three of them were as all McAteer had was the banter! But, from what we heard, they all had a very good strike record with the women in London. So, in that respect, maybe they were a bit Spice Boy-esque. The problem was that every single member of the squad was tarred with the same brush, which always used to rile me and Razor. We didn't want any part of the London scene and instead preferred going to our local boozer in Formby, The Grapes, on a Saturday night. For a start, we knew we wouldn't be ripped off – unlike in London, where the prices in the clubs Jamie liked to go were astronomical. We liked nothing more than getting absolutely smashed on Guinness in The Grapes, with a few shorts on the side. We also liked a drop of port or three, meaning a typical night involved sinking 20-25 pints of Guinness, a bottle of port between us and a few shots. Razor, who lived in Formby, would then get himself off home to the Missus, while I would go home to my new house in Birkdale. Then, we would meet again Sunday morning for another session.

Razor was a great drinking partner. We got on brilliantly and both knew the local was where we belonged. The Grapes was a great boozer as well and the manager, a fella we called 'The Chief', really looked after us. At closing time, he would usher all the regulars out, lock the doors and then we would settle in for the night. The great thing about The Grapes was we never got any bother. Everyone knew us so we were just treated like everyone else, apart from the lock-ins of course. They were great fun. I would be sitting there with a pint and a cigar with the fire roaring away, just enjoying the craic. The session might go on until 5am. Then, as he got up to leave, Razor would be looking at his watch and saying, 'Right, I can't see the time right now but I'll see you at 10am for a champagne breakfast - and don't be late'. At first, I thought Razor was joking but he never was. So, come 10am, I'd be back in The Grapes after about four hours sleep and ready to go again. We would then drink for another 12 hours before heading home. By later in the evening, we would often be arguing over something ridiculous. He always won the argument, as it would be a brave, brave man who stood up to Razor when his back was up. I have seen him in action and, believe me, he would take someone's head off if riled. Have you seen how big his forehead is? Take it from me, he can hurt you and hurt you badly. As I almost found out one night. A long session was drawing to a close. I was inside the pub and Razor outside. I was teasing him through the window about something, I can't even remember what but, suddenly, he was trying to smash his way through the window to get at me. I sobered up quickly and realised I was in danger, so gave him my puppy-eye look in the hope it would calm him down. Thankfully, for me, it did or I might not be here to tell the tale.

The odd drunken spat aside, we really looked out for each other. Razor had a few personal problems during his time at Liverpool, while for a lot of the time I was worried about my own career. We also both had issues with drink. But Razor still took me under his wing. People may say that might not have been the best thing for me in terms of all the drinking we did together, but I could have said 'no'. I was, though, quite relieved we never went away on holiday, like I did with Robbie or Carra. It was out of the question anyway as Razor always said he went away with his family, which knowing how flash he was probably involved a week in Butlins!

Mind, we may not have gone away in the summer together, but we did make up for that during the season when our big sessions weren't just confined to Formby. There was one particularly mad weekend that has since become known to us both as www, due to it involving us getting absolutely steam-boated in Warrington, Windermere and Wigan on consecutive days. This marathon drinking session actually took place during the season, on a weekend when we were both out of the team injured. The plan, when we set off on the Friday after having treatment at the training ground, was to nip over to Warrington to see a couple of Razor's friends who were up from London and enjoy a couple of pints. We would then head back to Formby and enjoy the rest of the weekend there. The reality, of course, was rather different with the Guinness going down so well in Warrington that we soon decided to hang around. As always happened if Razor was out, a crowd of locals soon started to gather around us and the craic was brilliant. Quite a few were Liverpool fans and, at first, they were not best pleased to see two of their team's players boozing on the afternoon before a game. But after we'd reassured them that we were both injured then they were fine. It turned into a great night, so much so that the time soon sped by and before we knew it the bell for last orders was being rung. We didn't have anywhere to stay but the landlord soon solved that by offering to put me up in the pub's flat and Razor in the pub itself.

Come the morning, we did feel a bit rough over breakfast and most people would have gone home at that stage. But not us. No, instead, Razor decided over breakfast that we should head up to the Lakes to visit a mate of his called Howard, who lived in Windermere. I didn't have anything else to do so thought, 'Why not?' So, off we headed up the M6 for another day/night on the booze but with the added ingredient of a trip round the lake on Howard's boat. The drinking began the moment we arrived so, by the time Howard suggested we head out on his boat before it was too late, I'd had a skinful. It didn't stop me water-skiing, though, which once I'd sobered up the following day suddenly struck me as probably having not been our most sensible idea. Can you imagine the stink it would have caused at Liverpool if they'd found out two of their injured players had been spotted careering round Lake Windermere on water-skis? They would have been even less impressed if they'd also been told that, at one stage, Razor pushed me out of the boat as we roared along at 40mph. Looking back, I don't know how he didn't kill me! It was after my impromptu dive into the lake that I thought it best we get back to dry land, where the drinking could resume. The night again went well and we were having a good craic when, suddenly, the mood changed due to a group of Manchester United fans having arrived in this particular nightclub. They took a real exception to Razor and words were exchanged. They then started acting the big 'un, which was a bit daft as all we wanted to do was enjoy a few more drinks and a laugh. The situation started to really go downhill when one of their lot started bouncing around like a jack-in-the-box. Razor just told him to 'piss off', which laughably these so-called hard men of Manchester responded to by running to the bouncers to complain. Even more ridiculous was the doormen's response – they threw us out! We couldn't believe it, as it had been these Mancs who had been trying to cause trouble. As daft as we found the situation, we decided to do as they asked and head back to our hotel to continue the drinking in the bar – which is exactly what we did.

It meant another hangover at breakfast but, again, there was no prospect of heading home once Razor's mate Howard had invited us down to Wigan to watch the Warriors rugby league team play at home. Howard sponsored the club's cars back then so had an executive box and we watched the game in there, predictably with a pint in our hands all the way through. Again, it turned into a good session and afterwards we met a few of the Wigan rugby boys. Razor was good mates with Kelvin Skerrett anyway, while Gary Connolly, Frano Botica and Joe Lydon – a fella who no-one in Wigan ever messed with – were all there as well. We ended up in a karaoke bar where a comedian mate of ours called Willie Miller was performing before finishing the night in a nightclub called Crystals in St Helens. We stayed there until 3am and then got a taxi home to bring an end to a weekend that me and Razor still talk about fondly today.

Dublin was another place where the two of us enjoyed many memorable trips, usually after Liverpool had played at Anfield on the Saturday and we would fly over straight after the game. We had a couple of top mates who lived over there called Alan and Chris. Alan was a taxi driver so would pick us up from the airport and take us round to see Chris, who would have a string of pubs lined up for the rest of the weekend. We had a great time, particularly on the Sunday afternoons after we had devised a challenge game. Basically, me or Razor would challenge the other to do something bizarre. It might be getting a bike or a moped from somewhere and then riding it into the pub, or it could be, as happened to me once, having to go on a sight-seeing tour of Dublin and come back with a load of souvenirs. The dafter the challenge, the more we found it funny. Then, after successfully completing the challenge and sinking a few more pints of Guinness, we would fly back to Liverpool on the Sunday night. On one occasion, though, we didn't make it after deciding to call in at a pub on our taxi route back to the airport that was holding a line-dancing competition. Garth Brooks, the country singer, was playing at Croke Park that night so the place was bouncing and we ended up missing the flight. That meant a mad rush in the morning to make sure we got the first plane out of Dublin in an attempt to get to training on time, which we did with about 20 seconds to spare.

Razor is a really loyal mate and someone who I will always be there for, no matter when he rings or where he is. I know Razor would say the same about me, as during our time at Liverpool he was always very protective when we were out. To be fair, most of my friends have always been like that. I am fortunate that I know a lot of people in, shall we say, high places so I never got too many problems. And if I did, then it was sorted out very quickly. Hassle is, unfortunately, a fact of life for someone who is in the public eye. I had first noticed how different people can behave around footballers when I broke into the Liverpool team. It was nothing like the attention Robbie or Macca got but people would be staring at me, which I found weird. I realised quickly that they were just curious. Some might be a bit jealous but, in the main, people were fine. Most just wanted a chat, which I was always glad to do. You ask anyone about me and they will say I am very sociable. I like people and always have. I have also always accepted that everyone is entitled to their opinion, so I never had a problem if someone said I wasn't a good footballer or anything like that. That is their opinion and good luck to them. I accepted that sort of thing as coming with the territory of being a footballer. But if they ever got personal or had a go at my family then I felt that was crossing the line and I would walk away. It has happened in the past. I never reacted in a violent way, I would just say, 'Look mate, fuck off'. Luckily for me, I didn't get too much hassle – probably because I didn't go into the centre of Liverpool too often due to living over Southport way. It was different for Robbie, Don Hutchison and

Macca, who had a few problems when out and about. Liverpool was also a place where if you crossed the wrong people then you could be in a lot of trouble, another reason why I liked to stay away and have my nights out in Southport. Despite that, I did enjoy going to Cream, the dance nightclub in Liverpool. I was good mates with the lads on the door. Alfie Lewis, Bobby Stein and Mally were the head doormen and they looked after me. Alfie, who was one of the top boys in the city at the time, would tell whoever was working to watch my back. One night, two Everton lads followed me into the toilet and were giving me some hassle. They wanted to fill me in but I didn't react. The next thing I knew, Mally had appeared and these lads were on their way out the back. He had these lads by the ears and was about to kick the living daylights out of them. One of them was still shouting at me, 'You're going to get it next time we see you'. I stepped in and prevented them getting a beating. I had only come for a quiet night out and didn't want anyone to get beaten up. So, I said to let them go and, thankfully, there was no comeback for me. I did see the lads again not long after the incident and nothing happened. So, the right thing was done.

The thing I never understand with idiots who want to pick a fight with footballers is why they would want to take on a sportsman? Or, in some cases, a couple of us. By nature, footballers are very fit – they have to be. So, if something happens, then they can usually handle themselves. But these idiots still think they can make a name for themselves.

Going out in Southport could lead to a few problems, though nothing on the scale of Liverpool where it is busier and a lot more people are out. I did, though, get bottled a couple of times in Southport. The worst came after Millwall had been playing at Tranmere earlier in the day and a few of their fans had come across for a night out. I was walking down the street on my way home and this Millwall lad came out of an alleyway and smacked me a few times, including with a bottle. I'd never met him before so the attack was completely unprovoked. I was a Liverpool player at the time but it wasn't a case of me being recognised. He was just some idiot out for trouble. I found out later that these Millwall fans had been causing bother all night, throwing pool balls at windows and so on. I was just in the wrong place at the wrong time. It sounds daft but I was actually quite lucky that night because a young girl jumped in to try and stop the attack. It is a good job she did, as I was out cold at the time and could have ended up in a really bad way. The worst part of it, though, came at the hospital later when I was treated like a criminal, as if I had been the one who had caused the trouble. I hadn't and I resented the suggestion I had.

Thankfully, there weren't many incidents like that. That was probably down to me developing a bit of an early warning system. I had a gut feeling about trouble, which helped a lot. And then, if that didn't work, thankfully all my mates were hard as nails. People seemed to realise who I knew and would stay away. If I was with Razor, that was definitely the case.

Like me, the Liverpool fans had taken to Razor very quickly after he had signed from Tottenham Hotspur. The diving header equaliser he scored against Manchester United in the 3-3 draw that led to the match-fixing allegations probably helped. Games against United were always the biggest of the season and, along with the derbies against Everton that during my time at Anfield bordered on real hatred, had the best atmospheres so Razor couldn't have picked a better game to be the hero. That equaliser against United came when Graeme was still in charge but Razor really prospered under Roy Evans, who I believe never gets the credit he deserves for the job he did at Liverpool.

Roy's appointment was a good one and he brought about an immediate improvement. We may have finished in our lowest position for three decades at the end of his first season, but we were still eighth and that was much higher than where we'd been when Graeme had left.

The 1994-95 campaign may not have been great on a personal level for me but the club fared a lot better, finishing fourth and winning the League Cup. It was during that year that Roy started to build his own squad. Certain players were moved on, while legendary players had to have their careers at Anfield brought to an end. Roy did it all quietly with the minimum of fuss. Getting rid of legendary figures is never easy and I doubt any other manager could have done what Roy managed. He had been there throughout all the trophy-winning seasons these players had enjoyed so was able to pull them aside and say, 'Listen, it's time for you to move on'. He made sure nothing came across as confrontational, which maybe hadn't been the case under Graeme. The older lads appreciated that and it turned into something of a quiet revolution at Anfield as he got rid of Bruce Grobbelaar, Steve Nicol, Jan Molby and Ronnie Whelan. Add in how he also ushered Mark Walters, Julian Dicks, Paul Stewart and Ronnie Rosenthal out the door along with Nigel Clough and that is quite a change of personnel. And all done with the minimum of fuss and aggravation. The changes that Roy made in those first couple of seasons are often overlooked when his reign is ever being assessed. He had to be ruthless and was, which doesn't quite tally with the impression the public have of him being quite soft. I certainly never shared that view, even though we all had a good rapport with Roy because he had been at Liverpool so long. If he needed to be tough, then he would be.

In the summer of 1995, Roy's squad continued to evolve with the big signing being Stan Collymore for a British record fee of £8.5m. Stan had scored 22 goals the previous season to help Nottingham Forest finish third, one place above us. His arrival generated a real sense of optimism around Anfield that we were going to have a good season. The players shared that sense of excitement, which was further fuelled on the opening day when Stan got the winner against Sheffield Wednesday. I was in the starting line-up, just as I was a couple of nights later against Leeds United at Elland Road. It was my reward for knuckling down in pre-season. I'd gone away at the start of the summer feeling sorry for myself but realised the only person who could turn things rounds was me. So, I'd come back and put a lot of hard work in. I then played in most of the pre-season games but it wasn't until I saw the team-sheet for the Wednesday game that I knew I would be starting. I did okay, as I did against Leeds when we were beaten by a wonder goal from Tony Yeboah. It was a volley from the edge of the area that flew past David James and into the net off the underside of the crossbar. The goal was so good that it is shown every time I go to a Leeds United dinner, which I don't enjoy seeing as I am the closest defender to Jamo as the ball whistles past us both. I am also sporting my ridiculous dyed blond hair from the holiday with Robbie. After losing to Leeds, we then went on a bit of a run by winning four of our next five games. Unfortunately, I didn't feature in any of them as I'd picked up an injury and that defeat to Leeds proved to be my last appearance until late March. My injured ankle kept me out for three months. Then, once fit, I couldn't get in the team because they were doing so well. That was the Liverpool way, anyone out of the side would only get a chance if someone had a couple of bad games. I understood that but it was still frustrating. I was, though, pleased to see Liverpool doing so well. Roy had built a decent squad with Stan having formed a good partnership with Robbie, who went on to score 36 goals that season. Older players such as Rushy and Barnesy were still contributing as well.

In the end, the Premier League title proved beyond us and we finished third, 11 points behind champions Manchester United. It meant United were chasing the double when we met at Wembley in the FA Cup final. Our run to the final had been relatively straight-forward. Only Leeds, who we beat 3-0 in a quarter-final replay after drawing 0-0 at Elland Road, put up much resistance and the team were in confident mood as we set off for Wembley in those white Armani suits. I had been fit again for quite a few months but managed just three appearances. The last of those had come a month or so earlier in a 2-0 win over West Ham United at Anfield so, in terms of playing in the Cup final, I was never really in the running. We travelled down to London on the Thursday and stayed at Sopwell House in Hertfordshire. The team was named that day and, as I'd always thought, I wasn't in. I hadn't been expecting to play so it wasn't a big disappointment or anything like that, even when Roy confirmed his three permitted substitutes would be Rushy, Michael Thomas and reserve-team goalkeeper Tony Warner. The big shock was that Razor wasn't playing. We were rooming together and Razor really thought he would be in the team. So, it came as a big shock when Razor heard he would not be involved. He was devastated and said we should have a drink together. It wasn't the time, though, so we decided it was a bad idea. It was the correct decision, as if anyone had found out then we would have been in deep trouble. Plus, bearing in mind all the fuss later caused by the suits, can you imagine what the fans' reaction would have been if it had later emerged two first-team players had been drinking before the final? There would have been uproar.

Once we got to stadium on the day of the final, however, we did decide to have a few beers. At the old Wembley, there used to be a bar in the corner of the dressing room so we had a couple after the lads had gone out to warm-up. We then made our way to our seats behind the dugout before kick-off. Along with everyone else in the country, I was looking forward to a cracking game. Both teams had enjoyed good years and scored loads of goals so it seemed a no-brainer that we would see a classic final. Sadly, it was anything but with plenty of players on both sides under-performing. There was only one decent bit of quality in the game and it came from Eric Cantona, when he drilled the winner in from the edge of the area. Losing a Cup final is bad enough. But to do so against your bitterest rivals makes it even worse, especially as Cantona's goal brought United their second double in three years and provided the springboard for further success in the future. The worst bit of that day, though, was that Manchester United were staying in the hotel opposite us in London so we could see them partying with the trophy. Across the road, we were sitting there looking miserable and drowning our sorrows as they danced with the Cup.

As the summer wore on and the criticism over those stupid suits started to fade, the disappointment of losing the Cup final started to ease. There were plenty of grounds for optimism where Liverpool Football Club was concerned. One big plus was that we were in Europe again. It may not have been the European Cup that had become such an important part of the club's history, but the Cup Winners' Cup, which we qualified for due to Manchester United entering the Champions League, was not to be sneezed at. Liverpool had reached the final once before in 1966 so the challenge was to go one better than Bill Shankly's team. We also fancied our chances in the Premier League after finishing fourth and third in the last two seasons so the season kicked off once again amid a sense of optimism.

The squad felt to be a very tight unit, with the dressing room packed full of strong characters. Jason McAteer was certainly one. He was thick beyond words and all the lads loved him for it. He always had something to say, though few took any notice. People would ask for him to pass the ketchup in the canteen and he would reply, 'Red or brown?' On his passport application, he wrote 'right wing-back' next to the word 'position'. By the time Jason arrived from Bolton, Rob Jones had already been nicknamed 'Trigger' in honour of the character from Only Fools and Horses. So, Jason became 'Dave', the name Trigger always used when referring to Rodney Trotter. Those two together would spend hours just laughing at each other, mainly because they were that thick! What they also were, though, were two great, great lads who were an important part of the Anfield team spirit. The great thing about our dressing room at the time was the mix of characters we had. On the opposite side to 'Trigger' and 'Dave' were the cool guys – Babbsy, Jamie and Scalesy, who all drove round in Mercedes convertibles and wore the top clothes. There is no better way of describing those three than the phrase 'wide boys'. Jamie was a really, nice guy who the women absolutely adored. Some would come up to him on nights out just to say how good looking he was, which obviously the lads all hated. Scalesy saw himself as a bit of a James Bond in the way he dressed and behaved, while Babbsy also thought he was a bit of a ladies man. The rest of us, in comparison, were like a rabble with lads like Steve McManaman just being really down-to-earth. Macca was a fantastic footballer but, off the field, he was never one to go shouting his mouth off. He preferred to keep himself to himself and definitely wasn't one for the bright lights. What I really admired about Macca was that he was never fazed by anything. If the attendance at a game had been 150,000, the one person who wouldn't notice was Macca. Add in to the mix lads like Robbie and it was no wonder we went out as a team so often. We all enjoyed each other's company. David James was another I always got on well with. He is a really intelligent guy with a bit of a mental streak running through him. We would go out for the annual Christmas Party and instead of pacing himself like everyone else, Jamo would neck ten pints in the first hour and be on his way home by mid-afternoon after having thrown up. As a goalkeeper, he was similar in that he could pull off the most amazing saves but then have a rush of blood to the head. I think if he had stayed on his line a bit more, he would have become one of the best goalkeepers around. I think maybe he was just that bit too confident and that led to him coming to try and win a ball he had no hope of getting. In that respect, his decision-making could maybe let him down but I still think he was great for Liverpool.

As exciting as the club's future seemed, my big concern in the summer of 1996 was the same as it had been during the previous two close seasons. Would I be able to force my way back into the team? In two years, I had started just seven Premier League games for Liverpool and one in the First Division with Sunderland. Leaving Anfield did cross my mind as, at 22, I knew I had to be playing more games. Leeds United, funnily enough, came in for me. Howard Wilkinson was the manager at Elland Road and made a £1million bid. There was also a bit of interest from a couple of other clubs and I spent a few days agonising over what to do next. I was desperate for first-team football but I was a Liverpool fan and wanted to make it with my team. It was a tough decision but, eventually, I opted to stay. I felt no-one had seen the best of me at Anfield and that I had to change that, rather than take the easy option and run away. I am so glad I did, as by the end of the year I was a regular in the team and dreaming about a Premier League title medal.

What changed everything for me was Roy deciding to employ a

sweeper system. And he wanted me to play the pivotal role. This was the chance I had been waiting for, not least as it meant playing in one position rather than filling in all over – something that I thought had, along with the injuries, been holding me back. The switch of tactics worked well for me and for the team.

The role of sweeper is an integral one as everything comes through you and I relished that responsibility. It was playing to my strengths. The new set-up, which saw me slot in between Babbsy and Mark Wright at the back, had a couple of teething problems on the opening day when we drew 3-3 at Middlesbrough and Fabrizio Ravanelli scored a hat-trick on his debut. But, after that, we went on a great run and won six of our next seven games to go top of the table. We also only conceded three times in those 630 minutes. A 1-0 defeat at Manchester United saw us knocked off the top but, by the end of the year, we were back in pole position. The signing of Patrik Berger from Borussia Dortmund had made a big difference. After smashing a couple of goals in against Leicester City early on, he never looked back. Patrik was a great player and gave us an extra attacking dimension that we hadn't had before. With Robbie and Stan forming a good partnership up front and Barnesy also having a good season, Patrik ensured the loss of Rushy, who had joined Leeds during the summer, was not as keenly felt as some supporters had initially feared.

On a personal level, I was loving my football again. I was in the team every week and our defensive record was decent as well. What could be better? My confidence was sky-high from getting a run of games and playing in a settled position. Everything felt right. I was never a left-winger, it was a position where I could fill in but it wasn't what suited me. Filling in across the pitch, as I did in those early years at Anfield, had probably led to all the niggling injuries I'd had. Different positions bring different demands and that possibly cost me in terms of the strains and knocks I picked up. By their very nature, utility players are always in and out of the team. Having my own position, however, meant that even when I missed a couple of games through injury, I went straight back into the team when fit. That did wonders for my confidence and I think it showed in my performances.

With things going well for me on the pitch, life had improved off it as well. I had started to get more used to living on my own. I'd bought my first house with a mortgage but, after I'd become a regular in the side, Liverpool offered me a new deal. It, basically, quadrupled what I had been on - making Roy again pull me to one side as I signed and say, 'Behave yourself with that kind of money'. I think he was still worried about how easily led I was off the field, even though I had cleaned up my act a lot. I appreciated the sentiment, as I did the club offering such a good deal without me asking for one. Liverpool's thinking was that all the first-team regulars were on at least that kind of wage and now I was in the team, I deserved the same. With Roy's words still in my mind, I paid off the mortgage – which was weird feeling in my early 20s. I started to feel more settled, even though I'd probably been happier at my Mum's house before I decided to move. I decided to make the effort and go the whole hog by getting an interior designer in. I ended up with chandeliers and all sorts of fancy things. It was better than a show-home. But, all I did was live in the kitchen, one bedroom and the massive TV room. It was all for show, really. But I did settle much better, particularly as I rarely spent much time in the house on my own. Instead, I would get all my mates round to watch football. It meant that, with me now living in the area I'd always wanted to and playing for the club I'd always wanted to play for, life really had become very enjoyable.

As our title challenge continued, I also started to get some good press. There were even a few comparisons with Alan Hansen. I wasn't in his league as a player but I understand why the comparison was made as a huge feature of Alan's game had been how he used to bring the ball out of defence, which was what I was doing. Basically, because we had Robbie and Stan up front, there was no point knocking the ball long as they didn't win many headers.

The manager had made it clear what my role was during the summer and some of the senior players reinforced that once the season got under way. Barnesy, in particular, encouraged me to collect the ball off the goalkeeper before bringing it forward. In fact, there were a couple of times when he had me by the throat in the dressing room at half-time if I hadn't done as I was told. Playing out from the back was the Liverpool way and I really felt to be part of things. It suited me, too, as I had been brought up to play the ball. As 1996 ended with us on top of the table, I couldn't help but look back to the agonising I had done during the summer over whether to join Leeds or not. Becoming a regular had fully justified that decision to stay.

We started the New Year with a defeat at Chelsea but responded by taking 10 points from the next four games. We were flying and all the talk among the boys as we headed off for a short team break in Marbella was of winning Liverpool's first title of the Premier League era. We were due to play Blackburn Rovers a few days after getting back from Spain and none of us could see anything but a win. Unfortunately, Colin Hendry and Tim Flowers had unbelievable games and it finished goalless. If we'd won that day, I really think Liverpool would have gone on to become champions. But, after that, we lost our way. We lost to Villa, had a mad game against Forest that we only took a point from and, in terms of the season, we never recovered. We went on to finish fourth, which was ridiculous considering it had been a two-horse race for the title between us and Manchester United for most of the season. Missing out like that is a big regret and is something I can't explain. Marbella wasn't to blame, even if our results did dip straight afterwards. We'd gone away in high spirits after beating Leeds 4-0 but it turned out to be a quiet trip, with the boys taking the chance to recharge the batteries. So, I don't blame the Marbella trip for us blowing the title. I think it was more that, as a squad, we didn't have the experience to finish the job off. As late as March, we were talking about winning it but, by then, the confidence had gone and Manchester United went on to finish top with 75 points, seven clear of Newcastle, Arsenal and ourselves.

It wasn't just in the Premier League where we blew our chances of silverware during those final few weeks. In the Cup Winners' Cup, we had been on a decent run and were through to the semi-finals. I had played in every game as we beat Finnish club MyPa, Swiss side Sion and Brann Bergen of Norway to reach the last four. Brann were a decent side who had knocked out PSV Eindhoven in the second round. They gave us a tough time, particularly in the first leg over there when a striker by the name of Tore Andre Flo was a real handful as we drew 1-1. In the return, two goals from Robbie and one for Stan saw us through to the semi-finals with a 4-1 aggregate win. We were then handed a two-legged tie with Paris St Germain, while Barcelona and Fiorentina met in the other semi. The first leg was played in Paris and we were shocking. They battered us 3-0 and it could have been more on a night that, at the time, felt like the worst of my career. Paris St Germain had Patrice Loko, whose name is very apt as he is a bit of a lunatic, in their team but it was Brazilian striker Leonardo who ran the show that night. We did come close to nicking a goal near the end but, in truth, we were well beaten. Our fans, probably out of frustration at how our challenge in the league was falling away, were not happy and booed us into the airport terminal before the flight home. To me, they were well within their rights. Those boys had paid a lot of money to get over to Paris on a midweek night and were determined to let us know how badly let down they felt. There was nothing we could do but put our heads down and carry on walking. In a situation like that, you can't go round saying 'sorry' to everyone – even if that is how you are feeling inside. The game has finished and you have to get over it.

A three-goal deficit was a lot to overcome in the home leg and we couldn't do it, though we did give it one hell of a good go. Because we needed goals, I was on the bench and didn't get on. The game was a thriller and we almost did it. We got the score back to 3-2 on aggregate but just couldn't get the extra goal that would have taken the tie into extra-time. We were all devastated at the final whistle, as the chance to play in a European final doesn't come along too often. It was also my first experience of being involved in a Cup semi-final with my club so I took the defeat badly. Unfortunately, by the time my career ended, I'd become familiar with that horrible feeling that comes with missing out on a place in a final and it never got any easier.

Nor does thinking about 'what might have been?' in terms of the Premier League title race that year. The Championship had been there to win. We all knew it, too. Instead, we went from hoping for the 'double' of the Premier League and Cup Winners' Cup to ending the season with nothing.

What was perhaps the most frustrating part was that some of the football we played that season had been among the best in Europe. So, to finish empty-handed was a big letdown. A consolation was that the team was clearly evolving and had improved. Plus, Michael Owen had made his first-team debut and already shown his ability by scoring against Wimbledon. Everyone at the club had been aware about Michael for years. It was a similar situation to Robbie in that it was a case of when and not if he made the first-team. Maybe Michael was a little bit more hyped because he had been at the National School so people had seen him on Sky in the Under-15s internationals and games like that. As a result, people were more aware of him than Robbie. But nothing fazed Michael, even though he was only 17 at the time. He had started training with us at an early age and always looked confident. He was certainly much more confident than I had been at that age. That self-belief, together with his blistering pace, meant he stood out straight away. Young players like that don't come along too often and, in my time at Liverpool, I was fortunate to see three – Michael, Robbie and Steven Gerrard. They all had something about them. The great thing with Michael is he was such a nice lad. He lived his life professionally from the start. Everyone thinks Michael was quiet as a young lad but he was quite a character, even at that age. He loved a game of cards and a bet. He also enjoyed the craic in the dressing room. Michael was very much a family man and they followed him to every game. He was similar to Robbie in the respect that he looked after every member of his family, buying them all a house on the same road and so on. That proved to me that Michael was a genuinely nice guy and it was great to see the success he went on to enjoy. That debut goal against Wimbledon, who were a hard team to play, was typical in that he showed no fear. After that, he was on his way and he started the 1997-98 season as Liverpool's number 9.

The emergence of Michael was probably a factor in the club deciding to let Stan leave for Aston Villa that summer. The fee was £7m, which meant we got back a good sized chunk of the money that had been paid to Nottingham Forest two years earlier. Stan was someone I got on well with. He could be a strange character and probably someone who you either loved or hated. He could be slightly cocky. Coming to Liverpool, I think Stan thought he would be the top man. But he soon found out that wasn't going to be the case. We still had people like Barnesy and Rushy around, so there was no way he was going to be above them. There were also people like Robbie in the team, plus characters like Razor. Stan also lived away from Liverpool so didn't really socialise that much with the lads and I think that was possibly why the move went sour in the end. He didn't make the kind of effort to mix in that the lads wanted to see. Stan was also someone who liked to tell you how good he was but, on the whole, I liked him. Above all, Stan was a very good player and very strong. It was just that at Liverpool, he under-achieved. If he had moved closer and really thrown himself into the move then I believe he could have become a great player for the club. Unfortunately, he only lasted a couple of years and his career never really reached the heights it had promised to in those first few months at Anfield.

As Stan headed out the door destined for Villa Park, Paul Ince arrived from Inter Milan. He was definitely someone we needed. Incey may have received mixed reviews for his time at Liverpool but I liked him. He was what he was and had a swagger about him. But I never thought that was a bad thing. The top players all have a bit of that in them. He had played in Italy and been a big success at Manchester United. During his career, he had won things and was a top player. So, why shouldn't he have an air of confidence about him? People who didn't know him may have mistaken that confidence for arrogance. But I never did. In fact, I considered him to be the opposite and I know a few of the younger lads really looked up to him. As a footballer, Incey was a winner and that is why we needed him after coming up short two seasons running. Apart from Incey, however, there wasn't too much transfer activity into the club. Stan may have moved to Villa but Roy didn't see much of the money, though he was able to bring in Karl-Heinz Riedle from Borussia Dortmund for £1.6m. Otherwise, the only 'new' additions were Michael Owen and Jamie Carragher. The promotion of two promising youngsters did, at least, bring a freshness to a squad that, during the opening few weeks of the campaign, would lose Razor on loan along with Barnesy, Mark Wright and Michael Thomas.

All things considered, we went on to have a decent season by finishing third in the Premier League – especially as we lost Robbie Fowler and Jamie Redknapp for long spells to injury. We also reached the League Cup semi-final, where we were drawn against Middlesbrough. We won the first leg 2-1 at home when Paul Merson scored a beauty but lost the return 2-0 at the Riverside so missed out on an appearance in the final. In the UEFA Cup, we knocked Celtic out in the first round but then lost stupidly to Strasbourg, while the least said about the FA Cup the better as Coventry City beat us 3-1 at Anfield in the third round. On a personal level, I'd had another good season and played in most of the games. The injuries that had been such a problem earlier in my career had also cleared up, which again I put down to me finally playing in a settled position. All in all then, I considered it to have been another decent season – even if the team had still not made the breakthrough we all craved in terms of winning trophies. I still, though, felt success was round the corner. Sadly, the board did not share my optimism for the future. Third place in the Premier League may today be cause for celebration but, to the Anfield directors back then, it was not good enough. Liverpool's proud history demanded we win trophies so, in their mind, drastic action was required to make that happen.

Chapter 8

The Odd Couple

One fact that my friends could never get their heads round when I was a player was that they usually knew more about what was going on at my club than I did. It didn't matter whether it was Liverpool, Leeds, Blackburn or Stoke, the players were invariably the last to hear about a new signing or the appointment of a new manager. That is just how football is. Usually, we only heard the rumours when fans or one of the Press lads inadvertently passed them on to us by asking things like, 'Is so and so signing?' My mates never quite believed this, thinking I was in someway playing dumb to try and keep a transfer or whatever under wraps. But I wasn't. I really did have no idea if what they were asking was true because players are always the last to be told anything. That was definitely the case in the summer of 1998 when the Liverpool board made one of the most ridiculous decisions of all time by bringing in Gerard Houllier to work alongside Roy Evans.

The first I heard of him possibly coming in was when one of the boys in the dressing room was told by a mate of his. Initially, though, we were told this French guy who I had never heard of was supposed to be coming in as Roy's assistant. That sort of made sense, especially as Ronnie Moran had left the club at the end of the previous season. Maybe bringing in Houllier, who one of the lads said had been the man behind France's World Cup win, was what we needed. In my mind, we were close to making that breakthrough in terms of winning trophies and this could be the key that unlocked the door. Unfortunately, whoever had heard the initial rumour had got his wires crossed. Gerard Houllier was coming to Anfield but not as Roy's assistant. He was coming in as joint-manager, a decision that was confirmed in mid-July by the board. Now, I really was uneasy. Joint managers had never been tried before in English football. It just wasn't part of our culture. How would it work? Who would pick the team? Did either of them have the casting vote on a signing? Had they ever even met? There were just so many questions that it was difficult to get my head round the appointment when it was confirmed on television.

What also became clear as Houllier was unveiled was that a few of the 'facts' that we'd picked up in the dressing room were not quite what they seemed. Okay, he had been the technical director of French football and France had just won the World Cup. But he had also been the manager who couldn't get France to the 1994 World Cup despite needing just one point from the last two group games. He had also fallen out with both Eric Cantona and David Ginola during his time as manager of the French side, something that didn't bode well for his man-management skills. What really set the alarm bells ringing in my head, however, was that Houllier had never played professional football and was regarded in France as a long-ball merchant. I'd never heard of the bloke when he was first mentioned as a possible assistant for Roy but now I was worried.

His first few days in the job did nothing to ease that concern, either. Straight away, he fell out with Razor. He spoke really badly to Razor, almost along the lines of 'Who are you?' Razor just looked at him as if to say, 'Who the fuck are you more like?' And that was the end of Razor, who was very soon heading out of the door. Houllier had made his mind up on Razor very quickly and, to me, never gave him a chance. Training was also something that changed, and it became apparent there was not much room for enjoyment in a session led by Houllier. He didn't like to see any of us smiling, while away from the training pitch the lads had all manner of new rules to live by. It was like we were back at school.

As strange as all these changes were and the atmosphere being affected for the worse, the real problem was that Houllier and Roy were joint-managers. A set-up like that is never going to work and, unsurprisingly, it didn't. People can dress it up how they want but having joint-managers causes nothing but confusion. Anyone at Anfield during those few months that the partnership lasted will tell you that. No-one knew who was making the decisions and there would be times when Roy, who let's not forget had been at Liverpool for more than three decades by then, would be undermined. Roy would tell us one thing and then half-and-hour later we would be told something else. It would be just little things, such as changing travel arrangements or Houllier saying we couldn't have a drink after a pre-season game after Roy had said it would be okay. But it was still bad for Roy. I really felt sorry for him because such a club stalwart deserved a lot better. Everyone knew the

Bonny Lad: Me as a baby -
and already smiling for the
camera.

Sad Day: With my
brother Victor, visiting
the grave of our sister
Fiorina. She died at
just a couple of months
old. I hadn't been born
and neither had my
brother Victor but we
still share our parents'
sense of loss.

A Proud Scot: Despite what my critics said later in my life, here I am proudly showing off my favourite football kit in our back garden in Dumfries.

Catching Some Rays: Me on holiday in Italy, where we went most summers to visit my Dad's family.

Proud Lad: Showing off my trophies at home in Southport

Big Stage: Playing for Birkdale United at my first 'proper' ground, Haig Avenue - the home of Southport FC.

Another Prize: More success for my school team

Meeting My Hero: Kenny Dalglish congratulates me on another successful season with Birkdale United. He would later sign me for Liverpool.

Boyhood Dream: Playing for Liverpool was all I ever wanted as a kid.
(©Yorkshire Post)

Pride & Joy: Visiting my parents' house in Ainsdale in my brand new Jag, which Mum had to capture on film.

Boys On Tour: Me, Steve Evason, Mike Atkinson and Robbie Fowler on holiday in Faliraki.

Three Lions: With Scotland showing no interest, I opted to play for England and did enjoy my time with the Under-21s and senior squad. (© Press Association)

Tussling with Bow: I keep the ball away from Lee Bowyer as Liverpool win 2-0 at Elland Road. (© Yorkshire Post)

No Way Through: Another Leeds player comes off second best, this time Paul Beesley. (© Yorkshire Post)

Partying With A Pop Star: The Liverpool lads on a trip to Marbella with Robbie Williams, who came along as a mate of Phil Babb.

Dream Debut: I couldn't have picked a better game to make my Leeds United bow - against AC Milan at home in the Champions League. (© Yorkshire Post)

Running on Adrenalin: I was only supposed to play an hour after four months out injured but lasted the whole game. (© Yorkshire Post)

Shortly after signing for Leeds United, I show off my new Bentley to Mum and Dad back in Ainsdale.

Big Night Out: Me and a few of the boys enjoy plenty of laughs on a night out.

Cool Finish: I score on only my third appearance for Leeds as we thrash Besiktas
6-0 at Elland Road. And then Alan Smith rushes up to congratulate me.
(© Yorkshire Post)

Get In: The goal that launched a thousand songs, I celebrate scoring against AC Milan at the San Siro. (© Yorkshire Post)

Job Done: I applaud the 7,000 fans who followed us to Italy as Smithy leads the celebrations as Leeds reach the second group stage. (© Yorkshire Post)

Camping It Up: Me, Rio Ferdinand and Michael Duberry have fun at a 'Back To School' party that was held in Leeds.

board wanted Houllier as manager but had bottled it and brought him in alongside Roy, who had basically become a dead man walking. If the board really believed a change of manager was needed then they should have had the guts to make that change. The problem was that a couple of the directors had grown close to Roy down the years so fudged it. I, personally, didn't think Roy needed replacing but they clearly did. If that was the case, they should have had the balls to do it. Instead, what we got were two managers who didn't agree on much at all running Liverpool and it paralysed the club. An indication of how successful it proved is that no other club in England has appointed joint managers in the 13 years since Liverpool tried it. The basic problem, and something the board should have realised, was we had two managers telling us two different things. I had a similar experience at Leeds later in my career when Eddie Gray came in as manager to work alongside Kevin Blackwell, who had been Peter Reid's assistant. The two of them never got on and it would lead to Eddie telling me, as captain, one thing and then Kevin Blackwell saying something completely different just a few minutes later. My head was spinning by the end of the six months Eddie and Blackie spent working together at Elland Road.

Credit to Roy, he stuck it out for four months before deciding enough was enough and quitting. He had tried hard to make it work. But, being so experienced in the game and Liverpool in particular, he knew things could not go on. He also didn't want to harm the club, which says all you need to know about Roy Evans as a man. There had been problems from the start with the two of them disagreeing over team selection, which did not come as a surprise to anyone but the Liverpool board. Robbie was dropped for one game against Roy's wishes. The same happened to Karl-Heinz Riedle against West Ham in early September after we'd won the previous two games and gone top of the Premier League. Predictably, changing a winning team meant we lost to the Hammers – even though Karl came off the bench to net a late goal. That defeat started a run where we won just one of nine games – and that was against a Nottingham Forest side who would finish bottom of the table with just 30 points come May. Roy quit on November 12 with us sitting 11th. I was sad to see him go, even if I knew the joint-manager experiment couldn't go on. Roy had been at Anfield for 33 years and deserved more respect than he got from the board and, later, from Houllier. What really started to annoy me after Roy had left was how

Houllier suddenly started to rubbish a lot of what had happened before his arrival. The way he started talking to the Press, you could have been forgiven for thinking Liverpool had been fighting relegation for the last few years and that he had been brought in to save us. Instead, we had finished fourth and third in the last two Premier League seasons and also reached two Cup semi-finals. And the year before that, we had got to the FA Cup final. Yet, listening to Houllier, it sounded like he had taken over a club on its knees. I didn't like that, particularly as it was designed to make Roy look bad and Houllier like some sort of hero who had ridden in to the city to rescue Liverpool Football Club. This blatant attempt at taking the pressure off himself at the expense of others really started to grate among the lads, and particularly those of us who saw Roy as a kind of father-figure after all he had done for us.

The upshot of Roy's departure was Liverpool now had a foreign manager, further adding to the high number already working in the Premier League. It was a trend that I hadn't agreed with, even before playing for Houllier. I have always thought a Premier League team should be managed by an English or British manager because, usually, they will know the club inside out. Houllier may have thought he knew all about Liverpool Football Club, but he didn't. Not at all. In fact, I never thought he 'got' Liverpool in the two years I played for him. Liverpool is a special club with the traditions of the place and the Boot Room. But Houllier never appreciated that. I also thought he had an arrogance about him. I never liked speaking to Houllier, mainly because it was impossible to get a straight answer out of him. He would get me in his office and try to tell me about Liverpool Football Club. I would be thinking, 'Hang on a minute, gaffer, I was watching this club when you lived in France'. I'd stood on the Kop and he was trying to tell me what a great history Liverpool had. But that was him all over. He thought he was the only person who cared about Liverpool Football Club but he couldn't be more wrong. When I made that point, he didn't like it. He started talking in French to me but I'd given up listening by then.

He just didn't 'get' the club. That point was brought home to the lads when we played Valencia in the UEFA Cup second round. The first leg had finished goalless at Anfield, meaning we were up against it in the return. Valencia went ahead in stoppage time at the end of the first half only for goals from Steve McManaman and Patrik Berger late on to put us in front. Claudio Lopez's free-kick then went in off David James to bring the scores level but, thanks to the away-goals rule, we went through. That should have meant the night was a special one for Liverpool, even allowing for both Macca and Paul Ince being sent off in the final minute along with Valencia's Amadeo Carboni after a bit of pushing and shoving. Emotions were still running high at the end and all our lads refused to swap shirts with the Valencia players, which they were perfectly entitled to do. They also had a few choice words to say to the referee and his two linesmen over Macca and Incey's red cards before heading back to the dressing room. Once there, the boys were able to reflect on a job well done as Valencia were a good side and one who would go on to reach the Champions League final a couple of years later. However, as the celebrations got going, one of the coaches was spotted rooting through the discarded kit and picking up a few of the shirts that, just a few minutes earlier, the lads had refused to swap. It turned out Houllier had ordered this coach to find a few shirts as he wanted to hand them to the officials, who just happened to be French. The lads went ballistic. Had he not seen how angry they had all been with the referee at the final whistle? Eventually, Houllier stormed out to leave all the players shaking their heads in disbelief. Incidents like that just don't happen if a manager backs his team. To the lads, he should have been sticking up for us – not worming his way round people outside the club, and especially not someone who had just sent off two of his players. Just over a week later and Roy had gone, leaving Houllier in sole charge. Phil Thompson was then brought back as his assistant, which meant at least someone with an understanding of Liverpool Football Club was still involved. To be fair, there was one member of Houllier's coaching team who I did enjoy working with and that was Patrice Bergues. He was a really good coach. They had worked together with the French Football Federation after first meeting at RC Lens in the mid-1980s. I always saw Patrice as the brains of the pair. I never thought Houllier was that great on the training pitch, he didn't do much that we didn't all know. In fact, his thinking was pretty basic. But Patrice was totally different and had some very impressive ideas, particularly in terms of diet and fitness.

Houllier, however, was a totally different matter. I never felt I knew where I stood with him, which is always a dangerous position to be in for a footballer. He was the sort of manager who was nicey-nicey with the Press, ensuring he looked good in the newspapers or on television.

Basically, Houllier liked the sound of his own voice and, judging by his few months in charge of Aston Villa recently, he still does. But, behind closed doors, he was totally different and I wasn't the only player who felt getting a straight answer out of him was impossible.

Another personality trait of Houllier's I didn't like was how he tried to take credit for things that were nothing to do with him. Stevie Gerrard had been brought to the club as a schoolboy by Steve Heighway and developed into a fine player. But the way the manager spoke about Stevie, you'd have thought he discovered him back in France! Houllier also reckons he introduced Stevie G to his agent but he didn't. I did. I used to sit next to Stevie every day in training and I recommended Struan Marshall, who had been brilliant for me ever since we'd first been introduced by John Barnes. Stevie took my advice and Stru still works for him all these years later. Houllier, though, seems to think it was him who put them in touch. Maybe he once did say something like, 'Yes, Stru is a good guy'. But someone else did the work. It was the same with the team Houllier inherited. People like Graeme Souness and Roy had done all the donkey work to get the club back in some sort of shape. And yet Houllier disregarded all that, instead giving himself all the credit when Liverpool did win three Cups in 2001. Anyone with a bit of class would have, at least, mentioned Roy's role after the FA Cup, League Cup or UEFA Cup success. But that was just not Houllier's style.

As disappointing as I found that reluctance to give credit to others, I think the biggest disservice Houllier did Liverpool was that he did not live up to his reputation of developing youth talent. That must have been in the board's thinking when they made the appointment in 1998. At Liverpool, however, he did the exact opposite and spent money on average players while not giving the young lads a chance. Eventually, a lot of them moved on. That is why I believe there was a lot of damage done during Houllier's reign, even though he did win those three trophies. So much so, in fact, that since 2000 not one player has come through the Liverpool youth set-up and gone on to become a regular. That may change now Kenny Dalglish, someone who understands the Liverpool way of doing things, is back in charge. But, for more than a decade, not one came through from a production line that just a few years earlier had seen Robbie Fowler, Danny Murphy, David Thompson, Michael Owen, Jamie Carragher, Stevie Gerrard and me break through to the first-team. Can you imagine how much that lot would have raised in the transfer market? I doubt there would have been much change out of £200m and that is all down to Steve Heighway.

The failure to bring through any decent young lads since then is something I put down to Houllier, and later Rafael Benitez, being obsessed with bringing in foreign players for transfer fees. They gave the impression of not being interested in the youth set-up, meaning many promising lads ended up being edged out. Every club needs at least a couple of youngsters coming through. Manchester United still do it, as do West Ham while Arsenal have perhaps produced the best of the lot recently in Jack Wilshere. At Anfield, however, not one has made it in more than 10 years and that is a shocking statistic – especially as Steve Heighway told me not long before leaving that many of the lads in the youth team and reserves were far better than a lot of the foreign lads that had been brought in by Houllier and Benitez. Seeing those lads overlooked in favour of the foreign imports was hugely frustrating for Steve and is probably why he left, which was a massive blow for the club. Houllier may claim to have brought Steve Gerrard through but he didn't. Stevie was already knocking on the door and destined to go on and be a top player, regardless of who the manager was. But that is typical of what Houllier was like at Liverpool, always trying to take credit for the things that went right and blaming others when they went wrong.

Chapter 9

Sweeping Change

Gerard Houllier's first summer in sole charge of Liverpool was when he really started to stamp his own mark on the team. Out went David James, Paul Ince, Jason McAteer and Phil Babb, while Steve McManaman had exercised his right to leave on a free transfer and join Real Madrid after his contract had run out. I was sorry to see them all go as they were decent lads and good players. Steve Harkness was another that left Anfield and those half dozen players represented the first wave of departures that would later include David Thompson, who joined Coventry City on a contract that was probably worth five times what he had been on at Liverpool. He was another one of the lads who came through the ranks but had to leave as Houllier packed the team with foreign imports. To be fair to the manager, the lads who came in during the summer that saw Jamo, Babbsy and Co leave were good quality players. Vladimir Smicer and Titi Camara joined from the French First Division, while Sami Hyypia and Sander Westerveld both arrived from Dutch football. German international Didi Hamann also signed after an impressive first season in the Premier League with Newcastle United.

The thinking behind bringing in so many signings from abroad as the homegrown lads left was that the manager wanted to change the culture at the club. He wanted us to stop going out and to eat better, which I admit was the right thing to do. I'd got to the stage of my career where I realised there was a need to be more professional. Where before, I'd be out two or three times a week, now I stayed in a lot more. I used my day off to rest and recharge the batteries, not embark on a 15-hour drinking session. It helped having lads like Smicer at the club. He was such a professional in everything he did that you couldn't help but learn from him. I think it also helped that Steven Gerrard and Jamie Carragher had broken into the first-team. They may have only been a few years younger than me but, in terms of footballing generations, we were poles apart. I was the last of a dying breed who had started out when drinking was acceptable. Lads like Ray Parlour, Trevor Sinclair and myself had grown up in a world where if you didn't drink, you were considered something of an oddball by people at the club. Stevie and Carra hadn't been subjected to that sort of peer pressure and it showed. They were thorough professionals, even as teenagers. It is why they have gone on to have such great careers. In a funny way, they probably benefited from the way fame changed the life of a professional footballer – especially once the big wages started to be paid. Both lads have been instantly recognisable round town since being teenagers. That could make things difficult when out for the night as I am sure there was always someone who was jealous coming up to say, 'You don't deserve all those thousands you earn every week'. When I started, we were closer to people working in normal jobs in terms of what we earned. Plus, in terms of needing to be more professional than I was at the same age, the amount of games people like Stevie plays with Liverpool in Europe and for England means there just isn't the scope to go out like we did. That probably isn't a bad thing.

In terms of my career, I would say what turned out to be my final season at Anfield was the first one where I started to live my life properly. And it is no coincidence that the 1999-2000 campaign turned out to be my best at Liverpool, as I nailed down the left-back position as my own. The niggling injuries that had dogged me in previous years disappeared, which was probably something to do with me not going out all the time and instead letting my body recover. I went on to play all but six of our Premier League games, which to me said the message about how I needed to live my life had finally sunk in – albeit after seven years! One thing that had helped me was the return of Steve Staunton to Anfield in the summer of 1998. 'Stan' quickly became a big mate of mine and was always ready to offer bits of advice. Included in that were a few home truths. Stan was from the generation of footballers who had gone out boozing all the time so he had already been down the road I was on. Stan drilled into me that there was a right time to have a drink and a wrong one. And that, in common with most footballers of my generation, I was usually choosing the wrong time to go out. Stan helped me realise that.

Mind, he wasn't always the sensible one – as I found out on a mid-season trip to Malta to play a friendly. We were told by the management that we could have a couple of drinks in the bar after the game but then must be in bed by midnight. I realised straight away it was a waste of time to ask for longer. Sure enough, as the clock struck 12, there was a roll-call of everyone in their rooms to make sure we had complied with Houllier's orders. I was sharing a room with David Thompson so when one of the coaches looked in on us, we were in our beds and looking ready to crash out. What this member of the coaching staff didn't know, though, was that we were fully dressed under the duvet so, the moment the door had been closed, we were up and heading out the window. Stan had also decided to join us so all three of us had to crawl on our hands and knees past Houllier's balcony. Once clear, we then jumped in a waiting taxi and headed off to the nearest bar. We were really pleased with ourselves as we walked in, thinking we had got one over not only Houllier but also our team-mates. So, you can imagine our surprise when the first people we saw in there were Sander Westerveld, Didi Hamann and Eric Meyer! They'd had the same idea and we all had a cracking night. The only problem was our flight home was an early morning one so after a few hours we all thought it best to call it a night. All, that is, apart from Stan who said, 'I'm staying out and I will take the consequences tomorrow'. Luckily, me and Didi managed to persuade him that wasn't a great idea and he came back in the taxi with us – so Houllier never found out about our little trip out.

That episode aside, however, Stan was a model professional once back at Anfield and his advice definitely led to my own attitude changing, which meant that during the 1999-2000 season there were very few problems between me and Houllier. I still wasn't over-keen on him as a person but we never had any bust-ups, probably because he didn't seem to have anything to say to me. I was living my life properly and playing well, so there was nothing for him to complain about.

An example of how the game was changing came in training. We would spend more time in the gym doing weights, whereas before we did none of that. It had been just football, football and football but now training had become more structured. A typical day during pre-season would involve a visit to the gym first, followed by some warm-ups and then a game of football. Lunch would then be followed by more work in the gym. The contrast with just a couple of years earlier, when I'd started every day with a bacon sarnie before heading out to train, could not have been more marked. Now, under Patrice Bergues, the approach was much more scientific and I certainly reaped the rewards of having a more professional attitude. I may not have liked Houllier very much but I could see things needed to change in terms of preparation due to the Premier League having got so much quicker following the influx of the foreign players and the emergence of fit young lads such as Steven Gerrard and Jamie Carragher. Anyone who wanted to stay involved and command the big wages that could now be earned had to change their attitude.

The season that had seen Roy Evans quit in November had ended with Liverpool in seventh place. Michael Owen had built on his impressive performance in the 1998 World Cup by netting 18 goals to finish as the Premier League's joint top scorer. Robbie Fowler had scored 14, which was an excellent return for someone who only started 23 games. Unfortunately, he also got himself into a bit of trouble that year, most notably at Chelsea in our 2-1 defeat and then in the derby win over Everton at Anfield. At Stamford Bridge, he'd been having a bit of a running battle with Graeme Le Saux. Eventually, after being clattered for the fourth or fifth time, Robbie snapped and had a couple of digs about Graeme's sexuality. Everyone knew Graeme was married and that the suggestions were nonsense. But Robbie decided to bend over as Graeme took a throw-in, something that earned him a yellow card. It was playground stuff. Whether it was right to do it in front of 40,000 people or not is debatable but all Robbie was guilty of was trying to wind up an opponent. Houllier wasn't happy afterwards and neither were the Football Association, who charged Robbie and ordered him to appear at a hearing. Before it could take place, however, we played Everton at home and Robbie landed himself in even bigger trouble when celebrating one of his two goals in a 3-2 win by dropping to his knees in front of the Everton fans in the Anfield Road end and pretending to snort the goal-line. Robbie had endured a disgusting whispering campaign down the years about him taking drugs, which was definitely not true. The Everton fans had latched on to this and given him awful abuse, singing about him being a 'smackhead' and stuff life that. They would also chant abuse about his family. Some of the stuff was criminal. There was one game we played at Goodison Park and Robbie told me to come over to stand in front of the Bullens Stand as we warmed up. I couldn't believe the abuse that was being aimed at him from the home fans. It was horrible. So, when he did that celebration, I could understand what had pushed him that far. Robbie was wrong to do it, though to the lads we just saw it as funny. We ribbed him about it for months. Even the Everton lads saw the funny side. I was at the other end of the pitch when it happened so I didn't realise what was going on straight away. But I was standing next to Everton defender Craig Short at the time and once it had dawned on us what had happened, we just started laughing. In terms of all the kids that idolised Robbie, though, it was definitely the wrong thing to do. Those kids would be asking questions of their parents such as, 'What did it mean?' As a Dad now myself, I know that is wrong. So, in terms of being a role-model, Robbie shouldn't have done what he did. But, in his defence, the abuse of Robbie's family had built up over the years and the chants aimed at him during the Anfield game had pushed him over the edge. Not that the FA saw it like that, though, as they handed Robbie a six-game ban at a hearing into both the Le Saux incident and the drugs celebration.

On a personal level, the 1998-99 season had been most notable for me finally scoring a league goal for Liverpool. It came in January against Southampton at Anfield, when I got the second one in a 7-1 victory. I can still picture it now, a corner coming in and me meeting it with a peach of a header that flew into the net. A split-second earlier, Incey had called for me to leave it and allow him a shot but there was no way I was going to do that. I wanted my first goal. I'd waited long enough. The best thing about that win over the Saints was that all seven goals were scored by local lads. Robbie had opened the scoring on his way to a hat-trick, while my goal was followed by Carra, Michael Owen and David Thompson getting on the scoresheet. It was a proud moment for the Academy and something that attracted a little bit of attention in the media, which was nice for Steve Heighway and all the coaches. Mind, an example of how quickly fortunes can change in football came just a fortnight later when I was sent off in a 3-1 win over Middlesbrough at Anfield. Mikkel Beck ran across me, I clipped his heels and he fell to the floor. It was an accident but the referee still showed me a red card for a professional foul.

Steven Gerrard was a substitute that afternoon and starting to make a name for himself. He had stepped up to the first-team squad earlier in the season and done well. It had quickly become apparent to the lads that Stevie could play anywhere. He even played at right-back a few times early on. I knew from experience how hard it can be to play in a lot of positions as a young player trying to make it so I had full admiration for how he made the step-up. What I also really like about Stevie, even now after the career he has had, is that you never hear him shouting his mouth off before or after games. That just isn't his style. In the 1998-99 season, Stevie was mainly used as a substitute, whereas Carra was first-choice in the centre of defence. Carra has gone on to enjoy a fantastic career but it was never as obvious as it was with Stevie that Carra would do so well. Carra was someone who had to work really hard at his football every day in training. In that respect, he was similar to me – whereas Robbie, Michael and Stevie were all players who had huge natural ability.

Both Stevie and Carra have gone on to be great servants of Liverpool Football Club. In terms of Stevie, though, I do wish he had tried his luck abroad. There were a couple of years when he was the best player in Europe and I would have loved to see him test himself in La Liga. Can you imagine how good he would have been at Real Madrid or Barcelona? Macca and Michael Owen went to the Bernabeu, which is a move that I believe would have suited Stevie – and I say that as a Liverpool fan.

By the time the 1999-2000 season kicked off, Stevie had joined Carra as a regular in the first-team. Robbie's ban for the Le Saux and Everton incidents had also ended with the final game of the previous campaign and he ensured we got off to a great start on the opening day with a win at Sheffield Wednesday. We were then a bit hit and miss for a few weeks before a run of six wins in seven games put us firmly in the race for a Champions League place. Qualification had, by now, been extended to the top three clubs in the Premier League and we really fancied our chances. Manchester United were already looking a shoe-in for the title but that still left two places up for grabs. Arsenal, Chelsea, Leeds United and ourselves were the four clubs battling it out. So, when Leeds came to Anfield in early February, we were all fired up. We'd beaten them at Elland Road in August but, during the build-up to the return, Leeds had still been giving it the big 'un about how all these young lads of theirs were going to dominate English football for years to come. David O'Leary also kept coming out with all his 'my babies' rubbish, which the newspapers seemed to be falling for. We were saying things like, 'Hold on, they're not all babies' but no-one would listen. Instead, they just fawned over Leeds as the next great thing. Leeds didn't help themselves ahead of the game at Anfield with a few of their 'babies' getting a bit boastful about what was going to happen. The year before, Alan Smith had scored with his first touch on his debut as Leeds won 3-1 and they seemed to think there was going to be a repeat. But we were adamant that was not going to be the case and we ended up giving Leeds a real going over in a 3-1 win. A week later, we also beat Arsenal and then followed that with a 1-1 draw at Old Trafford. We felt unbeateable, a feeling underlined when we took 17 points from the next seven games to move up to second in the table. With just five games remaining, we looked certainties to claim one of the Champions League places. The team had gelled really well, with Steven Gerrard, in particular, having had a great season. Even though still a teenager, he had proved capable of winning games on his own. Usually, an ability to grab a game by the scruff of the neck comes later in a player's career but Stevie started doing it almost straight away.

With our confidence sky-high, we headed to Everton on April 21 believing a place in the Champions League was ours for the taking. A goalless draw, therefore, was not a bad result. It meant that even after we lost to Chelsea in our next game, we were still overwhelming favourites to finish in the top three due to a run-in that involved back-to-back back home games against Leicester City and Southampton and a final day trip to relegation-threatened Bradford City. One of our main rivals, Leeds, were struggling with the murder of two supporters in Istanbul before their UEFA Cup semi-final against Galatasaray having understandably had a traumatic effect on not just the players but the club as a whole. As a result, they had just lost a fourth straight game – 4-0 at home to Arsenal, who leapfrogged us into second place on goal difference. Arsene Wenger's side also had a game in hand on us, while we were two points ahead of Leeds and seven in front of Chelsea. It was ours to lose, which is exactly what we did. Leicester were the first to inflict a blow to our hopes with a 2-0 win at Anfield. On the same night, Leeds beat Watford 3-1 to move up to third. We then reclaimed the last Champions League place with a goalless draw at home to Southampton only to then be dumped back down to fourth 24 hours later when Leeds drew 1-1 at home to Everton. By now, Arsenal had sealed second spot – meaning ourselves and Leeds were left to scrap it out on the final day. Leeds were due to go to West Ham United, while we headed for Valley Parade. The place was rocking. Third-bottom Bradford needed to better Wimbledon's score at Southampton to stay up – both clubs had 33 points but Wimbledon's goal difference was superior so if we won, Bradford were down. More importantly, three points for us meant Leeds would also have to win at Upton Park.

The early stages at Valley Parade were quite cagey, as you would expect with so much being at stake for both clubs. All that changed, however, on 12 minutes when David Wetherall put Bradford ahead with a bullet header from a corner. The place erupted and a couple of their fans ran on to the pitch. Even though we were behind, I wasn't unduly concerned as we had plenty of time to get back into the game. I still felt confident at half-time, even though by now I was in a lot of pain after injuring my foot in a challenge. I was on the side where the dugouts were and told Houllier I was struggling but he said, 'Stay on'. He gave me the same message at half-time, even though I said there was no way I was going to be able to get through another 45 minutes. I eventually came off with about ten minutes to go, by which time we were getting more and more desperate as Bradford defended for their lives. News had also come through that Wimbledon were losing 2-0 at Southampton so the Bradford players and fans knew just how important a win would be. We continued to press but never really looked like scoring as Bradford held on for the win.

At the final whistle, what seemed like all of Bradford piled on to the pitch in celebration and it took me ages to get to the dressing room. I was in total agony but no-one from Liverpool was around to help. The moment the whistle had blown, it had been a case of 'every man for himself' due to the dressing rooms at Valley Parade being down in the corner of the pitch. It meant a mad 50-yard dash for everyone involved with Liverpool, apart from me who could only hobble down the touchline. It is always the same with a pitch invasion.

When I finally reached the dressing room, everyone's heads were down as we knew a great chance to play in the Champions League had been blown. Leeds had qualified. They had only drawn at West Ham so if we had won at Bradford then we would have qualified, news that just made the dressing room even more depressed. Another season of promise had ended on a sour note and that meant the summer was difficult. Even going away to Barbados with my then girlfriend couldn't raise my spirits, especially as I still had my leg in a pot after breaking a bone in my foot on the final day. I just couldn't enjoy myself. Liverpool, with all our fantastic history in the European Cup, had never played in the Champions League so it was devastating to miss out. What I didn't realise, however, as I sat there in agony at Valley Parade was that I was destined to play in next season's Champions League after all. And, for that, I had Gerard Houllier to thank.

Chapter 10

"Leeds United want to speak to you…"

It must be some sort of record. On the Monday, I was a key part of the future at Anfield and signing a five-year deal that, by the standards of the day, was a lucrative one. But, just four days later, I was on my way out of Liverpool after being told that the best I could hope for in the coming season was a place on the bench. The transformation in my fortunes had been triggered by Liverpool signing Christian Ziege from Middlesbrough for £5.5m. I found out about the transfer in a 'phone call from one of the staff at Liverpool, not Gerard Houllier as you might expect. The call was very matter-of-fact, in that I was told Ziege was signing and that he was going to start the season in the team at left-back, the position I'd made my own during the previous year. I was in shock. How could things change so quickly in just four days? On signing the new contract, I really thought I would see out my career at Liverpool. I couldn't have been happier at the prospect, either. Liverpool were the club I had supported as a boy and I genuinely loved going into work every morning. I also felt I had made the breakthrough during the previous two seasons. Before then, I'd had a few years where I was in and out of the team and no-one had seemed to know what my best position was. But all that had changed – or that is at least what I thought when signing my new contract. What I didn't know at the time, of course, was that Houllier was determined to sign Ziege, who'd had a decent first season in English football with Middlesbrough after earlier spells at Bayern Munich and AC Milan.

Once I had got over the initial shock, I tried to make sense of the news. But I couldn't. Being relegated back to the bench was hard to take because I'd had such a good year. I felt really disheartened and I just couldn't accept it. Even today with my career having been over for several years, I still can't understand why Houllier wanted to bring someone else in. I had been one of the best players at the club during what turned out to be my final year at Anfield, particularly during the second half of the season. Didi Hamann even said to me when the news about Ziege broke, 'Listen, Dom, don't go because you'll do a better job than Ziege'. I just replied, 'But the manager has told me Ziege is going to play and that isn't fair on me because I've had such a good season'.

The thing that most upset me was Houllier never even saying I could stay and fight for my place. I did go in to see him and try to get some answers. At that meeting, I made it clear how unhappy I was. Football is a ruthless world and I could have accepted a new player coming in if I'd been told I still had a chance of getting in the team. But I was told Ziege would start ahead of me regardless of how well I might be playing. That was something I couldn't accept. I had played well the previous season and had been at Anfield a long time, so I felt I deserved more respect than I was being shown. I didn't want preferential treatment, far from it. That has never been my style. But I did feel I deserved some respect. Unfortunately, I got none off Houllier and that helped to make up my mind that my future lay away from Anfield. Even then, though, it was not an easy decision to make because I considered Liverpool to be my team. It was why I had been so pleased to sign a contract a few days earlier that, I thought, would take me beyond my 31st birthday. Leaving meant it wasn't just a case of saying goodbye to my team-mates. There were also the dinner ladies, the groundsman, the guy at the training ground gate – I had known them all since I was a boy. The thought of leaving them behind was an upsetting one. But, for the good of my career, I needed a fresh start. So, I went.

It meant I missed out on all the trophies that Liverpool won the following season. I'll admit that seeing the lads pick up the FA Cup, League Cup and UEFA Cup was difficult as I had been one of those players who had put in the years of ground work when Liverpool were in transition. I had played my part in the revival of the club but not been there at the moment when the trophies started arriving again. In a way, that is a regret. But, in other ways, leaving Liverpool is a decision I don't regret as it allowed me to join a wonderful club in Leeds United. Now, I consider myself as much a Leeds fan as I do Liverpool, so the move can't have been a bad one. In fact, I often get asked which team I support by fans and I always say, 'Both clubs'. I really do mean it, too. I was only at Leeds for four years but the club made such a big impact on me.

In many ways, I consider myself fortunate that Leeds were the first club I spoke to after making my mind up to leave Liverpool. A few had been lined up by my agent, Struan Marshall. He had put my name forward to every Premier League club, even the big guns, and there was plenty of interest. I had said to Stru right from the very start that I wanted to join a big club. It is often said that the only way after leaving Liverpool is down but I felt, at 26, that I could do well at a big club elsewhere. Happily for me, Leeds were one of the first clubs to show genuine interest and, after what had happened with Ziege, the news gave me a big lift. Leeds were a club on the up. Their last trophy may have been eight years earlier when the League Championship had come to Elland Road, but, in recent seasons, Leeds had made big strides – as had been proved just the previous May when David O'Leary's side had claimed that final Champions League place. O'Leary had taken charge after George Graham had returned south to manage Tottenham Hotspur in 1998. Many had expected O'Leary, who was Graham's assistant, to do the same but he had wanted to strike out on his own. It proved a wise decision with youngsters such as Harry Kewell, Jonathan Woodgate and Alan Smith coming through to bring genuine quality to an already decent side.

So, I travelled over to Yorkshire and met Leeds chairman, Peter Ridsdale, at a city centre hotel called the Malmaison. My agent was still waiting on 'phone calls back from other clubs so we travelled over with an open mind. Peter really sold the club to me that day. Of course, I knew they were in the Champions League because they had qualified at Liverpool's expense. But the vision Peter outlined to me and Stru suggested that was only the beginning. Peter also went through the squad, saying how strong it was and how I would not be the last addition as Leeds were determined to become a major power in English football. I knew the squad was very, very strong from playing against Leeds over the previous couple of seasons. We had done the double over them in 1999-2000 but the previous year they had beaten us at Anfield and then been unfortunate to only draw 0-0 with us in the return at Elland Road. During those games, I had felt the Leeds lads were a cocky bunch but I also knew they had a lot of talent. When I met Ridsdale, Leeds had only just broken their transfer record to sign Olivier Dacourt for £7.2m from Lens, while Mark Viduka had also joined from Celtic in a £6m deal. I took both signings as huge statements of intent by the club. Clearly, something was being built at Elland Road and that really appealed to me. As a player, I wanted improvement all the time and that was what Leeds seemed to be doing as a team and as a club. There was some proven experience mixed in with the young lads who had, despite their age, already played a lot of Premier League games. The move just felt right and I signed that night. Peter had been keen to get the deal done. And because I was happy with what I heard, that was just what we did. Peter was someone I always got on well with during my time at Leeds. I know people will read that sentence and think, 'I'm not surprised you liked him, he was the one who was so generous to you all financially'. That is a fair point. But, personally, I found him a really enthusiastic fan. Sitting with him at that first meeting in the Malmaison was just like sitting with someone who loved Leeds United. Whether that ended up being a good thing for the club in the long-run is open to debate but, at the time, I found Peter to be a big positive about joining Leeds.

The Leeds lads were actually on a night out when I met Peter to discuss the deal. So, after we'd sorted it, he drove me to the Flying Pizza restaurant in Leeds to meet the boys. Lee Bowyer had been fined for something or other so had offered to take the boys out. The thing that struck me the most about that night was that I didn't feel awkward in any way. Sometimes, when you go into a situation where you know no-one, it can be a bit weird. But there was none of that at the Flying Pizza. It was a good vibe and I headed back into the city centre from the restaurant thinking, 'I can see myself settling in well at Leeds'. Of course, me being me, I couldn't then call it a night. I had to carry on drinking with my new team-mates, even though my medical was due to take place the following morning. I didn't get back to the hotel until about 3am, and this after having drunk plenty of champagne with Peter earlier in the evening at the Malmaison. I suppose it showed that I wasn't worried about the medical, when as things turned out I probably should have been.

At Liverpool, I had come through pre-season okay. The bone I had broken in my foot on the final day when we lost to Bradford City had healed so that wasn't going to be a problem. I'd had a bit of a nagging pain in my knee from time-to-time in training since returning for pre-season but thought it was nothing more than a niggling injury, the sort every footballer will have played on with during his career. So, when I came in to be put through my paces by assistant manager Eddie Gray, I had no worries – other than that I felt a bit rough after my night out. In many ways, it was a re-run of when I first joined up with England under Glenn Hoddle when I'd gone out on the lash. I don't know if Eddie could sense I'd had a bit of a session or not but he really did work me hard. I felt fine but then my knee started to hurt halfway through the running exercises. Basically, every time I turned at the end of a sprint, it would become painful. Something was catching in my knee so I went with Dave Hancock, the club's physio, to have a scan at Leeds General Infirmary. I still didn't think it would be a problem but, in the end, I failed the medical. The scan showed that I had torn a ligament in my knee without anyone realising. It could only have been during the Bradford game that had seen me break a bone in my foot.

Dave was really, really apologetic about the result as he knew that a failed medical usually breaks the deal. Dave knew the damage to the ligament would take some time to heal. But all I could say was, 'That's a shame, as I signed last night'. Peter Ridsdale had insisted I sign for five years, there and then. So, regardless of whether I had failed the medical or not, I was already a Leeds United player. Dave was not overly happy with the situation but that was how it was.

As a club, Leeds were brilliant. They stuck by me despite the original prognosis that I would be out until October. Peter Ridsdale, in particular, gave me a lift when he said, 'Dom, we are signing you for five years and not five months so just concentrate on getting yourself fit'. I really appreciated Peter's words. It was a great feeling to know I was really wanted, and quite a contrast to how I'd been made to feel at Liverpool just a few days earlier. To be fair to Liverpool as well, on hearing about the injury they did agree to Leeds' proposal whereby an initial fee of only £100,000 was to be paid as a down-payment with the rest of the £4.25m fee being due once I was fit. Liverpool didn't have to do that and could have insisted the fee be paid as originally agreed, which could have made things a bit more difficult. But they didn't and I appreciated that.

It was only after the deal had been struck that I first met David O'Leary. David may not have had a lot of fans in the Leeds dressing room by the end of his time as manager but I always liked and respected him. Right from the start, David was very understanding about the knee injury and, again, very supportive. I have also never forgotten his first words to me, mainly because they were exactly what I wanted to hear. He said: 'Dom, you are going to have to work hard to get into my team because these are a very good group of players'. I liked that honesty. If Houllier had said something similar when Ziege signed for Liverpool then I would have stayed. But, instead, it was made clear to me that I wasn't going to play if Ziege was fit and that was no good to me. Another way David gave me a lift was when he explained my role. He said that, while at the start, he may use me in a few positions due to the injury problems Leeds had, long-term he saw me playing in central defence. That was music to my ears. I wanted to play there anyway and, at last, someone agreed. Now, I just wanted to get myself fit as soon as possible and start to pay back the faith Leeds United had shown in me.

Chapter 11

Oh Matteo, Scored A.....

When I agreed to sign for Leeds United, one of the big attractions was the chance to play Champions League football. At Liverpool, I had been fortunate enough to play in the UEFA Cup and reached the semi-finals of the European Cup Winners' Cup. But, as enjoyable as playing in both competitions had been, there was nothing to compare with the big one. The Champions League has an aura all of its own, right from the theme tune that welcomes the team out on to the field through to the Who's Who of European football that doubles as the list of past winners. Everyone who has played in either the Champions League or its predecessor, the European Cup, said the same thing – nothing compares to playing in club football's most prestigious competition. Joining Leeds meant I could at last share in that experience. Or that was what I hoped, at least, when I put pen to paper on a five-year deal on August 16, 2000. By then, Leeds' involvement was already under way. As the side finishing third in the Premier League, they had to negotiate a qualifying round before reaching the first group stage. Usually, this involved the English club in question having to get past one of Europe's lesser lights over two legs. In the two years that preceded our involvement at Leeds, for instance, Chelsea had progressed at the expense of Latvian champions Skonto, while Manchester United started the season that ended with them winning the treble by knocking out Polish side LKS Lodz to qualify. A similar sized task would, of course, have done everyone at Elland Road nicely. Instead, what Leeds were handed was a daunting two-legged qualifier with TSV 1860 Munich, who in 1999-2000 had finished fourth in the Bundesliga behind champions Bayern Munich, Bayer Leverkusen and Hamburg. They were a good team and Leeds would have all on to go through. The first leg took place a week before I signed, so I had taken only scant notice of a 2-1 win for the home side at Elland Road. I, therefore, didn't appreciate how the tie had swung the way of the Germans in dramatic fashion courtesy of a Paul Agostino goal in the third minute of stoppage time. Not only that, but with Oliver Dacourt and Eirik Bakke having been sent off by inexperienced referee, Antonio Ferreira de Sequeira, it meant Leeds were in real danger of missing out on the Champions League place they had fought so hard for throughout the previous season. Of course, I realised this the moment it became clear that Leeds wanted to sign me and the worst thing was I could do nothing about it due to the knee injury that had shown up during the medical. Having signed after the first leg, I wouldn't have been able to play in Munich anyway. But I would, at least, have been able to travel with the lads and offer my support from the touchline. Instead, I had to stay at home and keep my fingers crossed that they could do the business in the Olympic Stadium. It was, though, a tall order thanks to an injury list that, together with Ollie and Eirik being banned, meant just one fit midfielder was able to make the trip, Lee Bowyer. David O'Leary's response was to push Lucas Radebe and Gary Kelly into midfield alongside a barely-fit Matthew Jones. It was a gamble but one David was forced into by a lack of bodies.

I decided to watch the game round at Eirik's. We had hit it off from the moment I signed for Leeds. We were very similar characters, both enjoying a drink and a laugh, and are still good friends today. So, I went round his house and watched the game with a couple of beers. We were both so nervous ahead of kick-off, there was just so much at stake in terms of Leeds United's season that we couldn't be anything else. The two of us ended up kicking every ball in Eirik's living room that night. There was a really nervous moment in the first half when Thomas Hassler curled a free-kick on to a post, which Nigel Martyn promptly kissed in relief. That made us both laugh. Thankfully, two minutes into the second half, Smithy settled our nerves by putting us in front on the night and we just knew the lads were going to do it. 1860 now had to score twice before the end of normal time to take the tie into extra-time and that was not going to happen. Sure enough, by the final whistle no further goals had been scored and we were through. My new team-mates had been brilliant and Leeds were in the Champions League proper.

The club had hit the big time, not just financially but in football terms as well – as was underlined just a couple of days later when the draw for the first group stage was made. We had been hoping to draw at least one of the big boys, as every professional footballer worth his salt wants to test himself against the best. But we didn't get just one, we got two – Barcelona and AC Milan. I was getting treatment on my injured knee when our name was drawn out in Group H so was one of the first to know. I am told the lads, on being told out on the training field, at first didn't believe the news. This really was the stuff dreams were made of, even allowing for the fourth team in our group being from Istanbul – where just a few months earlier, two Leeds fans had been murdered on the eve of the club's UEFA Cup semi-final against Galatasaray. Thankfully, it was Besiktas who we would play and not Galatasaray, who instead had been drawn in Group D with Sturm Graz, Rangers and Monaco. But, even so, a return to Istanbul was something that no-one at the club, and especially those who had been in Turkey the previous April, had wanted. It was a different story, of course, with Barcelona and AC Milan as everyone was relishing the prospect of a trip to two of European football's most famous stadiums. On a personal level, much would depend on how the fixtures were scheduled as, at the time of the draw, I was still a few weeks away from a possible return. As it turned out, I missed just the first group game - the visit to the Nou Camp. Unfortunately, I wasn't the only one to miss the trip to Spain with injury also meaning Harry Kewell, Jonathan Woodgate, David Batty, Jason Wilcox and Eirik had to stay at home. Mark Viduka was another notable absentee due to being away with Australia at the 2000 Olympics. It meant David had to send out something of a makeshift team and the boys got a bit of a going over as Barcelona won 4-0. Patrick Kluivert got a couple of goals and Rivaldo was outstanding on a night when we just didn't get going. It seemed the worst possible start for a team making their Champions League debut but, in a funny way, losing so heavily probably did us a favour in the long-run as it opened everyone's eyes to the size of the challenge. I had played in Europe several times for Liverpool but not at Champions League level and there is a big difference. That fact was brought home to the lads that night in the Nou Camp. Thankfully, we learned such a harsh lesson in our first game and that gave us time to turn things round, which is exactly what we did. I believe losing as heavily as we did in Bareclona made everyone at the club, even those of us who had been watching at home on television, doubly determined we'd never suffer such an embarrassing result again.

There was no let-up in our schedule with AC Milan due at Elland Road just a week later. When watching our Nou Camp defeat in Eirik's living room, little did I know that I would be making my debut in such an important match. The game was on Tuesday night, but even on the previous morning I had no idea that I would be involved. That was when David called me into the office to ask how I was feeling. I said, 'Okay thanks, the injury feels okay and I will probably be ready to join in with training this week'. David just looked at me and said, 'How do you fancy playing tomorrow night?' I was gob-smacked, but said 'yes' straight away. It was only then that it dawned on me I was about to face AC Milan, one of the best teams in Europe, despite having not trained for six weeks. Not only that, but David wanted me to play on the left-wing because Harry Kewell was still injured. It probably wouldn't happen now.

David said he wasn't bothered about me getting forward too much but he wanted me to do a job on Thomas Helveg and help our full-back out. Milan were an attacking team and, after what had happened in Barcelona the previous week, David wanted to send out a solid team. Come the night of the game, the rain absolutely lashed it down. If we had been playing a normal Premier League game, it might even have been off. But, with millions watching across Europe and Elland Road full, the game went ahead. Milan's team was a formidable one, with Andriy Shevchenko up front and the incomparable Paolo Maldini at the back. So, I don't imagine many outside our dressing room gave us a chance of getting a decent result. But that is exactly what happened thanks to Milan's goalkeeper Dida making a complete hash of trying to catch a 20-yard shot from Lee Bowyer. In such wet conditions, he should have beaten the ball away. Thankfully for us, though, all Dida could do was divert the ball into the back of the net to, literally, hand us a last minute winner. I was still on the pitch when Bow scored, even though I was only supposed to play an hour at most. The game was so tight that the manager didn't want to make a change and I'll admit that by the final whistle I was fit to drop. It was only the adrenalin that got me through. I am glad it did, though, as that night was the start of the huge connection I still feel towards Leeds United. Everything about the Milan game was memorable, from the opposition to the result and the atmosphere inside Elland Road. I came off the pitch thinking, 'This is where I belong'. I'd had the same feeling at Liverpool, mainly because I'd grown up as a fan and had been at the club for such a long time. But, at Leeds, the connection was instant. I can't explain why being at Leeds just felt right, even now. But that night proved to be a turning point in my career. I fell in love with Leeds United.

The night had an almost surreal feel about it, probably because just over 24 hours earlier I'd had no inkling I would be playing. That feeling continued afterwards when I was interviewed by a journalist from *Gazzetta dello Sport*. Usually, a player making his debut would be interviewed by the local newspaper, which in Leeds' case was the *Yorkshire Evening Post*. But there I was, speaking to Italy's main sports paper. My Dad couldn't believe it when I told him. I also did Italian TV, who wanted to know more about me and why I had an Italian name. Perhaps the best thing about the night of my debut along with the result was that my team-mates seemed to appreciate me, which is always important. They could see I was hard-working and honest. They appreciated I was playing out of position on the left wing and had not trained for six weeks, but still given everything for the cause. Some of the lads were even laughing about it afterwards. I felt accepted.

The victory over Milan may have been fortuitous in that their goalkeeper was at fault for Bow's winner, but, on the balance of play, I thought we deserved the win. The team's performance, coming a week after that disappointing night in Barcelona, was testament to the spirit that existed at the club. I'd seen the strength of that for myself, once the boys had flown back from Spain. The key after a defeat like that is to lift each other. I was still the new boy so didn't think it was my place, especially as I was yet to make my debut. But I watched with interest as the manager and the coaching staff went about the task of lifting spirits. They did a good job, as did the big characters at the club. Gary Kelly was definitely one of them throughout my four years at Leeds. I always liked Kells, even though sometimes the Irish lads could be a bit cliquey and go off together on their own. If you were ever invited along on one of the Irish lads' nights out, as happened to me a few times, then it was a real badge of honour. Kells loved Leeds United with all his heart and never wanted to play for anyone else, which of course is how his career panned out. Michael Duberry was another who was a loud presence in the dressing room and a real funny guy, the sort who can be invaluable after a heavy defeat as he puts a smile back on your face. Other strong characters included David Batty, even though during my first few months he was injured, plus Nigel Martyn and Jason Wilcox. As the older lads, they would knock about together. They had their own banter, while I hung around with Eirik from the start, and then also Smithy. The three of us stayed really, really close throughout my four years at Leeds.

It was a good squad, and I am certain that strength of spirit was how we managed to turn things round after losing in the Nou Camp.

After coming off the field having beaten Milan, we were then given another unexpected lift by the news from the other group game in Istanbul. Besiktas had beaten Barcelona 3-0 so all four clubs were level on three points, the Turks having lost 4-1 in the San Siro in their opening game. That meant victory at home to Besiktas the following midweek would leave us in one of the two qualifying berths at the halfway stage. And few would have had a bet on that being the case after the opening round of fixtures!

The night of the Besiktas game turned out to be the moment when people started to sit up and take notice of Leeds United. We were absolutely superb and thrashed the Turks 6-0. I am not exaggerating when I say we could have scored ten. Even I scored a goal, which bearing in mind how few I scored in all those years I played for Liverpool might have surprised a few people at Anfield. I was proud of the finish, too, with the ball having broken to me in the box, I knocked it to the side and rolled it in the net. I doubt my old team-mate Robbie Fowler could have finished any better, or at least that's what I told him later by text! Such an emphatic scoreline meant no-one could ignore us now, not least as we had gone to the top of the group thanks to Milan beating Barcelona in the Nou Camp. After such a memorable 90 minutes, the entire team went out together that night and had a great time. We ended up in the Majestyk nightclub and got lashed up together. It turned into a crazy night, as not only did all the blokes want to buy us all a pint but the girls were all over us. As a single boy, I lapped it up. I woke up in Headingley the following morning at a student's gaff. That was a night when I had a good result on the field and an equally good one off it! On the way home, I then made sure I bought all the newspapers to see what they had to say about Leeds United. Unsurprisingly, they were all complimentary and I still have them at my parents' house.

With the Champions League put on hold for a few weeks, we were able to take stock of the season so far. In Europe, everyone was understandably delighted. But, in the Premier League, it had been a stuttering start with Manchester City and Ipswich Town having already won at Elland Road. Clearly, we were going to have to learn how to cope better with the demands of playing in two high-profile competitions.

Back-to-back wins over Tottenham Hotspur and Charlton Athletic did, though, lift us up to fourth in the table ahead of the Champions League resuming in mid-October with the return against Besiktas. It was always going to be an emotional trip after the tragic deaths of Kevin Speight and Christopher Loftus six months earlier. I hadn't been at the club back then but, obviously, I was well aware of what had happened in Istanbul. For two family men to die for nothing more than supporting their football team abroad is terrible. The boys had also told me what it was like playing against Galatasaray in that UEFA Cup semi-final first leg and it sounded awful. They had lost 2-0 but no-one really cared as football meant nothing compared to what had happened to the two supporters.

I could tell the lads had been badly affected by what had happened and, for some, it was a really emotional experience to go back so soon. The big difference this time was Besiktas, as a club, made a real effort to establish decent relations. Agreement had also been reached on limiting the number of away supporters that could attend the two games. In the end, Besiktas cancelled their official supporters' trip due to lack of demand, while just 138 Leeds fans made the trip to Turkey after independent travel was banned. The upshot of the two clubs' efforts and the restrictions on who could travel was that there was none of the nastiness that had gone on the previous season in the UEFA Cup. Even so, we did have armed guards outside the players' rooms throughout our stay. It was quite unnerving, and I remember looking at one of the policemen on our floor who had a machine gun and thinking, 'What is this all about? We are footballers not the president of some country'. It was a real eye-opener for me, as Liverpool had not had to deal with anything like that. I have to say, though, that as players we felt totally safe throughout our stay in Istanbul.

In terms of the match itself, the trip to the Inonu Stadium was a bit of a non-event. Their fans did make every effort to intimidate us. In Turkey, the culture is to get to the ground about three hours before kick-off. It meant that when we arrived, there were already thousands inside, chanting away. It is all very different from England, where the majority of fans seem to arrive at two minutes to kick-off after a mad dash from the pub. As we expected, the noise levels were cranked up the moment we went out for our pre-match warm-up. The locals were determined to make it as hostile as possible for us and we were left under no illusions as to how unwelcome we were in Istanbul. But, once the match kicked off, we blocked all the noise out and just got on with our jobs. Because of what had happened in April, we didn't want to let anyone down back in Leeds. Chances were few and far between and the game ended up goalless, which was just about the right result. With Barcelona and Milan drawing 3-3 in the San Siro, the point was enough to keep us on top of the group. Sadly, that is not what is probably best remembered from our draw in Turkey. Instead, it is the truly horrific Achilles injury that Michael Bridges suffered. Just 23 minutes had been played when Bridgey's studs seemed to stick in the turf and he went down, clearly in terrible pain. He was then stretchered off. None of us realised, however, just how bad the injury was until we got back into the dressing room. Bridgey was, unfortunately, never the same again. The previous year, it had been Bridgey's goals that had got Leeds into the Champions League. He was also a smashing lad around the club, always having a joke with the boys. But, after that injury, he didn't manage to score again for the club. He eventually went on to play for several teams, including Newcastle United and Sunderland. But he was never the same player and was forced to retire at the age of just 32 after a couple of years in Australia. It was a real shame, though I do remember the Leeds physio Dave Hancock saying to me once, 'Bridgey just isn't built to be a footballer in terms of his physique'. I could see what Dave meant, though I didn't necessarily agree as we are all different shapes and sizes. There isn't just one prototype of a footballer. But, it is a fact that Bridgey was never the same player again after that night in Istanbul.

The injury to Bridgey meant Dave Hancock had another long-term patient in his care. It also meant we made the trip to Manchester United the following weekend without a full starting XI of players. Just for the record, that 'team' was: Nigel Martyn; Danny Mills, Lucas Radebe, Michael Duberry, Ian Harte; Eirik Bakke, Olivier Dacourt, David Batty, Jason Wilcox, Harry Kewell and Bridgey. Quite an XI, I'm sure anyone would agree. Our subsequent 3-0 defeat at Old Trafford did not, therefore, come as too much of a shock. With Barcelona next up just three days later, clearly Dave was in for a busy time in the treatment room as he tried to rush a couple of the lads back. In the end, four were passed fit – Hartey, Millsy, Ollie and Eirik. Seeing those lads in the dressing room before the game along with Smithy, who had passed a late fitness test, gave everyone a lift, especially as we knew victory would be enough to book our place in the second group stage with a game to spare. With such a huge prize at stake, the atmosphere was even more highly-charged than usual. Bow then put us 1-0 up after just five minutes to crank the noise levels up even further. Barcelona, to their credit, came back at us almost immediately but Paul Robinson was having one of those nights that every goalkeeper dreams of. No matter what Barcelona tried, Robbo was their equal. Eventually, after what seemed like an eternity, the fourth official indicated there would be four minutes of stoppage time. We were almost there, or so we thought. Unfortunately, with just 20 seconds remaining, Barcelona launched one last attack that saw Gerard head Philip Cocu's cross against a post and Rivaldo fire the rebound into the net. Elland Road was stunned into silence, as were the players afterwards. No-one said a word in the dressing room due to feeling so deflated. Now, don't get me wrong, Barcelona put us under a lot of pressure and but for Robbo they would probably have won. I know getting any kind of result against a team like Barcelona is an achievement. But, even so, to concede an equaliser in the fourth minute of stoppage time was hugely deflating for everyone from the manager down and one that took a few days to get over. Once the dust had settled, however, the important thing was that qualification was still in our own hands. We may have lost top spot to Milan, following their 2-0 win in Istanbul. But we were still three points clear of Barcelona, meaning as long as we got at least a draw from the trip to Milan then we would go through to the second group stage. Simple, eh?

Some sides may have been daunted by a visit to the San Siro. But not us. We had really started to enjoy the European trips. I saw a similar thing in the Tottenham Hotspur boys when they competed in the Champions League for the first time in the 2010-11 season. Spurs were visiting these great places, not knowing if they would ever play at them again in their careers. So, they were determined to soak up the atmosphere and enjoy the entire experience. We were exactly the same at Leeds. What I particularly enjoyed about the trips was the night before a game, when we got a chance to train at these great stadiums. They were usually light-hearted sessions, where we would run through who was playing and what the team shape was. This would then be followed by a game of a five-a-side or whatever and a bit of fun. Milan was no different, though the first thing that struck me was just how awful the playing surface was. In parts, there was hardly any grass at all, while we noticed that the ball bobbled a lot. A few of us knew about the history of the San Siro and that a lack of light had always meant the surface suffered. But, even so, we were surprised by just how bad it was during that training session. The dressing rooms were a bit of a let-down, too. I expected them to be a lot better.

Maybe our view of the San Siro was tainted by the amazing standard of not only our hotel on Lake Como, but also the fact we had flown out to Italy on a private jet. We were told it was the one that usually ferried the rock band U2 around. I don't know if that was true but it really was the height of luxury. The plane had showers and sofas, and was beautiful. It was so nice, in fact, that even we, as footballers, found it a bit excessive. There was one thing I didn't like, though, and that was the seating arrangements, in that the chairman and the directors sat in the best seats down the front whereas the lads were at the back. Don't get me wrong, our seats were great and we wanted for nothing. But they weren't the best ones and didn't have the most leg-room, which as we were the ones flying out to play a vitally important game did strike me as being the wrong way round. The first class standards extended to our hotel next to Lake Como. It really was amazing. I'd been there as a kid and the whole area is beautiful. As footballers, you don't usually get to see much of a city so the coach ride from the airport to the hotel was a bit of a treat for the lads. Everyone was staring out the window, taking in the amazing view. A few of the lads commented that it was a step-up from our usual matchday journey from the Malmaison to Elland Road for a home game and it was hard to disagree. Once at the hotel, the food was also out of this world. In fact, it was so good that Mark Viduka didn't want to leave at the end of dinner! He would be saying things like, 'This is the best lasagne I have ever tasted in my life'. As Premier League players, we'd got used to staying at the best hotels but this was something else.

I was down to share with Eirik and, once we had got to our room, we settled into our usual routine. The one negative with playing in European competition is the amount of time there is to kill on the away trips. The only thing that breaks the time up is training on the eve of the game. For the rest of our stay, we were supposed to sleep or relax. But me and Eirik would be too excited to sleep, especially on the day of the game, and that was why we would take along things to keep us occupied. In terms of the essentials, our luggage for a typical away game was one tracksuit, some pants, our boots and that was about it. The rest of our luggage was made up of all the things we needed to keep ourselves occupied, such as the Playstation and a portable DVD player. We would then be able to while away the hours playing Tiger Woods on the Playstation or a football game. If we went for football, it was always Scotland v Norway - even though that did put me at a disadvantage as Scotland were always minging, while Norway weren't too bad. That was my excuse back then, anyway, and I see no reason to change it now!

Once the day of the game arrived in Milan, I felt good. I had a feeling the night was going to go well. I can't explain why, I just did. It might have even been because I knew all of my Dad's family in Italy would be watching due to the game being shown live on television in their own country. Whatever the reason, I just felt confident from the moment I woke up that morning. That feeling never left me all day as we counted down the hours to kick-off. Thankfully, my confidence did not turn out to be misplaced as the team produced a magnificent display to claim a point. Even when Milan were awarded a penalty midway through the first half when Kells was adjudged to have handled the ball, we didn't waiver – though I must admit to feeling relieved when Shevchenko struck the penalty against Robbo's right-hand post.

Just before the break, the moment that has come to define my career at Leeds arrived when I managed to nip in at the near post to head Lee Bowyer's corner into the net. The song that Leeds fans still sing to this day suggests it was, 'A fucking great goal'. I can't claim it was quite that 'great', but there was no doubt the goal was important. Milan did equalise midway through the second half when Serginho scored but, in truth, we were quite comfortable in the closing stages. Having said that, I was still relieved when the final whistle was blown to signal we were in the second group stage of the Champions League. A few moans came out of the Barcelona camp later, some even questioning how much effort Milan had put in. But we didn't care, what mattered was that Leeds United were through and Barca were heading for the UEFA Cup. For obvious reasons, I get asked about the San Siro all the time. I also find it amazing to hear some of the stories that fans have. One lad told me how he broke his arm celebrating my goal in the away end. I also met someone recently who lost his job because he stayed on in Milan for two days after the game, celebrating the fact Leeds had qualified for the next stage.

As memorable as my goal was, however, what really stands out from that night is what happened after we had showered and changed. About 7,000 Leeds fans had made the trip to Italy and were being held in the ground by the police so the streets outside could be cleared. We had been asked to go out and wave to the fans. The lads didn't need asking twice as we all wanted the celebrations to go on all night – which, as it turned out, is exactly what happened! Anyway, I wandered out after a few minutes with a couple of beers in my hand. Quite a few of the boys were already out there and having a great time. Suddenly, a chant of 'Leeds team, give us a song' began. Everyone looked at each other, wondering who was going to step forward. Unsurprisingly, Kells was the one. After being cheered by the fans, he then gestured for everyone to be quiet. Suddenly, the San Siro fell silent and I was thinking, 'What is he going to do now?' Quick as a flash, Kells started singing, 'Let's go fucking mental' while bouncing up and down on the spot. The fans didn't need a second invitation and, within a couple of seconds, all 7,000 of them were copying Kells. It was an amazing sight. All the lads joined in as well. Everyone was loving it. As the noise died down, Kells again asked for quiet before putting his tracksuit top down on the pitch and sitting on it. Again, I was wondering what Kells was up to but then he started singing, 'Sit down if you hate Man U'. Again, every single fan followed his lead.

By now, quite a few of the lads wanted to have a go. Smithy sang, 'We're Leeds and we're proud of it'. Again, it went down well. Unfortunately, the same can't be said about Bow's effort. No-one in the crowd had a clue what he was singing, prompting the response of 'What the fucking hell was that?' The lads were in stitches about that and Bow, who scurried off to the other end of the field, got a lot of stick afterwards. Peter Ridsdale also had a go, playing it safe with a rendition of 'Marching On Together' and, once again, all the lads joined in. I was later asked by a few mates why I hadn't had a go, but it wasn't for me. I was too busy supping my two cans of lager at the back. All that was missing was a cigar in my hand and I would have looked the perfect picture of contentment! The impromptu karaoke session was brilliant, though, and something that I can't imagine every happening again, anywhere. You wouldn't see, for instance, the Manchester United boys or the Chelsea boys doing that now. Or Arsenal. It could only have happened with that Leeds team and those wonderful supporters. I later found out that BBC Radio Five Live commentator Alan Green had described the scenes as the greatest example of fan-player bonding he had ever seen and I have to agree. None of us wanted it to end, even when the police came on to the field to try and get us to leave. The boys were enjoying themselves too much. It was brilliant. A sing-song had, in fact, become part of the European trips for the boys. On the coach after games, we'd all sing along to a tune called, 'I am a music man, I come from far away...' I think Black Lace recorded it, though that wasn't why we loved singing along. We loved it because it was fun. All the lads would mime playing a different instrument. Another song the boys enjoyed was the theme tune to the kids' television show 'The Littlest Hobo' and that got quite a few airings on the coach trip back to Lake Como.

Once back at our hotel, the celebrations continued as we all headed straight for the bar. The boys, the chairman, the staff...everyone was there celebrating what had been a memorable night. I didn't want the night to end, so even after the rest had sloped off to bed, I decided to get myself a couple of bottles of wine. It was about 6am by now. Unfortunately for me, as I walked towards the lift, who should be coming the other way but Peter Ridsdale. We were all staying another night as a reward for getting through to the next stage but the chairman had an early flight to catch so was on his way to the airport. He just looked at me, laughed and walked on without saying a word. Mind, Peter was so happy at Leeds qualifying for the next group stage that he probably wanted to high-five me – but couldn't as my hands were full. It was a funny end to an unforgettable day and night.

That trip was what the Champions League was all about – playing a top, top team in one of the most famous stadiums in the world, while travelling on U2's private jet and staying in an amazing hotel. And, to top it all off, I scored our goal.

Chapter 12

On The Lash With Figo and Raul

Hotels are a big part of life as a footballer, whether for overnight stays ahead of matches or when they provide a temporary 'home' after moving clubs. Most players, and particularly those with young families, try and limit the amount of time they spend 'living out of a suitcase', often deciding to rent somewhere until they find the right house to buy. For me, however, I loved life in the hotel so much I ended up staying for nine months at Oulton Hall in Leeds after signing from Liverpool. Situated on the outskirts of the city, it was a luxurious place and the staff really went out of their way to look after guests. The club put all the new boys up at Oulton Hall, which during the season I signed for Leeds meant there were quite a few of us staying there. None of them lasted as long as me, though. Even the lads who joined later in the year, such as Rio Ferdinand and Robbie Keane, were gone long before I got round to finding my own place. It is a proud boast of mine that I saw them all off. I just enjoyed life too much there to move out. I had two rooms throughout my stay – one for me and one for my clothes, which may sound excessive but was actually practical.

When I first moved in, Mark Viduka, Olivier Dacourt and Eirik Bakke were already staying so you can imagine what a laugh we had. 'Fancy a beer?' became our catchphrase during those first few weeks. Eventually, they moved on after finding houses out near the training ground but the catchphrase lived on when Rio and Keano arrived. Another thing I liked about the hotel was the staff. I became good mates with lads who were nothing to do with football. I've always liked to have mates from outside the game. I'd been like that at Liverpool when me and Razor had gone to The Grapes with our mates rather than into town or down to London with the rest of the team. One of my first real mates in Leeds, for instance, was a lad called Hav, who owns a hairdressers in the city centre. I went in one afternoon, got talking and ended up really getting on. Before long, we were having a few beers at his local in Seacroft called The Gate. Through Hav, I got to know a lot of people in Leeds and that helped me settle.

My long stay at Oulton Hall meant I remained there throughout the entire Champions League season. I only left in the end after the club had seen my bill, which by then had reached about £200,000. I'd had up to 20 mates staying at a time while i was there, which explains the huge amount. The club were not overly impressed and said I had to get out, which was fair enough. I paid the vast majority of the bill with the club chipping in a bit. The next question was where to go. Most of the lads lived in the villages that surround the training ground near Wetherby. But I didn't fancy a house in the middle of nowhere after having felt a bit isolated when I first moved out of my parents' house in Southport. If I'd had a wife and kids then it would have been different but, as I didn't, the city centre was the only place for me. In the end, I bought a flat at the bottom end of town – not far away from where my bar on Call Lane stands today. Unsurprisingly, it quickly became a bit of a party pad. A lot of the lads made use of it. Smithy stayed there a lot, which was great for me as, in those days, he had a lot of success with the ladies. It meant I could survive on his knockdowns - showing the value of going out on the town with the young, good-looking one!

As good, though, as it felt to be in town I did miss Oulton Hall from time to time. I'd had some cracking nights there, with probably the most memorable coming when we played Real Madrid in the Champions League. Back then, the structure of the competition was very different to today with the last 16 going into a second group of four, rather than a knockout stage as they do now. All the remaining teams would then compete for a place in the last eight, which was made up of the top two in all four groups. As we looked through the names in the 'paper before training on the day of the draw, it was clear there were a lot of top, top teams. Mind, after being drawn against Barcelona and AC Milan in the first group stage, we thought it couldn't be as tough again. We were wrong, as a Group D that included holders Real Madrid, Lazio, Anderlecht and ourselves showed. We were on the training pitch when the draw was made and one of the staff came out to tell us. Again, the lads thought he was pulling our legs. It wasn't that we wanted an easy draw after already having survived one 'Group of Death'. More that we thought we couldn't be that lucky again and get the chance to play against even more of the best teams in the best stadiums. Others may have expected us to be gutted by such a tough-looking group but we were delighted. The feeling was, 'Let's keep enjoying it'.

For me, the draw was great on another level as it meant a chance to see my old mate Steve McManaman, who had done really well since signing for Real Madrid from Liverpool in 1999. I was even more pleased when the fixture list came out and Real were to be our first opponents at Elland Road. And, as most visiting teams in either Europe or the Premier League stayed at Oulton Hall, that meant there was a good chance Macca would be staying in my hotel. It meant we would be able to have a good catch-up during his two-night stay. When Real arrived, the first thing that struck me was just how relaxed they all looked. This was the Galacticos era when Luis Figo, Raul, Roberto Carlos, Iker Casillas, Claude Makelele and so on were playing for the club and yet they all strolled around without a care in the world.

The biggest shock for me, though, came on the night before the game when I walked down to the bar area and ordered a coffee. I was sitting there on my own and reading the 'paper, when I suddenly looked up and saw all the Madrid lads had arrived and all of them had a pint in their hand. They didn't stop at one, either. I was stunned. Here were the very best players in the world getting stuck into the ale on the eve of a match. I hadn't thought they even drank alcohol before then. But, here they were, supping pints like they were going out of fashion. Macca told me later that, back in Spain, beer is served in smaller measures so they had been really taken by these pint glasses. The worst thing for me – and perhaps the most surprising part of the night to anyone who knows me – was that while all these star names were sinking the beer, I was sipping coffee. It didn't feel right at all!

The next day, the relaxed mood among the Real boys continued as they all went into town to do some shopping. We were in bed at our city centre hotel, trying to sleep and get some rest before a vital Champions League fixture. Yet, Real Madrid's Galacticos were out buying some new clothes or whatever. Again, very bizarre. Macca introduced me to their team doctor the night after the game so I asked him why things were done in such a relaxed manner. His reply was, 'We let the boys do what they want'. His reasoning was that the players were producing the goods on the pitch so deserved to be treated like adults. I thought, 'What a refreshing attitude'. It clearly worked too, as they played us off the park at Elland Road just a few hours after their shopping trip into Leeds. Basically, we were left chasing shadows for 90 minutes. It was a real footballing lesson and our fans knew it, as they showed by applauding the Madrid boys from the field at the final whistle. The final score was 2-0 but it could have been a lot more. Macca had a great game and showed what a quality player he had become since leaving Liverpool for La Liga. Afterwards, I was selected by the drug-testers along with Fernando Hierro so we sat and had a bit of banter. Unfortunately, neither of us could go to the toilet so, eventually, I said to him, 'Do you fancy a pint?' He nodded so I went to the players' lounge and bought a case of Carlsberg. I came back, plonked it down and said, 'Right, get stuck in'. It did the trick and before long we were on our way.

By the time I got back to the hotel, the Madrid lads were already in the bar. After having to watch them sink a few pints while I stuck to the coffee the previous night, there was no way I was not joining in this time. I ended up staying up with them all night. The entire squad were there and they were all really nice guys. By the end, we were all quite merry with Roberto Carlos being the drunkest. He was absolutely steaming on Jack Daniels. My mate Rob had decided to stay over that night at the hotel and we both said afterwards what a brilliant night it had been. Mind, Rob did nearly cause a diplomatic incident when, later on, he decided to 'borrow' Claude Makelele's trainers. I don't know why Rob wanted a pair of smelly, old trainers but he did. Unfortunately for Rob, his hopes of a memento were dashed the next morning when Claude knocked on his door and asked for them back.

I still look back on that night fondly, not least as it served as a real eye-opener as to how these top players operated. It also gave me an insight into just what a special club Real Madrid is. Earlier in the night, I'd spotted two old guys sitting in the corner of the bar and wondered who they were. They kind of looked familiar but I just couldn't place them. So, I asked Macca. His reply stunned me. It was only Alfredo Di Stefano and Ferenc Puskas, two of the greatest footballers of all time. I knew all about them from my Dad, who had shown me the Real Madrid v Eintracht Frankfurt European Cup final from Hampden Park on video countless times when I was a kid. Macca told me that Madrid took both Di Stefano and Puskas all over and made a real fuss of them. I was really impressed. It proved to me that Real, as a club, is not just a class act on the field but off it as well. Anyway, I made sure I got their autographs for my Dad and he was absolutely made up when I passed them on. He still has the autographs at home.

As enjoyable as my night in the bar with the Galacticos had been, I was well aware that losing our opening fixture 2-0 meant we were, once again, up against it in the Champions League. Lazio were our next opponents in Rome and another defeat would make it very difficult to qualify. Managed by Sven-Goran Eriksson, Lazio had won the Serie A title the previous season but were someway off the pace this time around. They still had plenty of quality players, though, with Hernan Crespo being the second most expensive signing in the world at the time after joining from Parma for £36m. Pavel Nedved, Alessandro Nesta, Juan Sebastien Veron and Diego Simeoni were also at the club so there was little doubt we were in for a testing night. Few gave us a chance, especially as on the Saturday before flying out to Rome we had been beaten 3-1 by Leicester City in the Premier League. Rio Ferdinand, our new £18m signing, had made his debut in a three-man defence alongside Jonathan Woodgate and Lucas Radebe but nothing had gone right for us at Filbert Street. I'd been delighted by Rio's signing from West Ham United, even if his arrival – and a request by Peter Ridsdale to myself and Mark Viduka, which I will reveal in a later chapter – did start me wondering about just how financially stable Leeds United were as a club. But in footballing terms, Rio's signing was a no-brainer for Leeds as he was a class act and I knew he would do well at Elland Road. That was why I knew the disappointing defeat to Leicester on his debut was nothing to be concerned about.

When we flew out to Rome a couple of days later, Rio was on the plane but unable to play having signed after the deadline. He would have to wait until February, when the group was set to resume with a double-header against Anderlecht. His unavailability meant David O'Leary was able to revert to our usual 4-4-2 formation with Woody, who had taken some flack over the Leicester defeat off the manager, alongside Lucas Radebe. I played at left-back with Jason Wilcox ahead of me on the wing. Harry Kewell was also on the bench after making his first appearance of the season as a second half substitute at Filbert Street after a spell out injured. I, of course, knew all about H from my games against Leeds for Liverpool. He was a special player. It meant I realised just how important it was to have him back available for such a big match. What I didn't realise, though, as we arrived in Rome was that H would be responsible for giving us all one of the biggest laughs of the season. The unfortunate incident came on the afternoon of the game, after David and his coaching staff had taken us for a stroll round the zoo. The gaffer wanted us to have an hour where we could stretch our legs and enjoy a bit of peace and quiet. It helped settle everyone down, though not as much as H inadvertently did a few minutes later when he decided to pop into a shop to buy a present for his Missus. He decided on a lovely leather jacket, which was on sale for what H thought was a few hundred quid. So, he went up and bought it on his credit card. The problem was he had messed up with the conversion rate between Lira and pounds. The jacket had actually cost £20,000 and H only realised on the coach trip back to the hotel. He was gutted. Worst of all, though, the tight git then decided to take it back and ask for his money back. How can you buy your missus a jacket and then take it back? The boys gave him some real stick over that.

H may not have been overly amused by the mix-up but it did the trick of relaxing all the lads. We knew the stakes were high following our defeat to Real Madrid, as they were for Lazio after Anderlecht had beaten the Italians in Brussels in the opening round of games. With Eriksson, who had already told Lazio he was leaving in July to manage England, also coming under pressure, we knew Lazio and their supporters would be pumped up. That was evident on the ride to the Olympic Stadium when home fans on mopeds were whacking our team bus with big sticks. They were clearly trying to intimidate us but it didn't work. In fact, my biggest worry once at the Olympic Stadium was whether I would be able to go through my usual pre-match routine. All footballers have them and mine was to go and sit on the toilet. I usually did this about quarter of an hour before kick-off. The problem in Rome was that the walk from the dressing room to the pitch took about 15 minutes, meaning I wouldn't be able to disappear into the toilet at my usual time. That proved to be the case, too, and I was worried not following my usual routine might, in some way, be unlucky. I know that will sound ridiculous to most people, but footballers are a strange breed. Thankfully, my fears in terms of the result proved unfounded as we turned Group D on its head with the Viduka-Smithy combination creating what turned out to be the winning goal with 10 minutes to go. In terms of the rest of the night, however, things did not go exactly to plan as I had my first big fall-out with David O'Leary.

It happened during half-time, when the score was still goalless. David had a real go at me over a tackle I'd made on one of their players. He accused me of trying to deliberately boot my opponent, when really I had just been going for the ball. I told David that but he insisted I'd gone in studs up to 'do' him. What had really got David's back up was the free-kick I conceded with the tackle had almost led to a Lazio goal. David continued to have a go at me until, eventually, I snapped and told him to, 'Fuck off'. As far as I was concerned, I had gone for the ball and not got it. End of story. The slanging match continued and then I was asked to leave the dressing room. Rio followed me out to check I was okay. However, once we were away from the dressing room, he just started laughing. He said he couldn't believe the row I'd just had with David. I wasn't in the mood to laugh along and just sat there. I was still adamant I had done nothing wrong and was furious with the manager. I presumed being sent out of the dressing room meant I was being substituted so I started to take my boots and shin-pads off. But then one of the coaches came in and said I was going back out. I still wasn't happy but I was relieved to be playing in the second half. Afterwards, I did apologise to David for how I had reacted – even though I still thought his accusation was wrong. I was expecting him to do the same but he didn't. That annoyed me a bit, though the most annoying part of our row was that it had all been so unnecessary. If David had said at half-time, 'Listen, Dom, we can't afford to give away any free-kicks on the edge of the box' then I would have accepted it. But the way he spoke to me was, I felt, totally out of order. Thankfully, the row didn't affect me or the team in the second half and we went on to get a great result thanks to Smithy's late goal.

Our win meant spirits were high among both the lads and the 1,000 supporters who had made the trip. Considering the fun we'd all had in Milan, there was another post-match sing-song with the fans, who had again been locked in by the Italian police. The usual suspects were leading the singing, with Smithy, in particular, enjoying the chance to be what he always has been – a Leeds United fan. Rio also joined in but, again, I opted out of leading the sing-song and decided to stick to my role as a backing singer. The lads saw it as our way of thanking the fans, who seemed to appreciate the gesture. After travelling back to our hotel, the boys had another sing-song and celebratory drink in the bar. Peter Ridsdale, who loved nights like this where he could let his hair down with the team, even played the piano and sang 'Lady in Red' to his wife. Surprisingly, he was quite a good singer. It was good fun, though my night was spoiled when I fell out with Eddie Gray and Roy Aitken. They thought I had reacted badly to David during half-time and told me so. Again, I wasn't having it so I defended myself. I was nearly fighting with them, by the end. I really did feel that passionately about David's initial accusation. Looking back now, Eddie and Roy were probably right in what they said. It wasn't professional on my part. But, at the time, I didn't agree at all and made that clear.

Our win over Lazio, together with Real Madrid 4-1 thrashing of Anderlecht, meant we were up to second in Group D. Less promising, however, was our league position. We were 11th in the table and, in terms of points, closer to Middlesbrough at the bottom of the Premier League than Manchester United at the top. By New Year's Day, we had slipped even further to 13th. It wasn't good enough and we knew it. We'd had a few good days, such as our 4-3 win over Liverpool in early November when Mark Viduka scored all four goals. We didn't play well as a team but Mark had one of those days when everything he touched turned to gold. I was close with Mark. He was so laid back that nothing fazed him. But the smile on his face that day said everything. What made it sweeter for Mark was he had supported Liverpool as a kid. On a personal level, it was satisfying to beat Liverpool. I'd only left three months earlier so I knew everyone in their team apart from Christian Ziege, the player who had been bought to replace me. It meant I could have plenty of banter with the Liverpool lads, and Robbie in particular. Mind, as good a friend as Robbie has been, he did try to boot me that day. I took it as a compliment for how we had come from 2-0 and 3-2 down to win 4-3.

As satisfying as that win over Liverpool was, our problem was we didn't have too many other good days in the league during that first half of the season – hence our lowly position come New Year's Day. Our main difficulty seemed to be getting ourselves up for a Saturday game in the Premier League after playing, say, AC Milan or Barcelona in midweek. For instance, either side of that win in Rome we lost against Leicester and Southampton. If you look at the results after the Champions League games, that was the theme of the first half of the season. We lost at home to Ipswich Town and drew at Derby County either side of beating AC Milan, while Bradford City held us to a 1-1 draw at Valley Parade just five days after we had come within 20 seconds of beating Barcelona. It is difficult to explain why this should have been the case, though maybe at times we were guilty of expecting to go places and batter teams just because we were in the Champions League. I certainly think there may have been an element of that in the League Cup when Tranmere Rovers knocked us out in the third round. That was a bad night, especially as we allowed Tranmere to come back from being 2-0 down to win 3-2. Injuries also didn't help. Any team would miss someone like Harry Kewell and David Batty, who like H only returned to the team in December.

In truth, we only really came to terms with the demands of competing in both the Premier League and Champions League when the Champions League resumed in February. By then, we had managed to go on a bit of a run and moved up to fifth. Robbie Keane's arrival from Inter Milan just before Christmas had helped, as had H and Batts being available again. For me, though, the big difference was Rio. The manager and chairman came in for some criticism for paying such a big fee as £18m to West Ham. But Rio had quickly shown Leeds had got value-for-money. He really is a great footballer. In training, we soon found out he could play anywhere: up front, midfield or at the back – it didn't matter to Rio. Off the pitch, he was a good bloke as well and I went on to have some great trips to Ireland with him and Michael Duberry. Rio was such a popular guy in the dressing room that even him being the manager's blue-eyed boy didn't cause resentment, as can happen at a club. Instead, all the lads used to laugh about how Rio couldn't do anything wrong in David's eyes.

Not long after Rio's arrival, I was moved to central defence – the position David O'Leary had said he saw as my best when I had signed a few months earlier. I'd enjoyed filling in on the left wing when H was unavailable and even scored a couple of goals. But I was more than happy to be back in defence and playing alongside someone as talented as Rio. We hit it off well, probably because we both hated to concede goals so much. Winning 5-2 didn't interest us, but clean sheets did. It became a real obsession – especially in the 2001-02 season when we set ourselves the target of keeping the most clean sheets in the Premier League. In the end, Manchester United just pipped us and I remember us both being absolutely gutted.

As a defender, I loved playing alongside Rio. I knew he was watching my back, just as I was his. I knew if I did make a mistake then, nine times out of ten, Rio would clear it up. I hope he felt the same with me.

I certainly thought our partnership was a good one. Rio got all the plaudits such as the man of the match awards, which was understandable considering the fee he had cost. That suited me as I have never been the sort who particularly enjoyed the limelight. I just liked doing my job, simple as that. What did make me happy, though, was what a lot of fans said to me when Rio got the Players' Player of the Year in his first full season at Leeds in 2001-02. They would come up and say, 'It should have been you, Dom'. I am not too sure they were right as Rio was outstanding and I, personally, voted for Smithy. But it was nice to hear that the fans realised what I contributed to the team.

By the time the Champions League resumed in February, not only had the partnership between Rio and myself clicked but also the team as a whole. A 4-0 win over Manchester City at Maine Road in mid-January had proved to be a big result. Confidence shot up after that and we went on a decent run. It quickly became clear that Robbie Keane's arrival had given us an extra dimension in the Premier League. Unfortunately, Robbie was unable to play in the Champions League after having appeared for Inter in the qualifying stages when they had lost to Helsinborg of Sweden in August. That meant that when Anderlecht came to Elland Road on February 13, Robbie had to sit the game out despite having scored six goals in our last nine games. Even without Robbie, however, we felt confident ahead of facing Anderlecht. That much was evident as we all met up on the afternoon of the game at the Malmaison hotel. We always stayed there before a night game in order to give the lads chance to get a bit of kip. David would then call us all together and name the team before running through a few things such as the opposition's likely line-up, plus their strengths and weaknesses. He would also outline how we might be able to get behind their defence or who needed to watch who at set-pieces. David wasn't a manager who said a lot before games, but what he did say was useful and made us believe we had a chance. There would be the odd time he might go overboard, such as when we were up against a superstar. In that first game against Madrid, for instance, he was going through the likely line-up when he reached Herero. We were waiting for some insight but, instead, David said: "He looks good, he smells good and he plays good....but he can't fucking run." We all fell about laughing. Sometimes, when you are playing the top teams you need a bit of a tension-breaker like that. On another occasion, David's team-talk amounted to him walking into the dressing room, pointing at the Nike badge on his coat and saying the company's advertising slogan: "Just do it!" It was very bizarre, but good in that we all felt relaxed afterwards. In that respect, I liked the way David did stuff. He wasn't a manager who liked to keep the players guessing as to who was playing, even if the actual team was not named until matchday. We all, basically, knew the team from how we had set-up in training the previous day. Personally, I always wanted to know if I was starting or not. I know it shouldn't be the case but I would prepare slightly differently if I was in or not. That is human nature. David also worked hard to keep us relaxed during the day, which I certainly appreciated. Then, once we had arrived at the ground, David would run through a few other things. Eddie Gray and Roy Aitken, who I always thought were real unsung heroes at Leeds, would also chip in with stuff and, after that, we would be chomping at the bit to get out there. That was certainly the case when we faced Anderlecht. As we had left the hotel, a few fans were there and were saying things like 'come on lads, get into them tonight'. It was quite inspiring.

One added complication for the visit of the Belgian champions was that the trial involving Bow and Woody was under way at Hull Crown Court. Sarfraz Najeib, a student, had been beaten unconscious in a street attack in January, 2000, on a night when both Bow and Woody had been out in Leeds. They were both subsequently charged with causing grievous bodily harm and causing affray in Leeds city centre. The same charges had been levelled at two of Woody's mates from Middlesbrough, while Michael Duberry was charged with perverting the course of justice. I hadn't been at the club when the incident took place but I could see the contrasting ways it had affected the two of them. Bow had kicked on and used his football as a distraction, whereas Woody had fallen apart. He didn't handle things very well and looked very thin. As a result, he didn't play in the final four or so months of the season. Bow, however, was completely different. He was flying, quite literally, a week before the home game against Anderlecht when a helicopter had taken him from Hull to Liverpool so he could play against Everton at Goodison Park. Bow wasn't training with us at all but natural fitness was getting him through. That fitness was one of the first things I had noticed about Bow when I signed for Leeds. That and his ability. He was a great footballer, who really stood out in my first year. By the following season, he was still playing at the same level but because the rest of the lads had improved he didn't stand out. But in that first season, he definitely did – it was why he got 90 per cent of the vote, including mine, in the Players' Player of the Year award.

The trial may have been going on seventy miles down the M62 during the day but there was no question of Bow not being involved against Anderlecht at Elland Road. In the end, we needed him too as it was his late goal that earned us a 2-1 win that our play probably hadn't deserved. Not that I cared much about that later in the night when I was out on the town with Jan Koller and Tomasz Radzinski, who said they fancied a night out. So, I took them to Majestyk for a few pints and made sure I thanked them for the three points. I was only joking, of course, and they took it in the spirit it was intended. The same, though, could not be said for the Anderlecht coach, Aime Anthuenis. He had been very bitter about the result after the game, telling the Press: "Leeds are not a good side. I was not impressed by them. Next week in Brussels is a different game. We will see what happens then. How can a home team create so few chances and win the game? One-nil is the right result, 1-1 just about acceptable." Anthuenis wasn't finished, either, as he continued to have a go at us in the Belgian 'papers during the build-up to the return game. Unfortunately for Anthuenis, Olly Dacourt, our French midfielder, translated them all for us and David hung them on the dressing room wall. One, in particular, was quite nasty about Mark Viduka and his performance in our win at Elland Road. I could never understand anyone having a go at Vidukes, who was a wonderful player for Leeds. It didn't matter how hard we fired the ball into him, he would always control it. And that allowed the rest of the team to get forward in support. I certainly knew his value, so I found it especially surprising that Anthuenis didn't.

By full-time in Brussels, I doubt anyone could have seen Vidukes as anything but a great player after his performance in our 4-1 win. We had gone out beforehand determined to ram Athuenis' words back down his throat and that was just what we did. By half-time, it was 3-0 thanks to two goals from Smithy and one for Vidukes. Ian Harte then added a penalty after half-time to end the proud home record – Anderlecht had won the last 21 in a row in the league and another nine in Europe – they had made sure we heard so much about during the build-up. I can't explain why but we went out that night just knowing we would end it. That belief and Anthuenis' unwise comments were all we had talked about on a short stroll around Brussels on the morning of the game. As satisfying as the win was, more importantly it meant we were through to the quarter-finals with two games to spare. The pressure was off, though the prospect of playing in the Bernabeu meant the boys were eagerly looking forward to the Madrid trip. Such was the level of excitement, in fact, that our training session on the eve of the game lasted for about three hours because no-one wanted to leave. In the end, the groundsman had to come on to the field and kick us off. The only Englishman not happy with our extended session was Steve McManaman, who had come down for a chat but had to hang around for ages before I was free.

The game itself was a cracker with Smithy putting us ahead. Raul then equalised with a blatant handball that the referee somehow missed before we were hit with more bad luck when an attempted cross by Luis Figo struck a divot and bounced over Nigel Martyn. Vidukes did equalise for us shortly after half-time but Real won it through a legitimate goal by Raul. If qualification had still been at stake, we'd have been gutted. But, as the result didn't really matter, the boys were not too upset – especially as we had put on a decent show. Our fans certainly seemed to appreciate our efforts, the 8,000 who made the trip to Spain giving us a standing ovation at the end. It was a similar story after our final group game at home to Lazio. Sven-Goran Eriksson had left by now to take up the England job, his departure no doubt being hastened by our win in Rome. We fielded a few of the fringe players but still came away with a point from a 3-3 draw. The only sour note for me was the penalty that Lazio were awarded when Fabrizio Ravanelli took a tumble despite there being no contact between us. Sinisa Mihajlovic duly converted the spotkick, much to my frustration. The important thing, though, was that we were through to the last eight and ready to take on whoever the draw threw our way.

Chapter 13

3-0 To The Weakest Team

"We have finally worked out why Dominic Matteo never gets a match for Liverpool," is how the article in the *Liverpool Echo* started. As an intro designed to get the readers' attention, it certainly worked. Or it did in my house, at least. That it came in the weekly column that my team-mate Neil Ruddock wrote for the *Echo* made me even more intrigued. So, I continued reading. As I did, I broke into a big smile. It was Razor being Razor and having a laugh. The article went on to say: "He is one of the most talented young defenders in the game and would walk into just about any other side in the country. But the problem is we do not have a chant for him. Whenever I come on the pitch, the crowd chant 'Razor, Razor'. When Ian Rush comes on, it's Rushy, Rushy'. But with Dom, it is 'Dom-in-ic Matteo'. It would take 90 minutes to just chant his name. So come on, the Kop – we are looking for a suitable chant so that Dom can get a game every week!" As far as I am aware, Razor didn't have one reply – at least not one that was printable – to his appeal, meaning I was destined to leave Anfield a few years later without my own song on the terraces. I can't say I was overly bothered by that, I've never been the sort to chase personal glory above the team. But, after what subsequently happened at Leeds when I had not one but two songs created about me, I do now wish the Kop had been a bit more inventive in the song-writing stakes during my time at Anfield. Only joking, lads!

The first song, which started a few days after Leeds' 1-1 draw against Milan in the Champions League, is the one that is still sung today. "Oh Matteo," it starts, "scored a fucking great goal, in the San Siro, in the San Siro." I must admit to always feeling very proud, if a little embarrassed, when the Leeds fans launch into that one during games. The second song about me may not have endured like the San Siro one, but it remains one of the special moments of my career – not least because it was first aired at Anfield towards the end of my first season with Leeds. The game took place on Good Friday and had been built up all week as a potential decider for third place, which in those days was the final Champions League spot in the Premier League. We were third but Liverpool had two games in hand. We had to win, there was no question about that. So, as I ran out of the tunnel before kick-off, I was totally focused on the three points. I did, though, want to wave to my Mum and Dad, who for the first time were sitting in the away seats at Anfield. It was while I was looking for them that the singing began in the Leeds end. "We've got Dom Matteo, you've got our stereo," made me laugh straight away, playing as it did on the stereotype of Scousers not being the most honest people in the world. My Dad told me later that both he and Mum did exactly the same, while even my Liverpool mates saw the funny side of it when we were chatting afterwards. It was a classic and one I really enjoyed. Whoever came up with that deserves a big pat on the back.

As for the football, I have to say we were brilliant that day. It was one of the best performances of my time at Leeds. The first 45 minutes of the game, in particular, were unbelievable. We were 2-0 in front thanks to goals from Rio Ferdinand and Lee Bowyer but it could have been a lot more. Liverpool were run ragged and didn't know what had hit them. They got a goal back through Steven Gerrard after half-time but we won the game quite comfortably. Having only left Anfield eight months earlier and not been overly happy at how things had ended, being able to go round chatting to people afterwards knowing we'd got the three points was great. Eddie Gray came up to me as we were about to leave and said, 'It's great beating your old team, isn't it?' Too right. It was only later that I thought, 'How does Eddie know?' He only played for one team in his entire career! But he was right, beating my old club was a sweet feeling. The only downer on the whole day was that I didn't see much of Gerard Houllier after the game. It would have been nice to rub it in that we'd won. Normally, I wouldn't have given him the time of the day – and I didn't on the times when our paths crossed over the next few years. But I was still upset about how I'd been treated and really wanted to bump into him. I wanted him to acknowledge he'd made a mistake in selling me.

As satisfying as my return to Anfield had been on a personal level, the main thing about our win was that it made us slight favourites to claim that third and final qualifying place. Liverpool still had two games in hand but had won only one of their last six. They also had to go to Goodison Park on Easter Monday and I knew just how badly the

Evertonians wanted to put a dent in Liverpool's bid for third. I couldn't see Liverpool winning, which meant I flew out to Spain for our Champions League quarter-final second leg tie in buoyant mood. Our promising position in the Premier League was not the only reason for my smile. We were also 3-0 ahead against Deportivo la Coruna and had one foot in the last four. Or so I thought.

When the draw had paired us with Deportivo, there were quite a few in the English media who said we were favourites. I couldn't have disagreed more. Don't get me wrong, I was confident we could give anyone a game. We'd shown that time and time again already. But I had watched quite a bit of Spanish football on the television so I knew they were a very good side with some top, top footballers. People forget today, when looking back at our Champions League run, that Deportivo were the reigning champions of La Liga. They had won it by some distance, too, with Barcelona five points behind in second place. An illustration of just how strong La Liga had been in 1999-2000 was that Real Madrid, who won the Champions League at the end of that season, only finished fifth. So, I firmly believed we were in for a tough night during the first leg at Elland Road. Happily, I couldn't have been more wrong as we blew Deportivo away to win 3-0. Ian Harte put us in front with one of his trademark free-kicks before Smithy added a second just after the break. Rio then rounded off the win midway through the second half before doing his guns celebration in front of the fans. Deportivo, who I sensed before kick-off thought they were in an easy 90 minutes, did rally late on but we never really looked like conceding to cap an amazing night. In terms of performance, that was our best at home all season with probably only Anderlecht away being a more impressive all-round display. The fans were also in fine form that night as they produced one of the best put-downs I have heard in a football ground. Before the game, Deportivo midfielder Victor had dismissed us as "the weakest side left in the Champions League". The Leeds fans' response during the closing stages was simple, "3-0 to the weakest team". The game was still going on but I had to smile. As with the 'We've got Dom Matteo, you've got our stereo' song from Anfield, whoever dreamt that one up deserves a medal.

The return in Spain was two weeks later on Easter Tuesday. Having just beaten Liverpool at Anfield, we flew out very confident of clinching a place in the semi-finals. Subconsciously, I think we thought the tie was over. We knew that if we scored just once, Deportivo would have to get five. Three-nil is a massive lead and I really didn't think we would come under much threat. Boy, was I wrong. Deportivo tore into us from the kick-off and we just didn't perform. They got it back to 3-2 with 20 minutes to go and I really did think we were heading out. Mario Silva was tearing us apart and we couldn't get near Roy Makaay. We were hanging on for grim death on a boiling hot night and the final whistle couldn't come quick enough. Deportivo gave it everything but, somehow, we held out. It was a big relief. I believe to this day that if Deportivo had got an equaliser during those closing stages then they would have gone on to win the Champions League. They really were that good. We knew we'd had a lucky escape, which is why the celebrations afterwards were more relief than joy on our part. It was certainly nothing like the nights in Milan and Rome, that's for sure. I almost felt sheepish going out to wave to the fans after we'd got changed. I felt we'd picked someone's pocket. It was like we had lost, even though we were in the last four of the most prestigious competition in club football. It was a weird feeling. I can't explain why we were so poor, especially after playing so well just four days earlier at Anfield. The main thing, though, was that we were through. Better still, just 24 hours later we were suddenly the only English side left in the Champions League after Manchester United lost to Bayern Munich and Arsenal had gone out on away goals to Valencia.

The draw for the semi-finals had been made at the same time as that for the quarters, so we knew Valencia stood in the way of us and a place in the final. It was another tough draw. Valencia had reached the Champions League final a year earlier and had finished top of both group stages this time around, a feat that included pipping Manchester United. The first leg was at Elland Road and it proved to be a tight affair. Chances were few and far between but one did fall my way in the very last minute. I was certain my header was going in only for the Valencia goalkeeper Santiago Canizares to pull off one of the most unbelievable saves I have ever seen. The ball was heading for the bottom corner and I'd set off celebrating, thinking it was in. But, somehow, Canizares clawed it away and the game ended goalless. It was a great save and I made a point afterwards of going up to Canizares on our way off the pitch to congratulate him. A 0-0 draw at home was not ideal but the one positive we took from the game was that Valencia had not managed to score an away goal. That meant that if we scored once, they would have to score twice to stop us going through. And I always fancied us to score at least once on our travels.

Unfortunately, it wasn't to be as Valencia ran out 3-0 winners on a boiling hot night in the return. The trip had started badly for us with Lee Bowyer being suspended by UEFA. They had a looked at video footage of the first leg and thought Bow had stamped on Juan Sanchez. I was in the treatment room with Bow I do remember feeling something just wasn't rightwhen he found out about the ban. He couldn't understand it. The referee for the first leg had been Pierluigi Collina, who was probably the top official in the world at the time. He had not seen anything wrong with the incident so why UEFA got involved was a mystery. I was gutted for Bow, who had been a major reason why we had got so far in the first place. It must have been bad enough to miss out on such an important game but with UEFA hitting Bow with a three-game ban, he would also be out of the final if we got through. Bow's suspension came as a bitter blow to the team as well. He was a lad with total confidence, creativity and real genius in his play. Single players don't make a team but losing single players can knock a team sideways. I certainly feel that happened to us ahead of the semi-final second leg.

I remember feeling something just wasn't right in the dressing room ahead of kick-off. The lads were unusually subdued and quiet. Usually, we were loud and bubbly. We were also very good at firing each other up ahead of a big game. But, in Valencia, the atmosphere inside what was a huge dressing room was almost eerie. Anyone wandering in would never have guessed we were about to play the biggest game of our lives. It was strange, as the camaraderie that had taken us this far had been there the previous day when we all decided to shave our heads. One of the lads had cut his really short a few days earlier so we all decided to do the same. Only Ian Harte didn't join in because he was getting married that summer. His Missus didn't want him looking like a thug in the wedding pictures, which of course gave us plenty of ammunition to tease Hartey with. So, our sprits were high. But, come the following night and those final few minutes before kick-off, we had gone flat. Things just didn't feel right and the team didn't look up for it. I did try to lift our spirits by indulging in a bit of mind games in the tunnel when I was standing next to John Carew. Eirik Bakke played with John for Norway and told me a few Norwegian swearwords, which I then passed on as we waited to go out. The phrase Eirik had given me was along the lines of, 'You're gonna get it tonight'. John didn't show a flicker of emotion, which considering the size of him is not a surprise. In fact, as I looked him up and down in the tunnel, I suddenly thought this might not been my smartest move. John ended up having a great game, as did most of his team-mates and Valencia ran out comfortable winners.

The second goal by Juan Sanchez just after half-time was the clincher. He'd scored with what Rio was adamant was a handball during the first half. But, at 1-0, we still fancied our chances – especially as if we equalised we would be, in effect, ahead on away goals. Once we were two goals down, though, any remaining belief completely drained away. Gaizka Mendieta, who had bossed things in midfield, added a third later on and that really was it. A bad night was then topped off by Smithy getting himself sent off for a daft challenge and our dressing room afterwards was not a nice place to be. There were bodies strewn all over the place and a few were in tears. A couple threw things around. The coaches were going round, trying to gee us up. But it didn't do any good. The lads knew we'd let ourselves down. Several had frozen and I maintain to this day that the game was lost before kick-off when we were unusually uptight. It would be nice to blame the referee or bad luck. But, in the cold light of day, I didn't perform and we didn't perform. Over the entire campaign, we had every right to be proud of what we achieved. But I am not proud of how it ended. We went out with a whimper, rather than a bang. I just wish it could have been different. In fact, that second leg in Valencia is the one game in my career where I would love to go back and play it again. Playing in a Champions League final would have been immense. I lost a lot of semi-finals in my career but that one was by far the worst. It is a huge regret that we didn't perform anything like we could have.

Our defeat to Valencia, who went on to lose the final to Bayern Munich on penalties, meant it was unlikely we would be competing in the following season's Champions League. Since losing to us on Good Friday, Liverpool had hit form and replaced us in third place. There were still two games to play but my old club were now overwhelming favourites to pip us to the final qualifying place. The damage had been done the previous weekend when we'd lost to Arsenal, a result that meant we were no longer in control of our own fate. We did what we could by winning our last two games – 6-1 against Bradford City and

3-1 over Leicester City. But Liverpool also claimed back-to-back victories, with a couple of goals from Robbie Fowler on the final day at Charlton Athletic meaning they finished a point in front of us. It was a role-reversal of the previous season: Liverpool got the prize of Champions League football and we had to settle for fourth place and the UEFA Cup. All I was left with were the memories and the shirts I'd swapped with opponents after games. Admittedly, I got some good ones. Macca gave me his when we played Real Madrid at Elland Road, while I swapped with Luis Figo over there. I also got Paolo Maldini and Alessandro Costacurta after the two AC Milan games, plus Pep Guardiola's. Mind, the funny thing with my shirts is I now have no idea where they are. I have looked all over in recent years but not been able to find them. I used to give them to my Mum to wash and she insists I got them back. But I have somehow lost track of them. It is probably because I decided very early on that I wasn't going to be one of those players who framed the shirts of famous opponents and hung them at home. I wanted to do things a bit differently and instead put up the shirts of players I played with. So, I have quite a few Leeds, Liverpool and Blackburn shirts hanging at home – though none from Stoke! I have shirts with Gerrard, Carragher, Ferdinand, Davey Thompson, McManaman, Fowler written on the back – all lads I grew up with. I also have my last Leeds shirt. It is all right having Maldini or whoever but I prefer to be reminded about all the great lads I played with.

Missing out on a place in the Champions League was devastating as we had all really enjoyed the experience and wanted more. I'd made 15 appearances in the competition – only Ian Harte (17) and Mark Viduka (16) managed more that year – so knew just how special it was. Everything was the best – the atmosphere, the players, even the music as you walk out of the tunnel. I understood after that season why players move clubs for Champions League football. So, it was gutting to know we wouldn't be taking part the following season. What I couldn't get out of my mind as I looked at the final league table was how we'd been denied two points at home to Manchester United in March through an awful decision by the linesman. The score had been 1-1 when Wes Brown put through his own goal in the last minute. The linesman immediately flagged for offside and the referee had no choice but to disallow our 'goal'. But replays showed he got the decision wrong and we were forced to settle for a 1-1 draw. Just imagine how different Leeds

United's history could have been if we'd got back into the Champions League, with all the millions that come with playing in the competition. Maybe it would only have delayed the inevitable and the club's finances would have collapsed anyway. I suppose we will never know. But it is a definite 'what if?' whenever the club's decline crops up in conversation between supporters.

The season had still been a good one, only Manchester United, Arsenal and Liverpool finished above us. Chelsea were back in sixth. On a personal level, it was the best season of my career. As a player, the pinnacle is being involved in the Champions League and I played in the vast majority of games. As we went away for the summer, we were gutted to have missed out but everyone was confident that good times lay ahead. I was really excited and couldn't wait to get back into training – and that's from someone who usually went away for the entire summer. I flew out to my pad in Ibiza firmly believing success was just around the corner.

Chapter 14

Flower of Scotland

The seed that led to me becoming a full Scotland international was planted when I was actually on England duty at a World Cup qualifier. Not only that, but it came in the old Royal Box at Wembley as well. The game in question was against Italy in February, 1997. I'd been part of the set-up since 1994, when I first joined up with the Under-21s ahead of the Toulon Tournament that England won. I had since graduated to the senior squad under Glenn Hoddle but was still waiting for my first cap. I'd come close in a friendly with Mexico only for injury to rule me out. It meant that, as I sat with Gazza watching England lose 1-0 to a Gianfranco Zola goal, I was not technically tied to the England set-up. So, when by chance I was introduced to then Scotland manager Craig Brown, I came to a decision there and then about my future in international football. On returning to Liverpool, I spoke to Roy Evans and asked him if he could find out if Scotland were interested. Roy knew I was starting to get a bit disillusioned as I hadn't played for England so said he would have a word on my behalf. It may sound strange to some people that I didn't mention anything to Craig myself. But I was on England duty and it would not have been very fitting to start asking about my chances of being called up to play for another country. I thought it best to play it cool and hope for the best.

Unfortunately, I probably played it a bit too cool and nothing happened for another couple of years. Even when I dropped out of the England set-up before the 1998 World Cup, Scotland never got in touch and I had started to think I was destined not to play for the country where I was born. All that changed, however, soon after my transfer to Leeds United early in the 2000-01 season. My name had been mentioned in the newspapers the previous year when Scotland had been due to play the Republic of Ireland in Dublin but my leg was in plaster so there was no chance of me being involved. Now, though, with my Leeds career taking off, Craig Brown got in touch and said he wanted to call me up for a friendly against Australia. I couldn't say 'yes' fast enough. Playing for Scotland had always been my dream and now, it seemed, that dream was finally coming true. Mind, it did come at a price as, in some people's eyes north of the Border, I became public enemy number one. My crime? Having represented England at Youth, Under 21s and B-team level a few years earlier. The Press had a bit of a field day at my expense, with one newspaper even ringing up everyone called Matteo in the phone book and asking them if I should be allowed to play for Scotland. Now, I don't mind getting flack – providing it is constructive. But some of the articles in the Scottish Press bordered on the ridiculous. One even wrote that because I wasn't born there and spoke with a funny accent, I didn't deserve to play for Scotland. What a ridiculous statement, not least as I was born in Dumfries. You can't get much more Scottish than that! Plus, my Dad was born in Scotland, is a proud Scot and he speaks with a broad accent. As for my scouse accent, what did people expect from someone who had lived in the Liverpool area for the past 20 years?

To me, I'd been doing well for Leeds United so felt like I could be a decent addition to the squad. But, instead, all I got was flack. Thankfully, my Dad didn't see most of the rubbish being written about me as he would have been very upset. Dad was as proud a Scot as you could wish to meet and yet even he was criticised by one journalist a couple of years later, something that left me seriously considering quitting international football. Criticise me, by all means, but don't involve my Dad. The flack that was aimed my way showed me just how fickle the Scottish media can be. They are certainly much more fickle than the English Press lads, probably because there is not a lot to write about in Scotland apart from Rangers and Celtic. Mind, as much as I hated what was being written about me by people who had no understanding of the facts, that week did show me just what a good group I was joining as both the lads and Craig Brown all took time to tell me not to read all the rubbish that was being written. I appreciated their support.

That first squad I joined up with was a strong one. Don Hutchison, Barry Ferguson, Colin Cameron, Billy Dodds and Brian O'Neil were all good players. Even better, they were also my kind of lads. As was Matty Elliott, the Leicester City defender who turned out to be someone I could really relate to. I loved being part of the Scotland set-up straight away and felt accepted – even if I did make the same mistake of getting leathered at the first meeting, just as I'd done with the senior England squad when first being called up by Glenn Hoddle. Craig was okay, though, as he didn't mind the lads having a few pints – providing we didn't go overboard. Craig's management style meant the atmosphere was relaxed and I remember thinking after a couple of days, 'This is for me'. On the pitch, unfortunately my debut wasn't the best of starts as we lost 2-0 to Australia. I didn't have a very good game, either. I'd picked up an injury the previous weekend when Leeds had drawn 1-1 against Chelsea and, for a time, it looked like I might not be able to play. After all the injury problems I'd had with England, I genuinely thought I might be cursed. Thankfully, though, the injury eased after a bit of treatment and I was able to start the game. Just walking out at Hampden Park in a Scotland shirt was enough to make me feel so very proud, as did singing the national anthem knowing that my mum, dad and brother were in the crowd. We may have been well beaten by the Australians but that night remains one of the highlights of my career.

As I'd not played very well, I came in for a bit of criticism in the newspapers. It was probably deserved but Craig Brown made a point of trying to take the blame by later telling the Press: "It was my fault he didn't do so well on his debut. The game against Milan in the San Siro had taken place a week earlier and he had also travelled to Stamford Bridge to face Chelsea with Leeds. I put him out wide left and the boy was tired. But I didn't want to take him off because he might have taken it the wrong way. He'd just turned his back on England to play for us and if I'd taken him off on his debut then he might have thought, 'What have I done here?' In hindsight, it wasn't fair of me to keep him on the park but I had to." Craig had no need to say those words and I really appreciated his backing.

That support was one of the reasons I stuck with Scotland – even after an unexpected attempt by England to nab me back. It came early in 2001, just after Sven-Goran Eriksson had been appointed manager. Sven and his assistant Tord Grip had made a point of watching as many Premier League matches as they could after taking over and, seemingly, had pinpointed me as a player they wanted involved. I didn't know any of this when I bumped into Sven at Anfield, where I had gone to watch Liverpool on an afternoon when Leeds weren't playing. We said 'hello' but I never thought anything else about it until a few days later when my agent had a phone call from Sven. I'd already played for Scotland but, seemingly, I could still switch back to England because the Australia game had been a friendly. It was a flattering piece of news but not an offer I was tempted to take up. Can you imagine what the reaction would have been if I had? I was public enemy number one in Scotland anyway. Going back to England would have probably got me shot. So, I told my agent to thank Sven but say, 'No thanks'. I have never regretted that decision, even if with hindsight I can see that accepting the offer would have been the best thing for my career. I was playing as well as any centre-half in the Premier League at the time and could have played alongside Rio Ferdinand for England as well as Leeds. There simply weren't many left-footed centre-backs around at the time, which was something Sven made a big point of when trying to persuade me. He wanted balance at the centre of the defence and saw me as a way of achieving that. But my heart said Scotland so I decided to stick to my original decision. I am glad I did, especially as I have always considered myself more Scottish than English. I had, for instance, cheered Scotland when they were playing England both in Euro '96 and the two play-offs to reach Euro 2000.

My decision to stay with Scotland meant that as England beat Finland at Anfield in a World Cup qualifier that Sven had said I would be involved in if I had accepted his offer, I was earning my second cap. Belgium were the visitors to Hampden in a World Cup qualifier so it meant any speculation over whether I would one day return to England could be put to bed for good. I was glad, as it had become a real distraction. Anyone who knew me realised what Scotland meant to me, as Kenny Dalglish wrote in his weekly column in the *Daily Mail* on the morning of the Belgium game. He said: "Make no mistake, the lad may speak with an English accent but his heart is with Scotland all the way." I appreciated Kenny's words.

Scotland had started well in Group 6, having won in Latvia and San Marino before drawing with Croatia in Zagreb. With the Belgians completing the five-team group, it meant we were in a healthy position. Things looked even better after half-and-hour of the Belgium game as Doddsy had scored twice to put us 2-0 up. Hampden was really bouncing by now as we tore into the Belgians. It looked like being a case of how many we would end up scoring rather than if we would win. Unfortunately, Belgium scored out of nothing around the hour mark through Marc Wilmots and then Daniel van Buyten, who went on to have a good career, scored with a header in the 92nd minute to rescue a point. I was gutted, especially as we had missed loads of chances before his late equaliser and I'd had what I now consider to be my best game for Scotland. We had battered Belgium but not been able to finish the game off and we eventually paid the price when they went to the World Cup as group runners-up behind Croatia rather than us. It was devastating, especially as we had only finished two points behind Belgium in third place – meaning that if van Buyten had not equalised at Hampden then we would have gone to Japan and South Korea instead. With hindsight and because of what it cost Scotland, the night of my second cap is one of the worst moments of my career. Watching the 2002 World Cup was difficult because I knew we should have been involved. Belgium went on to be drawn in a group with Japan, Russia and Tunisia. I hated watching their games on television, especially as they went through to the knockout stages and ended up playing Brazil. How good would it have been to play for my country against Brazil in a World Cup?

I went on to play in four of our qualifiers – the costly draw with Belgium, a 4-0 win over San Marino, a goalless draw with Croatia and the 2-0 defeat in Brussels that all but killed off our hopes of reaching the finals. I missed the final game, a 2-1 win over Latvia that came as Croatia beat Belgium to clinch top spot, through injury, which was pretty much the story of my career with Scotland. In all, I had to pull out of between 15 and 20 squads due to injury. Sometimes, it would be Leeds asking me to miss international duty after picking up a slight knock. As they were paying my wages, I didn't feel I could argue so did what the club asked. Most of the time, though, I was simply not fit enough to play. In fact, my injury problems had become so acute during my days at Leeds that they eventually sent me across to Munich to meet a specialist called Dr Hans Mueller-Wolfhart. He was also Bayern Munich's doctor and all the top sportsmen in the world went to him, such as Michael Schumacher. Funnily enough, while I was there, my old Liverpool team-mate Didi Hamann popped in and we had a good catch-up. After looking at my knee and back, the Dr painted a very clear picture of what state my body was in and it wasn't good news. He tried everything to ease my problems. I had goose liver, calf's liver and juices from a turkey's head injected. I also saw a chiropractor to try and get to the root of what was wrong. At one stage, I even had radiation treatment – which shows just how bad things had become. I did feel a slight improvement after my four days with Dr Mueller-Wolfhart but before long I was back in pain. It meant something had to give and that was my international career. So, I retired from the Scotland set-up. Berti Vogts had, by now, taken over as manager. I'd played in Berti's first game – a 5-0 thrashing by France in Paris. It was the team that had won the 1998 World Cup and Euro 2000, and they ripped us apart in front of a full house. Thierry Henry and David Trezeguet were on fire and we had no answer to them. I ended up playing in three different positions during the 90 minutes and nothing we did could hold the French. In the end, I lost my head a bit and had to be told to calm down by Henry. He was right, as I'd got so wound up that I was going round kicking people for no reason. It was stupid and I am grateful to Henry for what he said. I always liked Henry when Leeds played against Arsenal because I felt there was a bit of respect there. I certainly respected him, while I had quite a few good games against Arsenal so like to think he felt the same towards me. Certainly, I always got that impression. I listened to him in the Stade de France that night and did calm down. I am glad I did, as what turned out to be my last international appearance could have ended in not only a 5-0 defeat but a red card.

As I travelled back to Leeds from Paris, I still wanted to play for Scotland. But, after speaking to the medical people, I realised Leeds had to come first. So, I 'phoned Berti Vogts and said my career had reached a stage where the injuries were starting to cause me problems. He listened as I explained about how I needed more and more injections just to get through games and that my knee was causing me all sorts of problems. I wasn't training a lot of the time and, after games, I would often be struggling to walk. Basically, I needed the rest of a two-week international break. I was honest with Berti, who did initially try to talk me round. Eventually, though, he accepted what I said and wished me all the best. He did say, though, that if I changed my mind then I should give him a ring. That was decent of him. It was something he didn't need to say. Berti was a good guy. Predictably, I got some stick up in Scotland but that didn't bother me. What mattered was my health and trying to extend my club career as long as possible. The pain-killing injections I was having all over my body before and during games had become ridiculous. I'd have one before the game, then possibly another after the warm-up and another at half-time. They were not particularly nice injections, either, but I had no choice. I needed the pain numbing or I couldn't play. The cortisone injections had actually started at Liverpool. They definitely are not good for you as all they do is mask the problem.

I wasn't happy at having to take them but went along with it. There are days today when I really regret just accepting the injections without complaint, usually when my knee is playing up. I can be watching the television at home and, suddenly, my knee will seize up. It is awful.

Berti accepting my retirement meant my international career was over after just six appearances. I wish it could have been more, especially as but for the niggling injuries I reckon I could have won at least another 15 caps. I did, though, fulfil my boyhood dream of playing for Scotland at Hampden Park and that is something no-one can ever take away from me.

Chapter 15

Babies Ready To Mature?

For Leeds, the 2000-01 season had ended on something of a low when our Champions League semi-final defeat was followed just 10 days later by Liverpool pipping us to third place. This double blow may also have left us all pondering a series of 'what ifs?' as our summer break got underway. But, by the time we returned for pre-season feeling refreshed, a real air of optimism could be detected at our Thorp Arch training ground. The reason was simple. We had a bloody good squad. Apart from possibly at full-back, we had two or three players vying for every position on the field. In goal, Nigel Martyn was quite rightly still considered to be our number one. But Paul Robinson, who had stood in so admirably for four months the previous season, had developed into a fine player and was now ready to push Nige all the way. The centre of defence was a similar story with myself, Lucas, Rio and Woody scrapping it out for the two starting places. The same could be said about the midfield and the attack, especially after Robbie Keane's loan from Inter Milan had been turned into a permanent transfer. It was a very strong squad, no question. Another encouraging fact was that we had shown the best form of any Premier League side since the turn of the year. Even being out of the Champions League was seized upon by some as being a possible help to our ambitions in that we would not have as congested a fixture list this time around. Personally, I would rather have played a extra 18 games like we had in 2000-01 if it meant more Champions League football but I could see the point people were making.

As the season kicked off with a home win over Southampton, I didn't necessarily think we would win the title. But I did expect us to claim a Champions League place, especially as there were now four up for grabs, and do well in the Cups. By that, I am not saying I had written off any chance of winning the title. Far from it, in fact. But, while I felt our squad was very similar to champions Manchester United in terms of quality, I still believed their experience of winning things would prove decisive in the Premier League. It had taken Sir Alex Ferguson a long time to get that formula right at Old Trafford and I felt we were maybe not quite at that stage. That was why I thought the Cups might be our best bet before we pushed on for the league in 2002-03. By the start of November, however, my thinking had changed. I thought the title was on for Leeds United. An unbeaten run of ten games was an excellent start, especially as it included a hard-fought win at Arsenal plus away draws against Liverpool and Manchester United. We had been particularly unlucky not to win at Old Trafford after Mark Viduka had put us in front near the end. We had played really well and looked set to claim all three points, only for Ole Gunnar Solskjaer to equalise in the last minute. The lads were gutted to concede so late on, not least as it meant Aston Villa were able to leapfrog us at the top of the Premier League. We did, though, manage to snatch pole position back a week later with a 2-1 win over Tottenham Hotspur.

Things were going well, with the only black spot on our season so far having been a 1-0 defeat to Maritimo in the UEFA Cup first round, first leg. We were poor that night, which might have been down to us not applying ourselves properly mentally. After having competed in the Champions League, the UEFA Cup was a comedown – a point that was brought home to us when we flew out to Madeira to take on Maritimo. Put it this way, their ground was no San Siro or Bernabeu with the capacity only being about 10,000 and the pitch surrounded by a running track. After visiting all those great cities the previous year, here we were on a little holiday island playing against a team we knew very little about. We weren't right mentally and deserved to lose 1-0. David O'Leary wasn't a big shouter after games like that. Instead, he would just give you this look that said, 'That wasn't good enough, boys'. We knew we'd had a bad game anyway so there was no need for David to have a go at us. A week later, we put things right with a 3-0 win in the second leg to go through to the second round. Troyes were then beaten 5-4 on aggregate after a nervy second leg in France, meaning that the season was shaping up nicely – especially as just three days later we beat Spurs to return to the top of the Premier League.

Looking at a league table and seeing your own team at the very top is a sweet feeling. But what gave me the most encouragement was that we were yet to truly play well. Okay, we'd taken points off all the teams we'd been expecting to mount a challenge for the title. But, no-one truly felt we'd got anywhere near to hitting the heights of the previous season. That had to be a positive, as to me was the way David O'Leary was running the playing side of the club. I found his man management skills very good. Other players may have different things to say on that subject but, personally, I found David great. I think he understood me, in that I was a bit set in my ways. I liked a drink, I liked a bet and I would be always trying to organise a team night out. But David knew that, when it came to the training field or a game, I would give everything. Eddie Gray was the same in that he would, from time to time, warn me about the drinking. But I got the impression both David and Eddie accepted it to a certain degree because the fitness levels of myself and the whole team were exceptional. Don't get me wrong, there were times when myself and David did have disagreements – such as that night in Rome when we beat Lazio. There was another time when David had been sent a copy of my bar bill by a certain hotel in Leeds. He called me into his office to discuss the matter. He wanted to know why it was so excessive. My response was to joke, 'I thought it was more, gaffer'. He just gave me a look, as if to say 'I'd quit while you're only slightly behind, son'. I never found out if David had asked for the bill or not. I lived in the city centre on my own back then so would often think nothing of popping out. I didn't see any harm in wandering out and having a pint, while reading the 'paper or having a bet. It was just one pint, not ten. But maybe David wanted to keep a check on me. My drinking was nothing like it had been at Liverpool, anyway. The game had changed and so, to be fair, had I. On joining Leeds, I had realised this was a new challenge and that the best way of doing myself justice would be to look after myself. Which, as far as I was concerned, was exactly what I did, with any nights out not being too excessive – no matter what the size of a bar bill might have otherwise suggested.

After beating Spurs, we had a blank week due to the international break. That meant by the time we were next in action at Sunderland on November 18, we had led the table for seven of the season's 12 weeks. Any hopes of staying there were dashed by a 2-0 defeat at Sunderland, which was followed by a 1-1 draw at home to Aston Villa after playing almost an hour with ten men following Alan Smith's sending off. Referee Neale Barry red carded Smithy for an alleged elbow on Villa defender Alpay, though from where I was standing he was harshly treated. It wasn't the first time we had been on the end of some

Macca in Madrid: Catching up with my old mate Steve McManaman on the night before we took on his Real Madrid side in the Bernabeu. (© Yorkshire Post)

A Complete Performance: We blew away Deportivo la Coruna in the Champions League quarter-finals with a 3-0 first leg win at Elland Road. Here, my defensive partner Rio ferdinand celebrates scoring our third. (© Yorkshire Post)

Breakthrough? I think my shot is heading in against Valencia in the Champions League semi-final first leg. (© Yorkshire Post)

I Don't Believe It: My reaction after Santiago Canizares somehow claws the ball to safety to ensure we head to Spain for the second leg with the score 0-0. (© Yorkshire Post)

A Dream Dies: Feeling distraught after we lose 3-0 in Spain as Valencia go through to the Champions League final, where they lose on penalties to Bayern Munich. (© Yorkshire Post)

International Farewell: Zinedine Zidane and co. give us a real runaround in Paris in what turns out to be my last game for Scotland. We lose 5-0. (© Press Association)

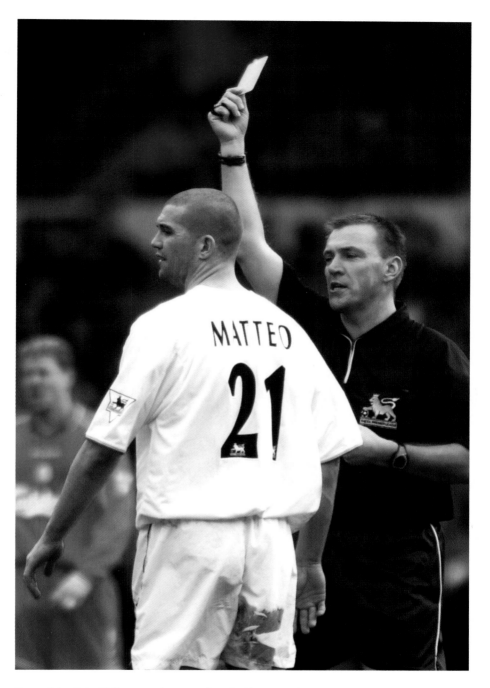

Part of the Job: Yellow cards are an inevitable part of any defender's career, here I am booked for a late foul on Michael Owen. (© Yorkshire Post)

Split Shorts: It's cold enough training in the Ukraine ahead of our UEFA Cup tie against Metalurg Zaporizhia without suffering problems with my kit. (© Yorkshire Post)

Swiss Roll: Leeds win again in Europe, this time 2-1 against Grasshoppers in Zurich. (© Yorkshire Post)

An Early Bath: Being sent off against Everton for two poor challenges on Kevin Campbell means an unhappy return to Merseyside. Brian Kidd ensures I don't get into any more trouble before heading down the tunnel. (© Yorkshire Post)

All Change: David O'Leary's sacking came as a real shock in the summer of 2002. Here we are put through our paces at the start of Terry Venables' time in charge.
(© Yorkshire Post)

A Familiar Sight: Injuries became an increasing problem for me during my final couple of seasons at Elland Road. (© Yorkshire Post)

Unhappy Return: I have to watch from the directors' box at Anfield with chairman Peter Ridsdale due to injury as we lose 3-1 to my old club Liverpool. (© Yorkshire Post)

Great Mate: I catch up with Leeds United fan and top radio presenter Chris Moyles at Radio One On The Road at Leeds Metropolitan University. (© Yorkshire Post)

Fun Night: Me and Alan Smith along with England cricket legends Michael Vaughan and Darren Gough at a Celebrity Question of Sport fundraiser at the Queens Hotel, Leeds. (© Yorkshire Post)

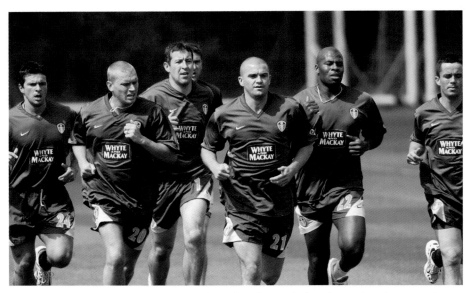

Doomed United? Pre-season is usually a time for optimism but, when I returned to training in the summer of 2003, I feared Leeds United were heading only one way and that was down. (© Yorkshire Post)

A Rare High: In what was a desperate 2003-04 for Leeds, I score the winner against Fulham to give us hope of avoiding the drop. (© Yorkshire Post)

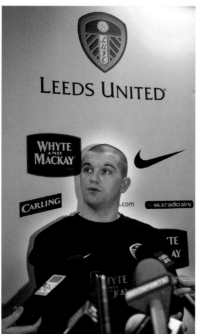

Facing The Media: Chatting to the press during the season Leeds were relegated from the Premier League made me an outcast in some people's eyes. (© Yorkshire Post)

Farewell to the Gentle Giant: As captain, I lead my team-mates into Leeds Parish Church for the funeral of John Charles in February, 2004. (© Yorkshire Post)

The Tears Flow. I try to console a distraught Alan Smith after Leeds have been all but relegated by losing 4-1 at Bolton Wanderers as Paul Robinson looks on. (© Yorkshire Post)

My Last Game For Leeds: I tussle with Chelsea's Alexis Nicolas as we lose 1-0 at Chelsea to end a truly horrific season for the club. (© Yorkshire Post)

Back...But Not For Long: I return to pre-season training in the summer of 2004 still hoping I have a future at Elland Road only to soon be on my way to Blackburn Rovers. (© Yorkshire Post)

A New Start: Rovers were a good family club but I missed the 'big city' feel of playing for Leeds and Liverpool. (© Press Association)

Live in Vegas: On holiday with a few of the lads in 'Sin City', plus me taking a dip with one of my best mates, Big Loz.

Final Call: Injury may have ended my time at Stoke City early but at least I left on a high - with the club in the Premier League. (© Press Association)

Columnist. One of the biggest pleasures I have had since retiring is writing a column, sponsored by sportingbet.com, for the Yorkshire Evening Post. (© Yorkshire Post)

A New Venture. Here I am with my co-owners of The Rock Bar in Leeds, Tony Hannan (left) and Rob Carlton. (© Yorkshire Post)

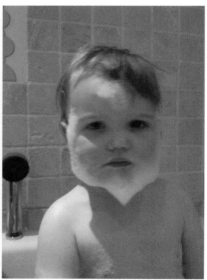

My World: My two beautiful daughters, Luisa and Elin.

questionable refereeing, either. There were times when we didn't help ourselves, me included. We would get embroiled in things that we should have walked away from. But, even so, I got the impression referees were treating us slightly different to the opposition. I was probably wrong but that was how I felt, almost as if the referee was waiting for one of our lads to get into trouble. Smithy suffered from that quite a bit, in my opinion. His game was based on aggression back then and that was what made him such a good player. Since breaking his leg playing for Manchester United against Liverpool, he hasn't had that aggression and I think his game has suffered as a result. For Leeds, he was a tough opponent – whether he was scoring goals or not. Smithy was also someone who got up the nose of opposing teams. I knew that from playing against him for Liverpool before I moved to Elland Road. I am sure Tony Adams and Martin Keown would agree with that as Smithy, even though he was still a young lad at the time, rattled them both during games between Arsenal and Leeds. They didn't like it, and neither did some referees. I think Smithy definitely suffered as a result in terms of the red and yellow cards he picked up. He wasn't the only Leeds player who, to me, was harshly treated by referees. One game, in particular, from that season stands out – our 2-1 win at Arsenal in August when we finished with nine men after Danny Mills and Lee Bowyer had been sent off for collecting two yellow cards. Neither deserved to go. The problem was both of them had a reputation for being fiery characters and tough tacklers. As a result, referees tended to clamp down on them when an identical tackle by someone else would not even bring a free-kick. Personally, I didn't think either Bow or Millsy tackled any differently to anyone else. I don't believe Bow, for instance, is a hard player. He is a good player but not a hard one. You wouldn't know that from how they were perceived, though. Maybe Bow's off-field antics didn't help him in that respect but I do think referees treated some of our lads harsher than they did other teams.

Smithy's dismissal against Villa meant we would be without him for three games, which was a blow. As was being without Mark Viduka and Harry Kewell around the same time. It meant we were a little bit short up front. No-one wanted our promising start to go to waste, not least our manager David O'Leary. So, he turned to God.

Chapter 16

Leeds United On Trial

At first, I thought I was seeing things. I'd just popped out of my flat in Leeds when, in the distance, I saw Robbie Fowler. Or, at least, someone who looked a lot like Robbie. I knew the 'real' one would be over in Liverpool, preparing for their game against Derby County. My old club had, like us, enjoyed a good start to the season and were on top of the Premier League. Robbie might not have started too many games but he had scored a hat-trick against Leicester City a couple of weeks earlier, and I still felt Gerard Houllier would see sense and give my mate an extended run in the team. So, there was no way the 'Robbie' I'd spotted near my flat in Leeds could be the real one. Or so I thought. A few minutes later, I was walking back towards my flat when who should I see but Robbie's Dad? Now I knew something was up, especially as Peter Ridsdale had a flat in the same block as me. I found out just a couple of hours later that Leeds had been trying to get Robbie for a while and that Liverpool had finally agreed to sell. For obvious reasons, the deal had to be kept secret. Hence, Robbie not having rung me. But, once the cat was out of the bag, he was firing questions at me about what it was like at Leeds. All I could say was positive things. To be fair, Robbie didn't need any convincing as anyone could see Leeds were an exciting, up-and-coming club. He had also not been getting on with Houllier so felt the time might be right to move on. I was well chuffed, especially when Robbie ended up moving in round the corner from me in the city centre. We had dinner most nights and it was just like the old times. I was excited by the signing in a football sense, too. Following on from big-name arrivals such as Rio and Robbie Keane, this was another signing that suggested something special was being built at Leeds. Now that we could count on Robbie's goals, I really did fancy us to last the pace in the race for the title.

By the time Robbie's transfer for £11m was agreed, David O'Leary had already signed Seth Johnson from Derby County. Seth's move may not have subsequently worked out but what tends to be overlooked today is that it was seen as a decent signing at the time. He had been playing well at Derby and was already an England international. So, if the money was there, why not bring Seth in? As important as the two signings were, though, a far more pressing matter for Leeds was that the second trial involving Lee Bowyer and Jonathan Woodgate had begun. The first trial had been abandoned earlier in the year after the *Sunday Mirror* ran a story in which the father of Sarfraz Najeib, the lad who had been badly beaten up in Leeds city centre in January 2000, claimed the attack had been racist. It had been established right at the start of the trial in Hull Crown Court that this was not the case but the *Sunday Mirror* ran the accusation anyway. I don't know why the newspaper did it. I know a lot had been made early on about race being an issue but, to me, Bow and Woody did not have one racist bone in their bodies. They just didn't. The content of the story was bad enough but that was not the biggest problem. Instead, it was the timing. The jury had still not reached a verdict and the *Sunday Mirror* story might prejudice their deliberations. There was a suggestion that the trial might be halted and, sure enough, on the Monday morning the jury were dismissed. A second trial date was then set for October. It was the last thing either the lads involved or Leeds United needed as, by then, the whole thing had been hanging over the club for a long time. Bow and Woody wanted to get on with their football and the club wanted to stop being in the headlines for all the wrong reasons. The re-trial meant that, by the time a verdict was due to be delivered, the matter would have been rumbling on for three seasons. As players, we had just become accustomed to it being part of life at Leeds United. But, for the club, I'd imagine it was a lot harder.

When the second trial started, the club management again copped a lot of flack. Not only did they have to wake up every morning to more negative headlines but hate mail was also sent to Elland Road, which can't have been nice for the office staff to read. On a personal level, however, I didn't encounter any hassle. We were instructed not to talk to anyone about the trial and that is exactly what I stuck to. I certainly didn't bother either Bow or Woody with it. As with the previous season, both of them spent all day in court so we trained without them. It meant we only saw them at weekends, when they would join up with us at the team hotel on a Friday night. I actually played a lot of three-card brag with Bow during those trips but the subject of the trial never came up. I was of the opinion that if he wanted to talk about it, he'd speak to me.

But if he didn't, then he clearly didn't want to discuss it. So I never once brought up the trial in his company.

As the trial continued, no-one seemed to know which way it would go. Everyone, it seemed, had a theory. But none of them really knew so the team soon learned not to take much notice. Eventually, after a couple of months of hearing evidence, the jury were sent out to consider their verdict. When they came back, Bow was cleared of both the grievous bodily harm with intent and affray charges. Woody, meanwhile, was found not guilty of the more serious charge but guilty of affray, and was sentenced to 100 hours of community service. The club responded by fining both players for being out drinking, four weeks' wages in Bow's case and eight in Woody's. The fine was immediately accepted by Woody but Bow, who let's not forget had not been found guilty of anything, wouldn't do the same. He did not think the fine was fair and refused to pay. It all blew up during the build-up to the home game against Everton shortly before Christmas when we won 3-2 and Robbie Fowler scored his first goals for Leeds. Bow missed the game so was sitting on the television gantry. When we scored the first goal that night, every single one of the lads ran over to him. The gesture wasn't pre-planned or anything like that, just our way of showing how tight we were as a group. It was totally spontaneous. The club probably didn't appreciate the sentiment but, to me, us being so close was a positive. By the end of my four years at Leeds, the squad had splintered and was pulling in all sorts of directions. It was part of the reason why Leeds collapsed as a club. But, at the time we played that game against Everton, we were all together and just wanted to show support for our team-mate. We played together and socialised together. Maybe the club also saw that as a positive, even though many of the newspapers claimed afterwards it was us having a go at the board. Certainly, no-one from the club ever said anything about it to us afterwards.

As relieved as everyone was that the trial was finally over, one man at the club did continue to suffer in the fans' eyes. Michael Duberry had been forced to give evidence for the prosecution in the second trial after admitting he had initially lied to police to protect his team-mates. Woody then said in the witness box that their friendship was over. It was really unfortunate and the fans took against Dubes after that. He carried the can in many ways, which from what I heard about that story wasn't justified at all. I will always stand up for Dubes when the subject of the trial and the fallout from it crops up in conversation because he did what was right and was harshly treated as a result. The bottom line is Dubes did nothing wrong, other than make a mistake early on out of loyalty to his mates. He had to change his evidence and knew that. He was trying to get custody of his kids at the time and had to do right by them by telling the truth, which is exactly what he did. Sadly, the upshot of him changing his evidence to tell the truth was his house being vandalised one night. When it came to Dubes, the Leeds fans got it badly wrong - and I don't say that very often. It was almost as if they were wrapped up in Woody and Bow being superstars. I felt Dubes deserved to be cut a lot more slack. Dubes was a good footballer as well, anyone who saw him against AC Milan at Elland Road in the Champions League will know that. He was outstanding in keeping Andriy Shevchenko, then one of the best strikers in the world, quiet. Don't get me wrong, there were times when he wouldn't have a great game but that is true of all of us. There was also the odd time when I thought he had a bit too much to say in the dressing room, usually after he hadn't played well. Sometimes, players who are too vocal are covering themselves a little bit and I thought Dubes was guilty of that once in a while. But, on the whole, Dubes was great and deserved better than being vilified by some supporters. He, along with the victim of the attack, is the one who I still feel sympathy for today.

With the trial over and Bow eventually settling his differences with the club, the focus was able to switch back to football. We'd not been on a great run since losing for the first time in the league at Sunderland in mid-November. But, even so, when we beat West Ham United on New Year's Day thanks to two goals from Mark Viduka and another by Robbie, it was enough to take us back to the top of the Premier League. Following on from what had been an excellent 2001, during which we had collected 86 points compared to the next best tally of 80 by Manchester United, the victory over the Hammers led us all to believe that we could make a real push for the title. Unfortunately, history now tells us that New Year's Day, 2002, was as good as it got for that Leeds United team. Just a few days later, we travelled to Cardiff City for a now infamous FA Cup tie that we lost 2-1. I missed the game through injury, which as it turned out was not a bad thing with Big Kev, the team's security man, having to drag a couple of our lads to safety at the end after the home fans had invaded the pitch. Being knocked out of the FA

Cup was a blow, though I did also think it might work in our favour because that left us with just the Premier League to concentrate on. With no distractions, we might have a better chance of landing the big one. And even if we didn't manage that, we would surely bag a Champions League place – especially as, for the first time, four teams would now qualify from the Premier League and not just the top three.

The reality, of course, was rather different with that defeat at Cardiff starting a run of form that saw our season come completely off the rails. We went almost two months and seven league games without a win, while we also crashed out of the UEFA Cup to PSV Eindhoven after losing the home leg. I'd been in a similar rut once before at Liverpool when we should have won the league in 1996-97. We couldn't buy a win for a month or so and it cost us the title. I am not saying we would have won the league at Leeds that season without those sticky two months. But we'd definitely have qualified for the Champions League, which was, as we later discovered, what the club's finances desperately needed. There were some really daft points that we dropped. We drew against Middlesbrough, Charlton and Everton, while Liverpool battered us 4-0 at Elland Road. To this day, I can't explain what went wrong. I know all sorts of theories have been put forward, from the fallout from the trial through to David bringing out his book *Leeds United On Trial*. But I don't think there was any one reason. Certainly, the book was not why our form collapsed. Okay, we all got a bit of a coating in the book. In my case, David had a bit of a pop over what had happened at half-time against Lazio the previous season when we'd had a row. He said a few things about the rest of the lads too but, as far as I am aware, no-one took offence. I certainly didn't, mainly because what he said about me was right. I had been out of order in the Olympic Stadium. The title *Leeds United on Trial* was a bit unfortunate. But I doubt David chose that. The timing was also not great, though only because it coincided with the results falling away. And not, as I have heard suggested on a few occasions, that the players had somehow developed a grudge against him for betraying a confidence. We were all grown men, and not the sort to take offence over a few words. I very much doubt many of the lads read it anyway. Maybe a couple of the older lads may have glanced at it, but I can't remember anyone else being interested. The only thing we read in the dressing room at Leeds back then was *Loaded* magazine and *The Sun*. We didn't care less about anything else and that is why I believe far too much has been made about the book.

The bottom line is we just didn't play well during those first two months of 2002. We did turn it round, in the end, and finished quite strongly to claim fifth place. That meant a place in the UEFA Cup again but, crucially, no Champions League, which as we all now know proved to be a disaster for the club's finances. The boys didn't know that then but we were gutted on a football level. We knew we had under-achieved. We were top of the league on New Years' Day and flying. Then, by the end of February, the mood in the camp had changed completely and we couldn't buy a win. That should never have happened. Even now, I look back at that squad and can't understand why we went so long without winning after that West Ham game. If we had won just two of those seven games, we would have pipped Newcastle United to fourth. Our problem, when compared to Manchester United or Chelsea under Jose Mourinho a few years later, is that we didn't really know how to grind out wins. If we played badly, we invariably drew or lost. The other top teams didn't do that, which is why we never really made a proper push for the title.

After such a disappointing end to the season, I wanted to get away for a good break. And where better than the World Cup in Japan? Of course, I wished it could have been as a player for Scotland but going as a fan was the next best thing. I went with my agent Struan Marshall and Andy Sterling, my financial adviser. We had a great time, the only sour bit coming when I went to the toilet at half-time in the England-Argentina match and was abused by a load of England fans. They were angry I had decided to play for Scotland. It was ridiculous. I was just there enjoying the football and these idiots wanted to have a go at me. I just laughed in their face. That apart, though, the World Cup was great. We based ourselves in Tokyo, flying in and out for the England games. While there, I also popped into the team's hotel as a few of my mates were in the squad. Me and Robbie Fowler had a great laugh. I even smuggled a few beers in one night for him in a back-pack. Robbie was bored and needed a bit of a release. It wasn't a major session or anything like that, just a few beers with a mate and a laugh for a couple of hours. We used to do this thing when staying in hotels before games where we would ring up other guests and slaughter them. It was an old favourite of ours. Paul Dickov loved doing it, too, as I found out when I joined up with Scotland. He would get quite nasty and properly slaughter people.

There were a few times when we were coming home from a night out in a taxi and going through each other's phone, looking for players to ring and abuse. Some didn't like it, I remember once at Stoke I did it to Andy Griffin. I told him, 'You've got a bad touch and can't play football'. It was just banter but he pulled me later on to say he hated things like that. Most were okay though. That night with England, quite a few of the lads had a phone call off Fowler and Matteo – including Sven! To be fair to Sven, he took it well. For Robbie, it was something that broke up the boredom – those World Cups are very, very long. He was missing his family badly so I think he appreciated seeing a familiar face and a bit of a laugh. Later, he gave me his shirt from the Argentina game when he came off the bench as a 'thank you'.

England got through the group stage and then beat Denmark 3-0 with Rio, who had been linked with a host of clubs by that stage due to having such a great World Cup, scoring one of the goals. After that, I had to come home because pre-season training was only a few days away so I missed the Brazil game when England lost 2-1. It meant I was back in Leeds when the bombshell news of the summer broke – David O'Leary's sacking by Leeds United. Like the vast majority of people in the city, I'd had no idea that it was going to happen. No inkling at all. I knew the club were disappointed to have missed out on a Champions League place again but I never imagined David would lose his job as a result. I was gutted, as I got on really well with David and respected him as a manager. He had improved me as a player, I was in no doubt about that. I just couldn't understand the decision or the timing. Fifth place may have been a disappointment but it wasn't too bad. Certainly, the club has not finished anywhere near as high since. It was a bad decision, end of story.

I am still not sure to this day why the board sacked David. There were suggestions in the media of some players going to Peter Ridsdale to say the manager had lost the dressing room. But that was not my view. Why would anyone go and say that anyway? David was doing a good job. If I had been the chairman and a delegation of players had come to see me, I'd have sent them away with a flea in their ear. I just can't see how anyone could claim David lost the dressing room. Not at all. All that happened, and this happens at almost every club, is that the ones who are not in the team maybe took against the manager. To me, they weren't big enough to try and get back in the team. So, they would mess about in training. That is all that happened at Leeds. The club had finished third, fourth and fifth under David, and reached two European semi-finals. To me, it was a crazy decision – a feeling that has been borne out by what has happened since. I definitely believe Leeds would not have fallen as quickly as they did if David had still been in charge. He could be a bit strange at times, such as that 'Just do it!' team-talk when he pointed at the Nike badge or the one when he said Herero 'smelt good but couldn't fucking run'. But, on both occasions, such an unusual approach worked as it broke the ice before important games.

Another theory as to why things went wrong that the fans, in particular, seemed to latch on to was David's decision to appoint Brian Kidd and promote him above Eddie Gray. Brian had come in to look after the Academy before I joined Leeds so our paths didn't cross too much during my first few months at Elland Road. But he then stepped up to the first-team early in 2001 to work alongside Eddie and Roy Aitken. Because of the rivalry between Leeds and Manchester United, our fans were a bit sceptical. But, as we were doing well and on our way to the Champions League semi-finals, not too much was made of the appointment. It was the same in the first half of the 2001-02 season when we were at or near the top of the Premier League. However, the moment we hit a bad patch in the New Year, Brian suddenly became the fans' scapegoat. It all came to a head during the last of those seven games that we failed to win in January and February. The game finished goalless and the Leeds fans made no secret of who they blamed. They chanted all the way through for Eddie, which is fair enough as he is a Leeds United legend. But the anti-Brian Kidd chants were well wide of the mark. Peter Ridsdale clearly agreed, as after the game he made his way over to the fans to explain why they were wrong. As someone who enjoyed playing under Brian, I was equally stunned as to why the fans were blaming him. The criticism he got was absolute rubbish. The fans just wanted someone to blame and because Brian was ex-Manchester United, he got the flack. It was nonsense. Brian was a brilliant coach and I doubt anyone at the club at the time will have a bad word to say about him. Certainly, all the lads he brought through at Manchester United absolutely love Brian Kidd. He had so many ideas. One of the first things he did at Leeds was to bring in a bag of mini-footballs, which were not much bigger than tennis balls. He then told us all to have a go at keeping the ball up for five minutes. I wasn't too keen, knowing that ball skills have never been my strongest point. The lads were also not too sure but, sure enough, after a few sessions with these mini-footballs our skills and touch had improved massively. It was the little things that made all the difference. He simplified things and that helped a lot. Footballers don't have the longest attention spans in the world so it is always best to get a point across quickly. Brian was great at doing that.

The only possible criticism I will make of the decision to move Brian from the Academy set-up to the first-team is nothing to do with Brian himself. Instead, what I felt David did get wrong was his decision to step away from training once Brian had joined the first-team coaching staff. When David was out there every day, training was a lot better. There was more intensity. But, as we started doing well, David spent more and more time in his office. I am not sure why, maybe the demands of the job got too much? Or maybe he brought Brian in so he could take it a bit easier. I really don't know. But I think if David looked back now, he would admit that was a mistake. Players want their manager to be there so they can impress him and the lads always used to comment on it. The thing was David was very good at coaching, probably the best I worked for on a one-to-one basis. He did a lot for me, improving my heading and so on. David had obviously been a quality centre-half so knew the position inside-out. Because of that knowledge, he was also able to really help the strikers. Mark Viduka learned a lot from David, for instance.

If I had to come up with an explanation as to why David was sacked, the only possible reason I can think is that David's desire to keep the squad together counted against him in the boards' eyes. As we all know now, Leeds were in big financial trouble during the summer of 2002 and players needed to be sold. But David, as you would expect of any ambitious manager, wanted to keep everyone together. David had built a good squad and we seemed on the verge of achieving things. I think Manchester United's interest in Rio inadvertently led to the sacking. They had made no secret of their interest in Rio towards the end of the previous season. An impressive World Cup then made Sir Alex Ferguson's mind up. He wanted Rio and with the Leeds board needing money fast, there was only one way it was going to go. But David didn't see it like that and, as far as I know, fought to keep Rio. That is why I don't believe the fact Rio left just a couple of weeks after David's sacking was a coincidence.

Rio's departure was, to me, a massive moment. Not because we didn't have the capability in the squad to replace Rio but because it sent out a message to all the other top players at the club that perhaps Leeds were on the wane. Okay, it was Manchester United and Rio wanted the move. But, in that moment, Leeds had suddenly become a selling club. As a professional, that is a worry. The lads started to think, 'Who's next?' Rio was a good captain and an excellent player, so his leaving unsettled everyone. At the time, we didn't know the true state of the financial problems so the decision made no sense – even if Rio's head had been turned by the prospect of playing Champions League football. The feeling was that things were being dismantled. Peter Ridsdale did himself no favours, either, by claiming soon after a £30m deal had been struck that Rio leaving was not a problem as Leeds already a better defender in Woody. Don't get me wrong, Woody was a great player. But, in my opinion, Rio was a better defender. His record in the game shows that. He had also just had an outstanding World Cup. Rio spent more time on the field, he was fit and oozed class. During my time at Leeds, I didn't see that much of Woody due to the trial and his injuries. So, for Peter to say what he did was wrong. I imagine Peter would take it back now. He was probably just trying to appease the fans. Certainly, the players were not fooled by Peter. Instead, we wanted to know what the club would do next. The key in a situation where a top player leaves is how the club responds. At Liverpool in January 2011, Fernando Torres being sold to Chelsea for £50m was followed by Andy Carroll and Luis Suarez arriving. That sent out a message and Liverpool went on to have a hugely impressive second half of the season despite losing a player many considered to be the star name. At Leeds, Rio leaving was followed by no new signing – again something that led to questions being asked in the dressing room as to what was happening. Looking back, that was the moment when it all began to fall apart.

Chapter 17

Warning Signs

A question I am often asked by Leeds United fans is, 'When did you realise the club was in big trouble?' The truth is that I probably didn't appreciate the size of the problems until the 2002-03 season, when the squad started to break up. But I do recall the moment when I first started to think that things maybe were not what they seemed and it was just a couple of months after I'd signed from Liverpool. It came just before Rio Ferdinand joined us from West Ham United. I had no problem with the £18m price tag, I'd seen enough of Rio in games and on television to know the club were going to get value-for-money even though they were breaking the British transfer record. But what did get me thinking about Leeds' financial state was a meeting myself and Mark Viduka had with the club just before the Rio deal was done. We had both been called into the office and wondered what was going on. It turned out the club had a proposal to put to us both, namely that they wanted us to be leased out to an American finance company. The money would then be used to fund the transfer of Rio. We both agreed as it was going to be a good move for Leeds United. So, we signed ourselves over to this firm, which now would not be allowed – as we saw with the Carlos Tevez affair at West Ham a few years ago. But back then there was nothing to say it couldn't happen. We were assured it was a routine thing for a club to do and we accepted that. I later found out that a few of the signings had been done this way. I do remember coming away from that meeting and being uneasy. Leeds United had just qualified for the second stage of the Champions League, which the newspapers claimed was worth an extra £10m or so to the club. So, me and Mark did ask each other where that money had gone. With the benefit of hindsight, it was of course an indication of where Leeds were heading. The club was over-reaching itself even then.

I put any sense of unease I had to the back of my mind, however, and continued to believe Leeds United were in a healthy state. It was the same when Seth Johnson and Robbie Fowler signed the following season. Once again, with hindsight, the two transfers just didn't add up. For a start, the wage bill was too high. Even lads who were not on the bench were earning £30-50,000 per week – that doesn't make any sense. Seth's transfer was a perfect example. On the face of it, he was a decent signing due to being a promising player who had already played for England. I also thought that David might have bought Seth to play at left-back, a position where we needed cover. If he had, Seth could have done well at Leeds. Instead, what he is best remembered for is the story alleging about how his contract talks were conducted. As most people in Leeds heard, the story goes that Seth and his agent walked in wanting a certain amount but Peter Ridsdale instead offered a lot, lot more. I never asked Seth if it was true but I have since seen Peter deny it. That is clearly the case. But by the very fact that I, who knew how negotiations were conducted at times by Peter, believed it could be true says a lot for how Leeds were as a club around that time. There were some crazy deals done. It wasn't so much the sums involved that were the problem, as big as they were in some cases. But the length of contracts did end up coming back to haunt Leeds. Everyone got five years. I can understand the club wanting to tie up players that other clubs wanted. But putting everyone on five-year deals smacks of no-one at Elland Road planning for the worst case scenario, which of course is exactly what happened. Peter must look back on that time and think, 'Why did I give these players so many big contracts?'

People blame Peter automatically. But I have to ask what the rest of the board were doing at the time? They must have discussed contracts with Peter. Okay, he dealt with the negotiations with a player and his agent. But he must have had to, first, get permission from the other board members. He can't have just been doing it himself. I imagine, in the end, he had the final say - but only after getting a broad agreement from the others. One area, however, where I do think Peter got it wrong was in his approach to any talks with a player. Negotiating a contract is like buying a house or a car, you start low and then negotiate upwards. With Peter, he started at the very top. It was a very strange way of conducting talks. He went in high all the time, and often with the wrong players. I am not going to name names but there were players at Leeds getting a lot of money when they weren't anywhere near the team. That meant the top players were saying, 'Well if he is on that, I should be on this'. People may say that is just greed but it is a natural reaction. The negotiations over my own first contract were pretty easy. I'd had a nice pay out from Liverpool for leaving. I had five years left on my Anfield contract and because I didn't ask for a transfer, I was due a settlement. Then, I got a nice signing on fee at Leeds and a good wage. I wasn't surprised by the wage I got at Leeds, as I knew roughly what the top players were on. But I was surprised by how easy it was to get. I thought we'd have to negotiate a lot more than we did. With Ridsdale, it was quite easy to get a new deal too. I would say things like, 'Bloody hell, chairman, how come these foreign lads are on all this money when I am not on anything like – where's my pay rise?' It was tongue-in-cheek, albeit it also being my way of getting my point across. Straight away, Peter would say, 'Tell your agent to come and see me to sort out a new contract'. I'd be straight on the phone to Stru and, soon, I'd have a new deal.

One area where the club definitely got things wrong in terms of the wages was the complete lack of a sliding pay scale. Usually, the top players at a club – invariably the strikers – get the biggest wage, the first-team regulars the next highest and so on. What instead happened at Leeds was that some of the lads not in the team would be on more than those of us who were playing every week. That is ridiculous. The regulars should have been earning what Seth was on, for instance. And the lads who were not in the team should have been on half that. The structure was all wrong, with no thought seeming to have gone into how much each player should be paid. I have seen it suggested in the past that the high wages Leeds paid were down to Peter just wanting to please people. I don't agree. But I do believe the wage structure was wrong right across the club. Fringe players being on huge amounts of money took the hunger away. Where was the incentive to better yourself? That is why I have always believed the best way forward for football would be to introduce some form of incentive-based contracts, certainly in terms of the young lads coming through or players who are coming in as squad members. It would be difficult to do it with senior pros who sign for a club. They have to be given what they are due. But for the others, appearance-based contracts would surely help improve the game's finances. It would certainly have helped at Leeds, where too many players on big wages didn't play a lot of games.

I have always believed someone has to earn their money, no matter what job they have. I certainly did at Liverpool. There was a proper wage structure in place at Anfield where, as you progressed, your wages went up accordingly. It might be from £300 to £2,000 to £8,000 and so on but everyone knew where they stood. At Leeds, young lads could go from a few hundred quid to a few grand without even playing a first-team game. There was no structure whatsoever. It is not the players' fault or the agents. It is the clubs themselves. Players don't ask each other what we all earn, though we do guess. The newspapers do the same but their figures are usually well wide of the mark. I remember one journalist showing me a supposed list of what everyone earned at Leeds and I knew it was wrong because mine was wrong.

The only people I told about my wages are my Mum and Dad. The first time I told my Dad what I earned at Leeds, he couldn't believe it. We were sitting in my garage at the time. My Dad had a business making overalls. It wasn't a big operation but he had some of them in my garage. I told him what I was on and he just said, 'You earn more in a week, son, than I'll earn from three years at doing these overalls'. I wasn't saying it to disrespect him, I just wanted him to know. It wasn't a nice conversation, to be honest. But I wanted him to know the family were going to be okay. And that we were going to have some nice things from now on.

The first thing I did was buy a place abroad and the main reason was so my parents could go there for some sun whenever they wanted. It is in Ibiza and, even now, they spend half the year out there. They are getting on a bit now so it is great to know that the sunshine will be helping them. Mum and Dad love it. They can sit in the sunshine, relax and chill out. My Dad is Italian and has quite dark skin anyway so the sun really suits him. Dad also loves chatting to people. He'll nip out for a couple of drinks while Mum puts the dinner on. Next thing she knows, he'll have brought back whoever he has just met for some food. He brought a female DJ back once. I also had Sky TV fitted so my Mum can watch Coronation Street every week. She'd be lost without Corrie, to be fair. If I ring when that is on the television, she won't answer the phone. That place is my way of saying thank you to them for all they have done. Even to this day, I give my Mum a few quid a week. My Dad still finds it hard to accept gifts, they don't like me treating them. But they love the holiday home. I have wasted a lot of money in my life on all manner of things, from drinking to gambling and cars. But the best thing I ever did was buy that holiday home in Ibiza. When they come back to England, they always look better for it. I love that and realise I am fortunate to have earned such a good living from football. I do believe, though, that I earned that money – something that maybe a few of those at Elland Road during my time probably can't claim.

In terms of Leeds United, I will always remember the moment when I knew for certain that the club was out of control. It came when I was listening to a couple of the young lads talking in the treatment room. Now, these two kids had never played for Leeds United and, in my opinion, were never going to. They just weren't good enough, as was proved later when they left Leeds and their careers faded away. Anyway, this particular day, one of them was complaining to the other about all sorts of things, including money. I wondered where he was heading with all this moaning, until eventually he blurted out to his mate, 'I'm only getting six grand, it's not right'. I couldn't believe what I was hearing. Neither of them were anywhere near being good enough to play for Leeds United and yet they were complaining about a wage that the vast majority of supporters could only dream about. I was having my leg iced at the time but I went red with rage. I launched into this kid. I told him, 'Six fucking grand isn't enough, how can you say that? When I was your age I was getting £200 a week and playing first-team football for Liverpool'. I nearly walled him up, I was that angry. The physio staff had to step in and this lad scuttled off. I took quite a while to calm down but once I had, it suddenly hit me just what trouble Leeds United were in. If that was the attitude of someone who was 17 and nowhere near playing for the first team then things could, I believed, only go one way.

I'd had an inkling the finances might not be quite what everyone thought a year or so earlier when the club had asked if it was okay to lease me and Mark Viduka to the American company. But, if anything, this kid's moans about being on 'only' £6,000 per week was even worse as it suggested the club could have an attitude problem within it. To be fair to the kid – which is not something I want to do – maybe he had picked up on the extravagant way things seemed to be done at Leeds United. For instance, most members of staff were driving top range company cars around. There were other instances of the club spending money like water too, such as flying back a few of the lads from international duty on a private plane. It cost tens of thousands of pounds but achieved very little. If they'd come back on a scheduled flight, they'd still have got back in time for the match. But that was how the club was run. Money was no object and there was too much extravagance, especially for a club who had not won anything. If we'd won a trophy or two then maybe such extravagance had been earned. But we hadn't and no-one at the top seemed to realise. People were getting a bit too cocky, far too early. The attitude seemed to be that the money would keep coming in and there was no Plan B if things went wrong.

Another example of the extravagance that went on at Leeds was the number of strikers we had. When Robbie Fowler signed in November 2001, it brought the total to six. That was crazy when the most we were ever going to start a match with was two. Plus, as is always the case in football, strikers earn the most money. I never had any problem with that, the game is about scoring goals, therefore, the quality ones earn very, very well. But for Leeds, having six top strikers meant the wage bill went up ridiculously. I'd love to know what Leeds paid just the forwards during that time. It must have been an eye-watering amount. I am not blaming the lads involved, far from it in fact. If you asked me then or now, for instance, who I wouldn't have signed then I couldn't tell you. They were all quality footballers. But did we really need six? I don't think so – especially as when Robbie Fowler signed, Smithy and Mark Viduka had just had the season of their lives during our run to the Champions League semi-finals. Stockpiling so many strikers also made the job a lot harder for David O'Leary as, all of a sudden, I don't think he knew his best team. David, of course, brought Robbie in. In terms of Robbie's ability, it was a no-brainer. But, maybe it would have been sensible to let one of the other forwards go? Eventually, of course, the club did sell Robbie Keane and then Robbie Fowler. But, by then, it was too late.

Chapter 18

El Tel

After David O'Leary's sacking had sunk in, I quickly realised Leeds United needed a big character as the next manager. Well, we certainly got that when Terry Venables was appointed. A former England manager who had also been in charge of Barcelona, he seemed to fit the bill perfectly. Certainly, Harry Kewell and Mark Viduka had only positive things to say about Terry from their time together with the Australian national side and that made my mind up. I was looking forward to working with Terry. Funnily enough, we were actually out in Australia on a pre-season tour when the news broke. Terry then flew out to meet us a couple of days later and I really did think we would go on to have a good season. My spirits were lifted even further when Terry arrived and he named me as captain. I think Eddie Gray had a say in the decision and it was a proud moment when I walked out before my first game as captain for a friendly against a team from Chile called Colo Colo. The venue was the Telstra Stadium in Melbourne but, to me, I doubt I could have been prouder had it been against Manchester United at Wembley in the Cup final. It was a great feeling. We won, too, with Harry Kewell scoring the only goal of the game. The only downside was that Rio had not joined us on the trip, his move to Manchester United was all but concluded so he had stayed at home.

Once we were back in England, our preparations for the new season continued. Missing out on the Champions League meant money was tight, even though Rio's £30m move to Old Trafford had smashed the British transfer record. Terry was, though, given a bit of cash to spend and he brought in Nicky Barmby from Liverpool for £2.75m, Middlesbrough's Paul Okon on a free and Teddy Lucic, who arrived on a season-long loan deal from Swedish club AIK. They were all decent lads but it was clear, to both the players and supporters, that the calibre of signing was already changing. We had gone from signing Rio Ferdinand and Robbie Fowler to bringing in Teddy Lucic. That is not meant to be disrespectful to Teddy, who had played in Italy and was a decent player. But he would never claim to be in Rio's class. Paul was the same, in that he was a great lad but the fans never really took to him and the signing didn't work out. The fans were asking where the £12m profit that had been made on Rio had gone, as only a fraction had been spent on the team.

Initially, our results were decent. We beat Manchester City on the opening day 3-0 at Elland Road. With Rio gone, I played alongside Lucas Radebe in defence and things went well. Jonathan Woodgate then came in for 'The Chief' at West Bromwich Albion a week later as we won 3-1 to become the early leaders of the Premier League. Our good start came to an end the following Tuesday when Sunderland won 1-0 at Elland Road, a game that saw Robbie Keane play his last game for the club before Tottenham Hotspur came in with a £7m offer a few days later. English football had introduced a transfer window for the first time during the summer so the board accepted, knowing they would have to wait until January to bring in any more transfer cash if the bid was rejected. It was a shame to see Keano go but with Mark Viduka, Alan Smith, Robbie Fowler, Michael Bridges and Harry Kewell still at Elland Road it was not as if we were going to struggle up front.

A 2-1 defeat at Birmingham City brought August to an end but we bounced back with a 2-0 win at Newcastle United to set us up for Rio's return with Manchester United the following Saturday. Unsurprisingly, Sky TV chose to show the game live so the cameras were there to capture a 1-0 win for us with H scoring the only goal of the game. We were third in the table and seemed set for another good season. Soon, however, any talk of challenging for the title or even qualifying for the Champions League was forgotten as we endured a bad run. In the next 11 Premier League games, we won just one – at West Ham United in November. Even then, we almost managed to throw it all away as West Ham fought back from 4-1 down at half-time to almost snatch a point. By December, we were fifth bottom of the Premier League and only three points clear of the relegation zone. We were also out of the UEFA Cup, Malaga having knocked us out in the third round with a 2-1 win at Elland Road after we had beaten Metalurg Zaporizhya and Hapoel Tel Aviv in the earlier rounds. The fans' patience was close to breaking, as was underlined by the 'Venables out!' chants that could be heard more and more after games. The players weren't happy, either. I certainly wasn't enjoying life. Because of all I'd been told about Terry, I had been expecting to work with a top coach. But after a few months together at Leeds, I didn't think his approach was right for either the club or the players. On a personal level, I wasn't overly close to Terry - despite one of his first decisions having been to make me captain. I didn't feel that I could go to him and voice any concerns I had.

Training was also very different under Terry compared to David O'Leary. We had started to spend more and more time working on shape, which the lads didn't really enjoy. It was a lot more technical than under the previous manager. David would always end a session with a long five-a-side game, whereas under Terry it was much more structured and the lads would end up standing around for long periods as he tried to get his point across. I am not saying Terry was wrong, any look at his record shows just what a top coach he had been. But the problem was a lot of the lads he inherited from David were not clued up on that side of the game. They couldn't take in the information Terry wanted to pass on. We'd played with natural flair under David but it soon became clear that was not the way Terry wanted to do things. It was a lot less relaxed under Terry. Later in my career, I experienced the same thing under Tony Pulis at Stoke City and it is not for me. Working on shape is fine but you also want to work with the ball. Terry also changed our shape in games and, again, that didn't work. The lads would just end up feeling confused. Maybe we weren't intelligent enough players to adapt and take on board the new information, I don't know. But the lads stopped enjoying training. The upshot was a few more fall-outs were happening behind the scenes.

I also got the impression that being awarded the captaincy had caused a bit of resentment towards myself. A couple of the lads seemed annoyed that I'd been asked to take the armband and not them. Others thought one of the more local lads should have got the job or possibly one of the older lads. To me, though, I'd played a lot of games in my first two years at Leeds and defenders often make good captains. That was possibly why Eddie had put my name forward in the first place. But a few of the others didn't seem to agree. I wasn't upset, I am not the sort to brood over things like that. But what had become clear to me as the season approached Christmas was that the squad had started to splinter. I didn't knock about with the lads as much as I had. The personnel had not changed that much, only Rio, Keano and the manager had left the club by this stage. But the craic wasn't the same. There were a lot fewer big team nights out together, for instance. The bond was not there that had so impressed me on that first meeting at the Flying Pizza. Certain cliques were forming and things were now being said behind people's backs. I am sure there were a few saying, 'Why's Dom been made captain and not so and so?' It just wasn't a good place to be. I did try to organise a few nights out but the manager was not keen. Terry was not as lenient as David when it came to the drinking. There were a couple of times after pre-season games, for instance, when I asked if the boys could have a few beers and the message I got back was, 'No'. Terry wanted to get his way of doing things across, which is fair enough. Following anyone who has been successful in any job is difficult, not just in football, which is why I think it would have been difficult for any manager to come in after David. The lads at the club had either been signed by David or had been introduced to the first-team by him. They had got used to how things were done, not just off the field but on it as well. Now under Terry, the style of football had become more cautious and the lads were finding it difficult to adapt. Our results were also poor and the fans were on the manager's back. Leeds United had suddenly become a very difficult club to manage. All I could foresee as we approached Christmas was a difficult time ahead. What I didn't know, though, was that things were about to get a lot worse.

Chapter 19

January Sales

The phrase Peter Ridsdale is best remembered for during his time as Leeds chairman is, 'We lived the dream'. He said those four words during a press conference held in the wake of Jonathan Woodgate being sold to Newcastle United towards the end of the January transfer window in 2003. Peter was sitting alongside Terry Venables and the body language between the two of them said all you needed to know about what was happening at Elland Road. It was a mess and the dream was well and truly over. Certainly, I couldn't see any way back to the top for Leeds United. Woody's sale just before the window was due to close had been the tipping point for supporters. He had come through the ranks and the fans loved him. They saw Woody as the future so his sale was the beginning of the end for many. To me, though, I had known for some time that the club was heading only one way and that was down. Woody's sale just opened everyone else's eyes to that fact. Over Christmas and New Year, the team had managed to paper over the cracks by taking 13 points from five games. We'd followed a 3-0 win at Bolton Wanderers with a 1-1 draw at home to Southampton before beating Sunderland, Chelsea and Birmingham City in consecutive games. The run took us up to 11th in the table.

The haul turned out to be vital as, without those points, we'd have been relegated come May. But, behind-the-scenes, there was a real stench about the place. There were constant murmurs in the dressing room about people leaving. Players wanted out, it is as simple as that. Life at Leeds had stopped being fun. Training was poor and we weren't doing things right. Meetings were held with the staff, as basically we wanted to know what was going on. But no-one had any answers. Every time we got money for players, it just disappeared into the black hole that was the finances. Two weeks before Woody was sold, Robbie Fowler had left for Manchester City in a £7m deal. Things had got so bad that, to get him out the door, Leeds had to keep paying a fifth of his wages for the next two-and-a-half years. It is bad enough to lose your top players but to then have to keep paying them shows just what a mess Leeds United had become. The situation was not Robbie's fault, he accepted a contract in good faith when other clubs such as Chelsea were making similar offers. He believed the promises Leeds made. He also had to look after his family. That may sound mercenary to some but anyone would do the same.

By now, I was getting more and more concerned. The dream was over and the club dying on its feet. Once Woody had gone, everyone knew it and I can honestly say that if the whole squad had been sold during that January transfer window then I don't think I would have been shocked. Things were really that bad. Almost overnight, Leeds had imploded and become a really dark place. I had gone from loving my football and relishing coming into training to wondering what was going to hit Leeds United next. My agent Struan Marshall asked me one day if I wanted out. But, because I was captain and took that responsibility seriously, I decided to stay. I just wanted Leeds United to somehow come through the mess they were in. I wanted to roll my sleeves up and try to lead by example. I would be chatting to Eirik and saying things like, 'What can I do to change this?' But we couldn't come up with any answers.

After Woody had been sold, midnight on January 31 could not come quick enough – especially as we had also lost Lee Bowyer to West Ham and Olivier Dacourt had gone on loan to Roma in Serie A. In that respect, I was glad the transfer window had been introduced as it meant no-one else would be able to leave once we had passed the deadline. Thankfully, midnight arrived and we still had a workable squad of players. Now it was up to us to get Leeds out of trouble. We were still in mid-table but there was so much negativity surrounding the club that I genuinely feared we would be dragged into the relegation trouble. Every newspaper was suddenly inserting the words 'cash-strapped' in front of Leeds United or 'troubled'. They were right, but it still made for uncomfortable reading. On the field, we continued to struggle with a 1-0 win over a poor West Ham United side doing little to lift the gloom, coming as it did in between a 2-0 loss at Everton and a very poor 3-0 defeat to Newcastle United at Elland Road. Where before we had been a team, now we were merely a group of individuals. Some of us would have a good game one week but not the next. There was no fluency about us and we played like a bunch of strangers. We still had lots of quality players but it wasn't clicking. The longer the season went on, the deeper we were being sucked into trouble. Confidence was rock bottom and no-one was happy. Even the big, loud characters in the dressing room had gone quiet. I had stopped enjoying coming into work. Deep down, though, I knew I had a responsibility to the club and fans. I wish I could say the same about everyone else, as there were others who were messing about in training. We were deep in trouble at the wrong end of the Premier League and yet some were tossing it off. As a result, there were plenty of arguments on the training pitch. The whole camp had gone sour.

There were plenty of low moments but the worst, by far, came in the FA Cup. Somehow, amid our struggles in the Premier League, we had managed to get through to the quarter-finals. Admittedly, we'd hardly faced a tough schedule as we beat Scunthorpe United, Gillingham (after a replay) and Crystal Palace to reach the last eight. The draw then handed us a Yorkshire derby against Sheffield United at Bramall Lane. We owed the Blades one, too, as they had knocked us out of the League Cup earlier in the season. I had missed that game through injury so was, thankfully, not there to see us go from being 1-0 up in the 91st minute to losing 2-1 at the end of normal time. Neil Warnock's Blades were in what is today called the Championship so our defeat had been a shock. It meant, though, that being drawn against them in the FA Cup was a chance for revenge. Unfortunately, injury meant I missed all of March so wasn't able to play. Instead, I watched it on television and I really couldn't believe my eyes at what I was seeing. The performance was awful, truly awful. There was no life in the team at all. Sheffield United went 1-0 up through Steve Kabba with 10 or so minutes to go and I was expecting us to throw everything at them. Instead, we barely got out of our own half. Talk about frustrating. I had a few mates in the away end that day and they couldn't believe a Leeds United team had surrendered so lamely. Unfortunately, I wasn't surprised as a malaise had descended on the club.

Venables was gone within a fortnight. It had been clear that there had been a fall-out between Terry and Peter Ridsdale at the press conference that followed Woody's sale, the one where Peter had famously spoken about having "lived the dream". The pair's body language told anyone watching on television that. They were almost sitting with their backs to each other, while Terry had his arms folded as he stared into the distance. Terry was not someone who spoke to me as captain and took me into his confidence so I don't know exactly what went on between him and Peter. But that FA Cup defeat at Sheffield United laid bare for the whole country just how much of a mess we were in. Terry's sacking came with us sitting 15th in the table and I hoped the club would move quickly to make an appointment. Thankfully, they did just that and Peter Reid was appointed a couple of days before we were due to play at Liverpool.

Reidy coming in was like a breath of fresh air. I knew enough about his personality to appreciate that he was exactly what we needed. Reidy is lively and people bounce off him. He is also someone who has never been scared of giving anyone a kick up the backside, which I felt a few of the squad needed. We lost that first game at Anfield 3-1 and, as a result, dropped another place in the league table. But it was noticeable within a few days of that defeat to my old club that people were starting to smile again at Leeds. Things became more light-hearted and the banter was back, which was something I had missed massively under Terry. The training ground had become too quiet but Reidy changed all that.

Mind, even Reidy's arrival could not bring to an end the turmoil behind the scenes with Peter Ridsdale deciding to step down as chairman a couple of days after our defeat to Liverpool. I think the pressure had just become too much for Peter to bear. Our paths have crossed a few times since he left Leeds and we always get on well. I bumped into him most recently at the 2011 Soccerex football conference in Manchester and we had a good chat about the old days. Whatever people say about Peter, he is a proper football fan who knows the game. The lads liked him because they could talk about football to him because he thought like players. With some chairmen, that isn't the case. I must admit I do feel sorry for Peter in how everything worked out at Leeds. He has carried the can for what happened to Leeds, a lot of which I feel is unfair criticism. He maybe lived life as a fan too much, he loved getting involved with the boys for instance. But I liked him as a guy. He was genuine and decent, and someone who was trying his best for Leeds United. It all went wrong but a lot more people are responsible than just Peter – including the players. I certainly feel responsible for what happened, never more so than at the end of what turned out to be my final season at Elland Road. Relegation was awful. It was the only time it happened in my career and I am glad because relegation is the lowest feeling for a footballer. There is a photo of me and Smithy after the Bolton game that all but confirmed Leeds' relegation and we are both in tears. As my family will no doubt agree, I am not that much of an emotional person usually. But that day my emotions got the better of me and I couldn't stop myself. I felt guilty about what had happened to a club I care about. That feeling stayed with me all summer, affecting both my personal life and how I was around people.

Peter leaving on March 25 meant the club needed a new chairman. I wasn't sure who would get the job, though it is probably fair to say that what I never expected was the new man would be a professor. I thought it was an early April Fools' gag when I first heard. I didn't know a lot about Professor John McKenzie, who had been drafted on to the board a couple of months earlier. We'd met a couple of times and he seemed a decent guy. But my immediate thought on hearing the news was, 'What is a professor going to know about football?' It was comical. Or it would have been if what was happening to Leeds United had not been so tragic. I was starting to get embarrassed with where the club had fallen to.

On the pitch, at least, we did start to click under Reidy. A week after losing to Liverpool, we bounced back by thrashing Charlton Athletic 6-1 at The Valley as Mark Viduka netted a hat-trick. I was delighted for Mark as Leeds' decline had hit him hard. Of all the foreign lads who passed through Elland Road, he was one of those who really cared. I know he was devastated by how things had gone. But, because he was such a laid-back guy, we didn't get a lot of out Mark apart from truly awful jokes. The lads would roll their eyes when he started one of them. No-one, though, doubted just how much he wanted to get Leeds out of trouble – which is exactly what he did with the type of purple patch that all strikers dream about. In total, he scored 14 goals in the final 10 games of that season – a phenomenal run and, undoubtedly, one that saved us. I can't explain why it just clicked for Mark during those final few weeks. Neither, probably, could he. But, thankfully, it did as without those goals we would have been in deep trouble.

The game where we preserved our Premier League status came on the penultimate weekend of the season at Arsenal. Our game had been moved for television due as Arsene Wenger's were side still in the hunt for the Premier League title. It meant all our rivals played the day before and the news was shocking, particularly at West Ham who beat Chelsea. I was sitting in my hotel room with Eirik Bakke and we were gutted when Paolo Di Canio scored the only goal of the game late on. The result meant we were only outside the bottom three on goal difference, ours being minus two compared to Bolton in 17th place with minus 11 and West Ham a further six goals worse off. All three of us had 41 points and it looked like being an almighty scrap to stay out of 18th place, Sunderland and West Bromwich Albion having already been relegated. A defeat at Highbury, therefore, and we really were going to be up against it. I didn't sleep a wink that night, which was not like me at all. Even before the Champions League semi-final against Valencia, I had slept fine. But this time I just couldn't stop thinking about the game.

We got to Highbury early and the mind games had already begun. With Manchester United having won the previous day, Arsenal also needed the three points to take the race for the title into the final week of the season. So, in an attempt to unnerve us, they had left the heated floor on. That would have been great in January but not the first weekend in May. They were clearly trying to wind us up. To escape the heat, I headed off to the toilet for my usual pre-match routine. The weird thing about Highbury was that the window from the toilet basically looked out on to the street. So, I could hear everything the Arsenal fans were saying outside and they were certainly very confident. I thought about those cocky comments when Harry Kewell put us in front with a cracker of a goal past David Seaman after just five minutes. They must have been stunned!

It was the perfect start and one I put down to Reidy relaxing us all before the game by saying, 'This lot are fucking shite' as he read out a team featuring Henry, Bergkamp, Pires etc. The comment really broke the ice and we went out feeling good, which is why I think we started so confidently. The game turned out to be a thriller with Thierry Henry equalising and Sylvain Wiltord having a 'goal' disallowed for offside before half-time. We went back in front early in the second half with an Ian Harte 'special' that gave Seaman no chance. Once again, though, Arsenal hit back with Bergkamp this time netting the equaliser. Needing all three points to stay in the title race, Arsenal poured forward and we had a couple of let-offs when Bergkamp shot wide and Henry hit a post. Maybe it was our lucky day, after all? Somehow, we kept them at bay and with just a minute remaining on the clock we seemed set to collect a precious point. Most sides would have settled for that, even if it meant we would have to beat Aston Villa on the final day to ensure our survival.

I'm not sure why, but we refused to accept the draw and pushed on for what would, at this late stage, undoubtedly be the winner. Our chance came when I dispossessed Jermaine Pennant on the right. I immediately looked up to see what was on. Mark Viduka, on seeing me claim the ball, had peeled away to the right of the Arsenal area so I found him with a chipped pass. I then set off racing forward, thinking Mark would square the ball as most of their team were up at our end of the pitch. I don't think I have ever run as fast in my life, I must have really wanted to score our winner! After what felt like a second but was probably nearer ten, I made it to the edge of the penalty area and was screaming for the return pass. So, what does Mark do on seeing me race forward unmarked? He only steps inside Oleg Luzhny and curls this unstoppable shot beyond Seaman and into the corner of the net. Any feelings of frustration on my part at Mark ignoring my run disappeared in an instant. We had done it. The lads went berserk and all jumped on top of Mark. A few minutes later, I was named Man of the Match and, for the first time in my career, I felt really emotional about the award. I knew what had been at stake and even said 'hello' to my Mum live on television. She was well chuffed.

That game at Arsenal is probably my favourite memory of being at Leeds. I know most people assume it must be the goal in Milan that put us through to the Champions League second group stage. But, because of what was at stake and with me being captain, I look back most fondly on that 3-2 win at Highbury. With hindsight, all we did was delay the inevitable as Leeds were relegated just a year later. But, at the time, it really felt like we had saved the club. No wonder the lads wanted to celebrate. After surprising the Sky interviewer by giving my Mum a name-check, I went back to the dressing room and the party was already under way. After enjoying a couple of drinks, we got back on the bus and Reidy immediately headed to the fridge at the back. He opened it but all he could find was a few chilled Lucozade bottles. That wasn't going to be any good so we stopped at an off-licence somewhere in London. I went in with Reidy and basically scooped up all their ale and wine. Only then did Reidy say, 'Would you believe it Dom? I've only gone and left my wallet on the bus.' I didn't believe him for a minute. But, I was so happy, I just bought it all and the journey was great fun. We had a sing-song and the atmosphere felt like it had in my early days at Leeds. It was like we had won a trophy. Reidy deserves a lot of credit for keeping us up. Not only did he lighten the mood significantly but he also brought a sense of belief back. Another smart move was getting us back to doing what we liked the most, playing football. We didn't spend hours working on team shape or anything like that, which had been a big problem under Terry.

We went on to beat Aston Villa 3-1 the following week with Mark Viduka again getting on the scoresheet to take his Premier League tally for the season to 20, a remarkable achievement in a team that almost went down. The win over Villa meant we finished 15th on 47 points, five clear of West Ham in 18th. It also meant the season had ended on a high. Once the euphoria had died down, however, an assessment of the campaign as a whole did not make comfortable reading. Basically, we'd had a good first two games, beaten Manchester United in September, done well over Christmas and then finished with back-to-back wins. James Milner, who has gone on to enjoy a good career, had also made the breakthrough during the season. But, other than those few positives, it had been very, very disappointing. Still, as I headed off on holiday that summer, I still hoped that by beating Arsenal and staying in the Premier League, we had somehow managed to turn the corner.

Chapter 20

The Not So Magnificent Seven

Pre-season is invariably a time of optimism for footballers. Anything seems possible, no matter how badly or how well the previous year has gone, as the squad returns to training after a few weeks recharging the batteries on a foreign beach. Usually, there will be at least a couple of new faces to welcome as we all get down to business. That sense of hope ahead of a new season was a feature of all my pre-seasons, whether I was at Liverpool, Leeds, Blackburn or Stoke. All, that is, apart from one. And that was the summer of 2003 when, from the moment we returned to Thorp Arch, I had a feeling we were in trouble.

It shouldn't have been that way. I had actually gone away on holiday believing the worst was over for Leeds United. Avoiding what would have been a catastrophic relegation should, I thought, be the springboard for the club to at least return to a sense of normality. Peter Reid being confirmed as our manager on a permanent basis a couple of weeks after the season had ended made me feel even more confident about the future. Reidy had deserved the chance to manage Leeds after the rescue job he had performed in keeping us up. He'd also proved his quality at Sunderland, who he had led to back-to-back seventh place finishes in the Premier League just a couple of years earlier. After Reidy's appointment had been confirmed, I thought, 'A few decent signings and we should be okay'. Unfortunately, as the summer wore on, it became more and more apparent that the money had totally run out and the club was in a real mess. How else could all the loan signings Leeds ended up making be explained away?

During that summer, we made one permanent signing – Jody Morris from Chelsea – and, eventually, seven loanees. Now, I have nothing against the loan market being used in football. It can work very well, particularly these days in the Championship where promising young Premier League players can make a big impact and possibly help a club to promotion. But the loan market is used best only in isolation, as the kind of large-scale influx that Leeds opted for in the summer of 2003 always runs the risk of flooding a club with unsuitable players with little or no feeling for who they are joining. I am not saying that is necessarily what we got with all those summer signings but I challenge anyone to name more than one of the arrivals from abroad whose move worked out anything but badly.

At least we brought in one England player - Jermaine Pennant, then 20 and a hugely-promising winger with Arsenal – to go with Lamine Sakho, Cyril Chapuis and Salomon Olembe from Marseille. Zoumana Camara also arrived from Lens along with Paris St German's Didier Domi, who did at least have some Premier League experience from his time with Newcastle United. The final loan signing is perhaps the one everyone remembers the most but for all the wrong reasons - Roque Junior, the Brazilian World Cup winner who joined us from AC Milan. The loanees, which one national newspaper laughably dubbed 'The Magnificent Seven' during the early weeks of the season, hardly represented the re-build I'd been hoping for in the wake of our win at Arsenal the previous May. The quality of the signings had come as a big disappointment, with perhaps the worst bit being that I'd never heard of a lot of the foreign lads. I appreciate Leeds didn't have the money to go out and bring top names in. But surely we could have done better than just get lads in for the sake of it. In football, if you're lucky, you might find one or two bargains during a summer transfer window, but not seven. The unease in the dressing room was only added to when we were told some of these new lads were on £40,000 per week. I don't know if that was true but, bearing in mind this was Leeds United, none of us found the claim to be too outrageous. The English lads, especially after seeing some of the loanees in action during pre-season, couldn't understand this. Why not, we asked each other, go for someone with proven ability in English football for £10,000 per week? It was as if nothing had changed in terms of the club over-spending on wages.

The huge number of loan signings together with Liverpool snapping up Harry Kewell, who had scored 16 goals the previous year, meant I started that season knowing we were in a dangerous place. Our results in pre-season, some of which I missed after undergoing knee surgery at the start of the summer, only added to my unease as we were held to a draw by a York City side who were destined to be relegated from the Football League the following May and beaten by Burnley, Hull City and Irish club Shelbourne. I am not one who usually pays too much notice to results in pre-season, which to me should be all about building fitness. But, on a daily basis in training, I and the rest of the lads could see the wrong players had been signed and that meant we were in for a long, hard season. Deep down, I knew that a 17th place finish would be a major achievement – a shocking state of affairs, really, when you consider that exactly two years earlier I had firmly believed Leeds were on the verge of making the breakthrough in terms of winning trophies. I couldn't, of course, let on just how worried I was in public as it would have shattered our already fragile confidence. So, in my programme notes for the opening day game against Newcastle United at Elland Road, I wrote: "I feel this season is going to be one of consolidation after everything that has gone on here in the past 12 months or so. We need to finish in a good position this season and then, next time around, we can start to push on once again." If only!

To be fair, we actually started okay and by the end of August were sitting 12th in the table with five points from four games. We had followed a 2-2 draw with Newcastle by losing 2-1 at Tottenham Hotspur on an afternoon when Aaron Lennon became the youngest Premier League player in history after Reidy brought him off the bench. Three days later, we drew 0-0 at home to Southampton and then Mark Viduka sealed a 3-2 victory over Middlesbrough at the Riverside Stadium with a stoppage time winner. So far, so good – especially as our next game was a trip to newly-promoted Leicester City. Roque Junior, our World Cup winner who had joined us shortly before the end of the transfer window, was also set to make his debut at the Walkers Stadium so what could go wrong? Unfortunately, a lot, as Leicester gave us a 4-0 hammering that started a terrible nine-game run that brought just one win – 2-1 at home to Blackburn Rovers – and eight defeats. By the end, Reidy had been sacked and replaced by Eddie Gray, whose first game was the last of those eight defeats as Bolton Wanderers won 2-0 at Elland Road. Reidy had been sacked after our previous game, a 6-1 thrashing at Portsmouth, another side who were new to the Premier League. We had slumped to the bottom of the table a week earlier with a 4-1 home defeat to Arsenal and that was an awful experience. But losing like we did at Fratton Park was, frankly, embarrassing. They battered us and our heads went down long before the end. It had only been 2-1 at half-time but, because the team spirit was so fragile, we just collapsed in the second half. I had become accustomed to us rarely looking like getting back into a game after falling behind but this was something else. That day at Fratton Park was a low, low moment for me and the five-hour coach journey back to Leeds the longest of my career. Reidy realised he wasn't going to survive a defeat like that and I felt we had all let him down. Sure enough, he was sacked the following day and, in a funny way, I would imagine the decision came as a relief to him. Life had become a grind at Elland Road and there seemed no way of lifting the club out of trouble. Reidy is someone I respect hugely and it is just a shame that he came to Leeds when it was an impossible job. He had very little money to spend and very little time to decide who to bring in. It must have been so frustrating but, credit to Reidy, he always tried to be positive around the lads, even though anyone could see the spirit just wasn't there. The manner of some defeats will have hurt him, particularly the 4-0 loss we suffered at Everton in September. After that, he told the Press: "We did not try and we did not turn up. We did not want to turn up. All I ask is for them to go out on the pitch and earn the right to play. It is not too much to ask, is it?" It was a fair question.

I still see Peter at the races to this day and he is someone I respect a lot. He kept us up in 2002-03 when, if things had continued under Terry Venables, we'd have gone down. I know Leeds suffered a lot of problems after being relegated a year later but had we gone down in 2003 I firmly believe it would have proved even more disastrous for the club.

After Reidy's sacking, Eddie Gray coming back as manager was, at least, a positive move. Eddie is an icon at Leeds United, where he has filled just about every position apart from goalkeeper and chairman down the years. Eddie also loves his football and he is someone who, even now, I enjoy chatting to about the game. All the ex-Leeds lads are the same. When he spoke to any of us about football, it was clear he was on the same wavelength as us. So, Eddie's return was, to me, a decent decision by the club – even though I was gutted Reidy had left. Eddie represented a safe pair of hands as he was someone the vast majority of the players were comfortable with. It was similar to what happened when Kenny Daliglish went back to Liverpool after Roy Hodgson had been sacked. The return of a legendary figure always gives a club a lift. And if anyone needed a lift, it was Leeds United in the wake of that defeat to Portsmouth.

The job facing Eddie was a tough one, especially as he had taken over a group of players feeling pretty shell-shocked and embarrassed. We were in deep trouble at the bottom of the Premier League with just eight points from 12 games – comfortably Leeds' worst start since the club had been relegated from the First Division at the end of the 1981-82 season. The first thing Eddie did was call the squad together and say: "We are Leeds United, lads. We can't be going to places like Portsmouth and getting stuffed. We need to get some pride back into this club and you are the people to do it." The words hit home.

For Eddie's first game against Bolton, he stuck largely with the team he had inherited from Reidy. But, after that defeat, he took the decision to dump the foreign lads and only Didier Domi of the six who had joined in the summer started more than one game during the rest of the season. It was a decision I was fully behind as the foreign signings just hadn't worked. Roque Junior was perhaps the most glaring example of how they had failed to settle in English football. When the news first broke that we had signed this former World Cup winner, I was really looking forward to playing with him. All the lads thought he must be some player but, straight away, he proved to be unsuited to the Premier League. Instead of tackling, he would dangle his leg out - an approach that was never going to work. His positioning was also all over the place, which was something we quickly discovered on his debut against Leicester. Watching him that night, I was not impressed by what I was seeing. He may have looked good on the ball at times but he just had no positional sense whatsoever. Maybe the formation Leeds played didn't suit him, I don't know. But, as a World Cup winner, I felt he should have been able to adapt. The one game that always sticks out in my mind as an example of how Roque Junior struggled was the 4-0 defeat we suffered at Goodison Park. He was up against Duncan Ferguson, who before long had literally wrestled the shirt off his back. He was a World Cup winner but looked terrified. He simply could not handle the physical demands of English football. After Eddie took over, Roque Junior never played again – not even in that first game against Bolton. Funnily enough, after he left, the lads had a shirt made up with 'Roque Junior' written on it that was given to the player who had been the worst performer in training. That shows what we thought about his stay at Elland Road. We'd all been expecting great things but he just wasn't built for the Premier League, either mentally or physically. To be fair to Roque Junior, after leaving Leeds he still kept being picked for Brazil. So, he must have had something about him. At Leeds, though, we never saw what it was.

Sadly, Roque Junior wasn't the only foreign signing who flopped at Leeds that season. Lamine Sakho, for example, started well but then quickly faded and seemed to lose interest. Salomon Olembe was another who never cut it at Leeds, so much so that throughout his time at Elland Road I was always amazed he even passed his medical. The worst bit of Olembe's stay at Leeds, for me, was that he was on big wages.

One foreign signing who doesn't deserve criticism is Didier Domi. His heart was definitely in it and he clearly wanted to help Leeds United. That was why he was the only one to make a decent number of starts under Eddie. As for the rest, though, I thought the right decision was made in binning them. They had only come in because we desperately needed bodies in the summer, even if that didn't stop the club handing them big wages. Eddie's decision to go with the lads he knew was reflected in the starting line-up for his second game in charge, against Charlton Athletic at The Valley. It read: Paul Robinson; Gary Kelly, Lucas Radebe, Michael Duberry, Ian Harte; Jermaine Pennant, Me, David Batty, James Milner; Alan Smith, Mark Viduka. The bench was even more telling with only Domi of the foreign lads present alongside Scott Carson, Jody Morris, Michael Bridges and Stephen McPhail. It was a step in the right direction, as was the result. A goal from James Milner meant we ended a six game losing run, which had included being knocked out of the Carling Cup by Manchester United, with a 1-0 win. I was delighted for James, who along with Aaron Lennon represented what I hoped would be a brighter future for Leeds. Coming into a struggling team at such a young age could have crushed them both. But, credit to them, it didn't and they have gone on to play for England and become established Premier League players. James, in particular, was a very mature lad, even at 16. He never drank, for instance, and always looked after himself. I wish I'd had his maturity, even when I reached my 30s! I could see straight away he would have a decent career, as I could with Aaron. It is a shame that couldn't have been with Leeds but I am still delighted for them both.

After winning at Charlton, we went on a bit of a run and took six points from the next four games. As these included home fixtures against Chelsea, Fulham and Aston Villa plus a trip to Manchester City, it represented a decent haul. It gave us hope. We were, though, still in deep trouble at the wrong end of the table. Being bottom of any league, never mind the Premier League, was a new experience for me and one I didn't like. I thought the previous season had been bad but this was something else. There was a dark cloud hanging over the club and training was poor. There was no intensity to it. When I'd arrived, training had been sharp and there was a real buzz. As a result, we had looked a lot fitter and physically stronger. But training had become lackadaisical. I didn't like that. I always wanted training to be like a game. Anything else was no good to me. Usually, I was the sort of player who couldn't wait to get in to the training ground but in what turned out to be my final year at Leeds I had started to dread it.

I was finding it so hard to be positive, especially when the initial run of decent results we had enjoyed under Eddie gave way to a string of losses. After the Boxing Day draw at home to David O'Leary's Aston Villa that left us just a couple of points adrift of safety, we rounded off 2003 by being beaten 3-1 at Wolves. January then turned into a nightmare as we followed a 4-1 thrashing by Arsenal in the FA Cup with defeats to Newcastle United, Tottenham Hotspur, Southampton and Middlesbrough. A few calls were made to bring back the foreign lads during that run of losses but I don't think that would have made any difference. By the start of February, we were back at the bottom of the table – a position where we remained after a 2-0 defeat at Aston Villa on the first Saturday of the month. Any feelings of optimism I'd had following Eddie's arrival were now long gone. One of my toughest tasks became trying to find something, anything, positive to say in my programme notes. Things really had got that bad. For those of us who had been at the club a few years, it was horrible. We'd had the taste of the good life and now it had been reduced to this - a mediocre, bottom-of-the-table team. I know a lot of people point to the off-field problems and I admit these did, at times, prove a distraction. But I don't think we can hide behind that when it comes to why Leeds were down the bottom of the table. We were just not playing as a team, at all. Sometimes, Vidukes would play well. Another game it would be Smithy. Or me. But, as a team, we just couldn't click. Collectively, we just weren't there. The effort was, by and large, being put in. But maybe it just wasn't channelled properly. It was almost as if everyone was trying to do too much on their own. With hindsight, I know I was.

That season turned into the slow, lingering death of Leeds United.

No-one was enjoying going to work, which is sad to say. I know this will upset the fans, who will say we were being paid a lot of money and wonder what we had to moan about. But it is true. I didn't enjoy anything in the entire season. I felt helpless as I could see the way the club was heading but was unable to do anything about it. No matter how hard we all tried, things just didn't get any better. Even now, it is hard to put my finger on exactly what went wrong. I wish I had known, as then I could have done something about it. But there was no one reason, more a combination of many factors – one of which was the team simply wasn't anywhere near as strong as it had been. It meant we had to go a little bit more direct in getting the ball up front to Mark Viduka and Smithy. We still had a lot of good players, probably a better squad than a few of the teams who did stay up. But team spirit was poor. There was also a lot of turmoil behind-the-scenes, with the change of managers and so on. The whole dynamics of the club were not right.

The relationship between Eddie and his assistant manager Kevin Blackwell was a strange one, too. Blackie had been brought in during the previous summer by Peter Reid and I liked him. He had a different way of doing things in training, but that wasn't necessarily a bad thing. Once Eddie came back, though, the impression I got was that the two of them simply didn't get on. I have no idea why that was the case. There was certainly no big bust-up that I or any of the other players witnessed. But, as captain, I would unwittingly end up getting caught between the two of them. I would often have a meeting with Eddie in one room and then Blackie in another. And often, they would be saying contrasting things. It was so wrong to me, and I made sure I didn't take sides - even though Eddie was someone who I had got to know very well. It did put me in an awkward position, though, as I would be coming out of these meetings and thinking, 'What the hell do I tell the lads?' Soon, though, that wasn't a problem as many of the lads had stopped talking to me at all.

Chapter 21

Down And Almost Out

As I looked around the room for support, not one of my team-mates would even look me in the eye. Not one. I couldn't believe it. The meeting had been a tense one from the start and I'd been in the firing line. But I still expected a few of the squad to listen to my explanation and understand where I was coming from. Instead, all I got was abuse. The reason for me being sent to Coventry by my team-mates was an interview I'd done with the Press a couple of days earlier where I'd said I would be willing to defer part of my wages to help Leeds United. The club had been put up for sale in December but no buyers had been found by the middle of January. The debt had by then shot past £80m and showed no signs of slowing down, something that must have been a factor in putting off any potential bidders.

To add to the uncertainty surrounding Leeds, Professor John McKenzie had stepped down as chairman towards the end of 2003, meaning Trevor Birch, who had only arrived at Elland Road a few weeks earlier, was in charge. The lack of a buyer meant the threat of Leeds becoming the first Premier League club to go into administration – or worse - was a very real one. I knew this because Trevor had done his best to keep me, as captain, in the loop. I liked Trevor and, as an ex-player who had started at Liverpool before moving to Chester and Shrewsbury Town, I respected what he had to say. We met one afternoon in the Living Rooms bar in the city centre and he outlined the situation. It was bad. The one positive was that Trevor had managed to buy the club a bit of time by agreeing a standstill agreement with the major creditors, whereby repayments could be put on hold. The problem was that the agreement was due to run out on January 19. It was as that deadline approached that a possible wage deferral by the players was first mentioned. The money that would be saved, we were told, could then be used to keep Leeds United going. No percentage was put forward at that stage of how much the players would defer and for how long, it seemed more that the club was floating the idea to see what the feeling among the lads was.

Personally, I was in favour and I said that to the Press a few days later when they asked me the question.

I just replied honestly. I made it plain that I wasn't speaking on behalf of anyone else at the club, just myself. What I didn't realise as I spoke to the Press lads was that as soon as my comments hit the 'papers, I would be cold-shouldered by my own team-mates. This became evident at that first squad meeting to discuss a possible deferral. The club wanted us to defer 40 per cent of our wages, which would then be paid at a later date – probably the end of the season. Trevor Birch had gone on record before the meeting to say the club needed £5m to keep trading until the end of the season so a 40 per cent cut would have been more than enough to help out. I felt it was the right thing to do, and I still do. Unfortunately, that thinking was not shared by many others in the dressing room – as I soon found out once the meeting began. The interview with the Press that I had done was brought up almost straight away. 'What right have you got to say things like that?' was one point forcibly made to me. As was how I had been 'out of order, blah blah blah'. I tried to explain, saying that I'd made it clear during the interview that I wasn't talking on behalf of the team, how I couldn't speak for anyone else and never would. But no-one wanted to listen and, instead, I had to just stand there as a few had a real go at me. As the tirade continued, I looked around the room for just one person to back me up but no-one did. A few did privately later. But, by then, it was too late. They'd not had the bottle to speak up when I was copping all the abuse so what use was their 'support' now?

I am not going to name which of my team-mates were involved. But they were senior players, not kids trying to make a cheap point. They didn't like what I had done and made that clear, which is fair enough. But it was no excuse for the way they had a go at me. Even as I tried to explain for about the fifth time that I had never said anything along the lines of, 'We will defer as a team', they wouldn't listen. I realised nothing I could say was going to appease them so I just sat back down in my seat and thought, 'If that's how it is, that's how it is'. That day, I lost a lot of friends. Maybe some of them were reluctant to say something because those having a go at me were such strong characters. But the bottom line is I was left to take all the flack, which is something I have never forgotten.

Along with the flack I took off my team-mates, what I also couldn't understand was why so many of them were against a wage deferral. It wasn't a pay cut or anything like that. We were going to get the money back, or at least we were 99.9 per cent certain of doing so – providing the club survived, which to me had more chance of happening if we helped out with a deferral. Football is unique in that it has a preferential creditors rule - whereby all football debts, be it transfer fees or players' wages, have to be settled in full. So, a deferral hardly represented a gamble. Plus, even if we hadn't ever got the money, what is a few weeks' wage to people who had earned fortunes out of the club? We were all millionaires. Okay, some of the lads were coming towards the end of their careers. And some were not going to get contracts at other clubs anywhere near as good as they were on at Leeds. But, even so, we were all set for life. I know some may feel that is easy for me to say - I was still 29 when all this was kicking off and, as was proved when I signed for Blackburn later that year, still able to command a good contract. Smithy was in the same boat, as we saw when he signed for Manchester United, while Vidukes also got a good deal at Middlesbrough. But none of those players at Leeds were on the breadline and struggling to pay the mortgage. Despite that, the club's request for a 40 per cent deferral was rejected. Understandably, the fans were not happy – especially when, a few days later, it was revealed the club had been forced to make around 75 of the club's office staff redundant over the previous few months in an attempt to cut costs. Everyone could see a saving like that was miniscule compared to what the players were being paid and yet we'd not been willing to help out. It meant we weren't overly popular in the city, which I understood. I thought the whole affair made us look mercenary. The club was in a mess and I felt agreeing to a deferral would have been our way of saying to the fans, 'We know where Leeds United is at and we are trying to sort it out'. But we missed that opportunity and I am not sure the fans ever really forgave us.

The thing with a decision like the rejection of the proposed deferral is that it has to be a collective one so I went along with the consensus - even though I didn't agree with it. It meant I copped for some negative comments in the street, though it was nothing compared to the going over I'd had from my team-mates.

Another element of that first meeting that I wasn't happy with was the Professional Footballers Association. Since I retired, I've had my problems with the PFA over my back operation and whether they felt able to contribute to the £25,000 cost. But it isn't just recently that I have fallen out with them, my unhappiness mainly stemming from the events of January, 2004. As we left the first meeting to discuss the wage deferral, the PFA told all of us, 'Don't speak to the cameras'. So, what happens? Straight afterwards, I saw the PFA speaking to the media and saying the players won't agree to a deferral. What I didn't like either was how what they were saying seemed to be slanted against the players. Now, of course, I didn't agree with the collective decision we had come to, but the PFA should still have backed us. I just got the impression they were too busy trying to help the club – even though it is a players' union, not a union for the clubs. I lost a lot of faith in the PFA after that.

What also changed hugely after that first meeting was the attitude among a lot of the players. Mine certainly did and things were allowed to fester. The jokes stopped around the training ground and the social side, which had been such a strong part of Leeds United in my first couple of years, ended almost overnight. We all started to avoid each other because no-one wanted to be around. I spent more and more time socialising with my mates outside football, with people like Shorty and Avs. I didn't want to go out for squad meals or anything like that, which before had been the highlight of the week for me. Maybe what we needed as a group was a big night out. A few drinks and a few laughs. It might even have helped if we'd gone out and cleared the air and said a few home truths. Some might have said, 'You're not a good captain' and then told me why. I would have taken that. I might not have agreed but I would have taken on board what was said. But it didn't happen. I'll admit I wanted nothing to do with most of my team-mates any longer. Before, I'd loved nothing more than going in to train and then hanging around for lunch with the lads. But now I got the hell out of Thorp Arch as fast as I could after training to go home. That is how bad things had got. My neighbours couldn't understand why I was home so early every day.

It wasn't just the OTT reaction at that wage deferral meeting, either. I had started to hear about comments that were being said behind my back. At one stage, I was told even a player who had left Leeds had been bad-mouthing me at a dinner. I know these 'he said' type reports should be taken with a pinch of salt but things had become so bad that I really believed they were true. I went from trusting everyone at the club, considering them to be really good mates, to not going out with any of them. It was an awful time and all caused by me saying publicly that I wanted to help Leeds United out. I still don't believe I did anything wrong. I didn't agree with what they were saying. And I didn't agree with how some of them had been acting in training. But that wasn't personal, just a difference of opinion. When it becomes personal is when someone is getting called all sorts behind their back. And I didn't like it. Things got so bad on a couple of occasions that I seriously considered stepping down from the captaincy. My thinking was, 'Give it to one of the local lads'. The only thing that stopped me was that it would probably have rocked the boat even more. It would also have given my critics more ammunition, as well. I hated those last few months. They were horrible.

After the initial rejection of the wage deferral, it was suggested that a player could be sold to find the £5m needed to keep Leeds going until the end of the season. The transfer window was open and that meant there was plenty of speculation, mainly over Alan Smith and Mark Viduka. A host of clubs were linked but Trevor Birch, to his credit, made it clear Leeds wanted to keep both players as they were our best hope of staying up. Trevor also negotiated a couple of extensions to the standstill agreement with the creditors, again buying vital time that he hoped would see someone come forward to take the club over. Eventually, though, it became clear that a buyer could not be found in time and, with the creditors starting to get uneasy, the club again approached the players about a possible wage deferral. The difference was that the percentage being asked for was 25 and not 40. A second meeting of the squad was called and this time agreement was reached. With the two-week delay and the percentage drop, it meant everyone had saved a few grand. Great! I left that meeting glad that we had done the right thing but still disillusioned over the whole saga. I just couldn't understand why lads who had earned so much money out of the club could bicker over such a small amount. Every single one of them got the money back when the new board came in, which to me made it worse in many ways. That proved we were always going to get the money back, it was just a case of lending it to the club for a few months or, as it turned out, about six weeks. Where is the hardship in that? All of us lived in big houses and drove big cars, so where was the problem. If we'd been at Rochdale and needed the money to pay the mortgage, then fine. But we didn't. I doubt even half of us had mortgages.

I look back at those meetings now and wish I'd said more, even though it might have led to things getting really nasty. A room of 15-20 lads arguing the toss over something can start to get personal. And maybe that would have happened that day. I don't know. But I do wish I'd said more, particularly to those who felt I'd abused my position as captain by speaking to the Press. In terms of how our season panned out, I doubt it would have helped. I would have felt a lot better, though.

The wage deferral may have been agreed by the end of January, which at least meant Leeds United could continue in business and, hopefully, find a buyer. But, to me, in terms of the Premier League we were as good as down. We had been in a mess on the field before, but now any semblance of team spirit had gone for good. There were people behind the scenes who didn't help matters, either. Some office staff even seemed to think they were qualified to pick the team. They thought they knew more than the manager or the players. In reality, they knew nothing. One member of staff even slagged me off to a local journalist. I over-heard him bad-mouthing not only me but a few of the other lads as well and I just snapped. He tried to say I'd mis-understood him but I was having none of it. I am not a violent man but I very nearly was that day. I had to hold myself back. I was fuming. From that day on, we never spoke again.

As all this was going on, we were having an awful time on the pitch. We were back to the bottom of the table and I couldn't see any way out of trouble, even though there were still 16 games to play after the wage deferral had been agreed. We had collapsed, end of story. Two years earlier, we had been top of the league. Yet now, here we were unable to buy a point, never mind a win. I became too embarrassed to go out in the city centre. If I did, people would be asking, 'What the hell is going on?' But I just didn't have an answer. I couldn't let on what was really going on in the squad, that would have caused all sorts of problems had my views somehow got out. The people asking were loyal supporters who absolutely loved Leeds United and it would have broken their hearts to know the truth. They didn't want to hear that training was a mess, that team spirit had evaporated and that our standards had not just slipped but collapsed. There was no pride. Rows were taking place on the training pitch. There was one day when Mark Viduka pulled a couple of the lads and said, 'Get your fucking act together'. It shocked a few players. But instead of the target of Mark's frustration taking some responsibility, their reaction was, 'Oh, so it is just me playing bad is it?' Too few were prepared to look at themselves and ask, 'What can I do to get Leeds out of this mess?' Part of the problem was members of the squad were taking their lead from the strong characters. And because they were messing about, the others followed. That was the point Vidukes had been trying to get across. Maybe, as captain, I should have been the one to say it. I certainly felt the same.

Mark was right as people were fucking about. To be honest, the manager should have nailed that down. It is okay saying it is down to the players but we had enough shit to cope with. I love Eddie to bits but just wish he could have stepped in. The place was out of control. Everything was a mess. It got so daft that one of our players, Nicky Barmby, was even pictured in the Sunday 'papers sitting at Hull City when we were playing the same day. I didn't think that was right, though in Nick's defence he was a Hull lad and is still with his hometown club now.

Mark Viduka wasn't the only one to voice his criticism, either. Smithy did the same, though he chose to do so in public when away on international duty with England. He had come off the bench in a 1-0 defeat to Sweden and then been stopped by a few of the lads who work for the national newspapers afterwards. Smithy, as a local lad, was hurting at what was happening to Leeds. He had come through the ranks and was the fans' favourite. He was also a very good player. So, he told the Press: "There have been too many games this season when we have just rolled over and accepted defeat. We lack a bit of fight. It has been missing all season. We roll over in games. At Everton, we let four in, at Portsmouth we got beat by six goals. You shouldn't get beaten by those scores. It is too easy to blame what's happening off the pitch. As a group of players in any sport, if things aren't going right that should make you stronger. People have been saying it's because we've got too many loan players but they've only played a handful of games all season and that shouldn't affect everyone else in the team, should it?"

Smithy felt it was right to go public with his thoughts, especially as at the time we still had a chance of staying up. It probably needed the fans' hero to say what he did, though I would have preferred if those things had been said in the dressing room to people's faces. Things were bad enough at the time without upsetting people even more. Smithy didn't agree and wanted to say it to the Press. That is his choice.

By the time of Smithy's outburst, Leeds United had new owners. Gerald Krasner, an insolvency expert, had led a consortium of six locally-based businessmen and been appointed chairman. The deal had been confirmed just a couple of days before we were due to play Manchester City – and my old mate Robbie Fowler – live on Sky. The takeover had brought to an end a four-month search for new owners by Trevor Birch that had seen all sorts of rumours sweep round Leeds. There had been a Sheikh, a Ugandan, someone from China - you name a country and, at one stage, I bet we were linked with a possible takeover by someone from it. The speculation became ridiculous. As players, we heard all the rumours – usually from supporters. That is often the way in football. I was being asked in the street who was buying Leeds but no-one would ever believe me when I said, 'You probably know more than me, mate'.

To be fair to Trevor, he had tried to keep me, as captain, informed as much as possible. We would have meetings from time to time, where Trevor would outline a few things. In fact, that whole season became one where I had meeting after meeting after meeting. There was Trevor, Reidy, Eddie and the PFA who all had to be spoken to when, really, all I wanted to do was concentrate on my football. I did, though, appreciate Trevor taking time to keep me informed. I remember one particular meeting when things were looking very bleak. Trevor went through the problems, not least the number of players who had left but were still being paid by Leeds. Some would remain on the books until 2007, despite the fact that by then they would not have played for the club in four years. I couldn't understand why it had been allowed to happen, both from the clubs' perspective and the players themselves. Most were moving on to good clubs and good contracts so why couldn't some form of agreement be reached? When I left, I was happy with what I was getting at Blackburn so didn't hold out for everything I was due from Leeds. After what the club had done for us, I felt it was the least I could do. Unfortunately, some of the other players didn't show any compassion to Leeds United. The flipside to that argument, of course, is that these players could have got an equally good offer from another club but chose Leeds, so why should they miss out on what they were due? I understand that point entirely. What I have never been able to get my head round, though, is why whoever was in charge of Leeds at the time - and let's not forget that in the 22 months between Peter Ridsdale leaving and Ken

Bates arriving, the club had four chairmen - did not try to give the players who had left a bit less money but quicker. Having the millstone of paying some ex-players until 2007 was only ever going to drag the club down, which is exactly what happened. It was almost as if whoever was making the decisions wasn't bothered what happened in two years' time because they were not going to be there and that it would be someone else's problem. That only really ended when Bates arrived in January, 2005, to bring an end to the short-term thinking.

The first I knew of Krasner's consortium taking over was when sitting at home watching Sky Sports News. My initial reaction was that it could only be a positive thing. The transfer window was shut but, hopefully, they would be able to throw a few quid in and help the club out in years to come. Unfortunately, that didn't prove to be the case and within 10 months they had sold the club to Bates. I never really got to know the Yorkshire consortium as people but what I didn't like about them was the directors would come in the dressing room with their families only ten minutes or so after a game. The lads would be getting changed and yet there were all these strangers walking around. I am all for the chairman or a director coming in half an hour or so after a match, that is not a problem. But not almost straight away. After a team has lost, the last thing the players want is other people coming into the dressing room. I didn't want to have to make niceties when relegation was staring the club in the face. It was unprofessional and I did one day say, 'I just don't want them here'.

You can't run a football club like they did. They were all successful businessmen in their own field but I didn't think they had a clue how to run a football club. Geoffrey Richmond was part of the new ownership team and I know some fans were concerned after what had happened to Bradford City, who had gone into administration after being relegated from the Premier League. But, to be honest, the players were past caring. We had enough on our plates trying to keep Leeds up.

Somehow, amid all the chaos surrounding the club, we gave ourselves a chance of getting out of trouble around Easter. The run of six defeats in January and early February had been ended with a 4-1 win over Wolves. We had then drawn at Manchester United and taken a point off Liverpool at Elland Road before losing 2-0 at Fulham. We were still bottom but a 2-1 win over Manchester City in Krasner's first game as chairman nudged us up to 19th. A 4-1 defeat at Birmingham City after

Mark Viduka had given us the lead early on was a setback but then we managed what we had failed to do all season – win back-to-back games. First, Smithy netted a late winner at home to Leicester City and then, on Easter Saturday, Vidukes was our hero when he sealed a 2-1 win at Blackburn by scoring in the 89th minute. Suddenly, we had a chance. We were still 18th but now level on 31 points with the two sides immediately above us in the table, Portsmouth and Blackburn. Those thrashings against Pompey, Everton and Leicester meant our goal difference was hugely inferior to them both but with six games to go we had every chance of getting out of trouble. Or so I thought on the coach home from Ewood Park. We were not due to play against until the Tuesday night at home to Everton, while both Blackburn and Portsmouth were in action on the Monday. They both won, meaning we had to beat Everton. Unfortunately for us, we came up against our former goalkeeper Nigel Martyn, who had left us just four games into the season after becoming frustrated at being kept out of the team by Paul Robinson. Since then, Nige had been in such good form that he was wanted back in the England fold by Sven-Goran Eriksson. Nige showed why Sven was so keen on recalling him with a string of superb saves to ensure the game finished 1-1. With a trip to Arsenal in store just three days later, dropping two points was a serious setback. The Gunners were seven points clear at the top and destined to remain unbeaten all season, so few gave us a chance. I was hoping for a repeat of the previous season when, against all the odds, we'd pulled off a 3-2 win to stay up. Deep down, though, I knew it was unlikely against a team that have since been dubbed 'The Invincibles'. Against us, Arsenal never looked like surrendering that proud record as Thierry Henry ripped us apart. We lost 5-0 with Henry scoring four of the goals. It could have been ten that night, which meant the coach journey home was, not for the first time that season, a quiet one. The following afternoon, Portsmouth and Blackburn again both won to move five points clear of us. We did, though, still have one team within touching distance, Manchester City, who were just two points ahead of us in 17th place. A week later, City stretched that advantage with a draw at Leicester City as we prepared to face Portsmouth at Elland Road the following day. A win and we were back in it, even though our goal difference meant City would keep us in the bottom three. Once again, however, we were unable to help ourselves as Pompey completed the double with a 2-1 victory that was a lot more comfortable than the scoreline suggested. The stuffing had completely been knocked out of us by now. I had gone off early injured early on and knew, deep down, that there was no way out of this – even though there were still three games remaining and nine points to play for.

Bolton Wanderers were our next opponents and, again, the game was moved to the Sunday to be shown live on television. It meant the trip to the Reebok Stadium came three years to the day since we'd taken on Valencia at Elland Road in the Champions League semi-final, something the media made a lot of during the build-up. Results the previous day, not least Manchester City beating Newcastle United at home, meant we had to beat Bolton to have any realistic hope of taking the relegation fight to the last two games. Mark Viduka raised those hopes by opening the scoring and we were still in front as half-time approached, even though in truth Bolton had battered us. I started to think, 'This might just be our day here'. A big blow came when Mark was sent off after collecting a second yellow card. Even then, though, I still believed we might get out of jail after getting to the break still in front. Sadly, within two minutes of the restart, Youri Djorkaeff had equalised and Bolton went on to run riot in the second half and win 4-1. Our fate had been sealed long before the end but, even so, hearing the final whistle was an awful feeling. We were down and it was no-one else's fault but our own. Even allowing for all the problems the club had, I still believe the players were the ones who got Leeds relegated. The squad was good enough to stay up but we couldn't manage it.

As relegation sunk in, I went to Smithy, who was in tears, and hugged him. I was close to Smithy and knew what relegation meant to him. I wanted him to know he couldn't have done any more. I said, 'Listen, mate, you've run your legs off this season. You can look at yourself in the mirror'. No-one really played well that season, apart from possibly Vidukes. But, as a professional, if you can look at yourself in the mirror and know you put everything into it, then you can live with yourself. He was, though, in a minority. There were a lot of players who, in my opinion, couldn't do that. We went over to clap the fans, and unbelievably they applauded back. I had a real lump in my throat then. Those supporters were the only positive thing about Leeds United at the time. I am not saying that to curry favour, it is simply the truth. The fans filled Elland Road, even when it became clear we were heading for relegation. They were probably the only people who did not deserve what happened. Never once did they let us down. I just wish we could say the same. I always think back to that game at Bolton and the television footage of the little lad crying at the final whistle because his team had gone down. I can still see his face now. It broke my heart watching that on the news later that night, it brought home to me just how much that football club means to the city. It is why I am as desperate as any fan to see Leeds restored to their rightful place in the Premier League as soon as possible.

After applauding the fans, I returned to the away dressing room at the Reebok and the scene was one of total devastation. There was just silence. If I'd wanted to speak, I don't think I would have been capable. I never thought during my career that I would ever be relegated and yet, here I was.

A week later, we drew 3-3 with Charlton in our final home game. At the end, Smithy got carried off the pitch, which I found a bit weird. Maybe the fans just wanted to say goodbye, as he had made it clear during the season that if Leeds went down then he would have to move on for the good of his career. The fans loved him and gave him a big send-off. But I still felt it strange that anyone could be lauded after relegation.

The supporters' feelings towards Smithy changed, however, just a couple of days later when it became clear Manchester United wanted to sign him. Immediately, he went from being the King of Leeds to public enemy number one. I suppose that is how football is, though that doesn't make it right. I know the fans were disappointed he was joining our biggest rivals. But in Smithy's defence, I don't think any footballer would have turned down the offer. You can be the biggest Leeds or Liverpool fan in the country, but if Manchester United come knocking after you have just been relegated then there is only one decision to make. You have to go. I know to this day some supporters won't accept that and, when Smithy's possible return was mentioned by manager Simon Grayson during Leeds' first season back in the Championship, there was an outcry. But, for what it's worth, I don't think any of the other lads would have made a different decision to Smithy's when he signed for Manchester United.

My own future was less clear once the season had ended with a 1-0 defeat to Chelsea, a result that left us 19th in the table. I still thought I would be part of Leeds United the following season, though the club were very non-committal. I did say to the club that I would take a wage cut. But, eventually, the answer came back that I was still on too much money. I understood where they were coming from on that score, relegation from the Premier League means a huge drop in income. The parachute payments that clubs get following relegation were nothing like the £48m spread over four years that they get today. What I have not been able to understand since, however, is that the club still kept others who were on big money on their old salaries. They would have been better keeping me than the ones who stayed. They were, in the main, those who couldn't get a move elsewhere so stuck around. The exception to this was Gary Kelly, he was Leeds through and through. There was no way he would play for another club. He might not have been born in the city but Kells was desperate to finish his career in Leeds. So, I understood completely why he stayed at Elland Road to the end of his career. But, as for the rest, they stayed because the money was not going to be as good anywhere else and that did Leeds no favours.

When Leeds were relegated, I had three years left on my deal and I am certain I could have played a big part in helping us get back to the Premier League. Certainly, if I'd been in the team that faced Watford in the 2006 Championship play-off final, I don't think we'd have lost 3-0.

In a way, my departure from Leeds turned out to be a repeat of what had happened to me at Liverpool. I didn't want to leave, but I had to. At Anfield, it was because I wanted to play first-team football and not be stuck behind Christian Ziege, whereas at Leeds the club just couldn't afford me. It was a real shame because I loved playing for both clubs.

The day I left Elland Road, I never imagined the club would be out of the Premier League for so long. I knew they'd spent eight years out of the top-flight in the Eighties but I couldn't see that happening again. Unfortunately, I was wrong. The play-off final defeat to Watford was the big one for the club, and in particular how they lost the game. Leeds were bullied out of it in the Millennium Stadium. Then, they dropped down another division and it was an awful time. More players left and the only constant from my time was that the fans stayed around. Leeds' crowds were impressive, even after three years in League One. I know Manchester City had big crowds when they were relegated to the third tier. But they only stayed down one year. Would those fans have stuck around for two or, even, three years? I doubt it, to be honest. But the Leeds fans did. I doubt there would have been many fans who would have stood by their club in such a loyal manner. I take my hat off to every single one of them.

Chapter 22

'What Was Dom Thinking? Arsene Wanted A Word'

When it became clear that I would not be staying at Leeds, I sat down with my agent and went through the options. I had been fortunate enough to play for two great clubs but, having just passed 30, my next move was clearly going to be the last big one of my career. There was no shortage of offers, which was pleasing after the difficult season Leeds had just had. Being relegated was a new experience and I hated it, so knowing that a few Premier League clubs were showing interest gave me a big lift. Graeme Souness, my old boss at Liverpool, was the first to get in touch officially. He had been at Blackburn Rovers since 2000 and done very well. After winning promotion from the First Division in his first season, Graeme had gone on to win the League Cup and lead Blackburn to a sixth place finish in the Premier League. Rovers had, though, since slipped back to 15th in the season that had just ended. Leeds had also done the double over them, which considering the season we'd had was not something anyone at Ewood Park could be happy about. I'd played really well in the second of those two victories, the 2-1 win at Blackburn on Easter Saturday that had suggested we just might have a chance of getting out of trouble. To be fair to Graeme, he had been keen on me long before that afternoon but I do think my performance helped to make up his mind. It also persuaded a few others at Ewood that I would be a good signing. John Williams, who was then Rovers' chairman, once told me that when Graeme said he wanted to sign me, it was one of the only times he never questioned the decision – and he said a lot of that was down to how well I'd performed for Leeds in that Easter game.

I'd played defensive midfield that afternoon and Graeme saw that as my best position, which I was happy about. I'd played a lot there over the past two years and had enjoyed it. I was available on a free transfer because Leeds were so keen to get me off the wage bill so Blackburn made me an offer. I knew there was interest from elsewhere but, because

I liked Graeme and had enjoyed playing for him at Liverpool, I said 'yes' straight away. Part of my thinking was that joining Blackburn was a chance to get a little bit closer to my family in Southport. Eventually, that proved to be the case with me moving to Hale in Manchester - though only after I had continued to live in Yorkshire for the first six months or so. During that time, I soon discovered there is simply no easy route to Blackburn so I ended up hiring a driver called Mick, who used to take me across every morning and then back again after training. He'd even bring me pillows so I could sleep on the way.

My transfer to Blackburn wasn't signed after I'd agreed to join because there was still a medical to pass and a contract to draw up. But I told Graeme I would sign and that was that. Or so I thought. A few days later, I was away on holiday in Ibiza when my mobile phone rang. The voice on the other end said, 'Hi Dom, it is David Moyes here'. I immediately sensed a wind-up by one of the lads so was quite stand-offish, not wanting to be suckered in to the joke. In fact, I was quite dismissive. Credit to David, though, - yes, it was really him - he didn't hang up and instead kept talking. After a couple of minutes, I realised I really was speaking to the manager of Everton so listened intently to what he had to say. 'I know you want to get back to the area and we want to sign you,' was the gist of what David said. I was interested, particularly as anyone could see what a good job David had been doing at Goodison Park. Like Blackburn, they'd not had a brilliant season. In fact, Everton had finished 17th and just six points above the relegation zone. But, the previous year had seen them finish seventh, and there were plenty of promising players at Goodison – as David went on to prove by leading Everton to fourth place in 2004-05 and the Champions League qualifying round. My problem was that I'd already said 'yes' to Blackburn. Even though I'd not signed anything, I'd given my word to Graeme and I am not the sort to go back on something like that. So, I had to tell David, 'Thanks but no thanks'. It was a shame, as I know I'd have enjoyed playing for David. Some Liverpool fans might not have been too happy had I signed for Everton. But I was never the sort of Liverpool fan who hated our neighbours or anything like that. Goodison Park was also one of my favourite grounds. I loved the tradition and it felt like a real place to play football. David was also someone I had always respected so it was with a heavy heart that I said 'no'.

Financially, moving to Everton would not have been as rewarding as

Blackburn. David was very honest about that. He said, 'I have heard what you are on at Leeds and we won't be able to come anywhere near matching that'. To be fair, Blackburn couldn't either, but they were a lot closer. So I signed a three-year deal. What I didn't know as I put pen to paper, however, was that there was one other club who were interested in signing me. And it was none other than Arsenal, the champions of England and the team who had just been dubbed the 'Invincibles' after going an entire top-flight season unbeaten. Unfortunately, I only found out about Arsenal's interest a few months later through my former Leeds team-mate Alan Smith. Gary Lewin, the Arsenal physio, was the person who let it slip to Smudger at one of England's get-togethers the following season. Gary also worked for England and he asked Smudger, 'What was your mate Dom thinking by signing for Blackburn? Arsene wanted him and was going to give him a year'. Now that did come as a bombshell. There is no reason for either Smudger or Gary to lie so I do believe Arsenal were seriously interested. Missing out on playing for Arsene Wenger is something I regret – even though, as a rule, I am someone who doesn't do regrets. Joining Arsenal would have been brilliant, especially as they were at their peak at the time. Even if it had been for only a year, those 12 months would have been something else. I can only think that the Blackburn deal was done so quietly that maybe Arsene never got chance to come in for me. I wish he had!

To be fair, signing for Everton or Arsenal would have probably have been better moves for me. Don't get me wrong, I enjoyed my time at Blackburn – or most of it, at least. But there was an unmistakeable difference to life at Ewood Park compared to Liverpool or Leeds. At my two previous clubs, there had been pressure and expectation from the fans. At Blackburn, there was none of that. In fact, it took me quite a while to get used to not being booed if we'd lost a game. In a way, I was a bit disappointed by that as there wasn't the buzz I had always associated with playing for clubs with passionate fans. It was almost as if Blackburn as a club was just too nice and too quiet. I also found it a bit weird that everyone lived quite a way out of Blackburn, in either south Manchester or Cheshire. The flipside, though, of there being less pressure and expectation surrounding Blackburn was that there was a nice, family feel to the place. They were a good club with good staff, who all cared deeply about Blackburn Rovers. All the office staff seemed to be fans, while I got on really well with Howlesy the kit-man and H, who was in charge of the boot room. I still see H when on holiday in Ibiza. Great guys.

Blackburn also had a very good physio called Dave Fevre, who I'd heard a lot of great things about. He'd been at Manchester United and impressed a lot of people. Because of the injury problems I'd had at Leeds, I felt having someone like Dave in charge of my fitness could only be a positive thing. Another big plus about Blackburn, along with Graeme being manager and the physio being another that I could trust, was that I knew a few of the boys. They were good lads and that meant the dressing room was going to be an enjoyable one. We had some good players, too. Lads such as Matt Jansen and Barry Ferguson were already at the club along with Garry Flitcroft, Lucas Neill, Brad Friedel and David Thompson. Paul Dickov, who I'd got to know with Scotland, also joined during the same summer as me so I fancied Blackburn to have a good season. Instead, we had a shocking start and only won one of our first 14 games. By November, we were rock bottom of the Premier League and I remember saying to Paul Dickov, 'I can't believe I'm in another relegation battle here'. By then, Graeme Souness had left. In early September, Newcastle United had asked him to become their new manager and it proved an offer that was too good to turn down. The season was only four games old and we'd got two points from draws against West Bromwich Albion and Manchester United at home but lost at Arsenal and Southampton. Funnily enough, Graeme's first league game for Newcastle turned out to be against us at St James' Park and we lost 3-0. Tony Parkes was in temporary charge that afternoon as the board searched for a replacement. Gerard Houllier was one name suggested in the 'papers, a prospect I found less than enticing for obvious reasons. But, thankfully, the favourite seemed to be Mark Hughes. He had finished his playing career at Blackburn and had done a great job with Wales, who had only missed out on a place at Euro 2004 after losing a play-off to Russia. Not for the first time, the bookies got it right and Sparky's appointment was duly confirmed four days after our defeat to Newcastle. I was happy with the appointment and looking forward to working with the new manager. Mind, just a few days later, my agent did receive an interesting 'phone call that, basically, said Graeme wanted to take me to Newcastle. And that if I wanted to go, the move could happen in the January transfer window. I'll admit to being half tempted. Graeme had been the reason why I had joined Blackburn in the first place, mainly because I had enjoyed playing for him at Liverpool so much. So hearing that he wanted to take me to the North East as well meant I had a big decision to make. I gave it plenty of thought but, in the end, I decided to stay at Blackburn. I'd only just signed and, to be fair, they had been very good to me in terms of my contract. With hindsight, maybe I should have gone. I know it didn't work out for Graeme at Newcastle and that he lasted just 18 months. But they are still a huge club and I think I would have enjoyed playing at St James' Park. Still, staying at Blackburn is not something I regret - unlike missing out on that possible move to Arsenal.

At Blackburn, Mark made an immediate impact. Training was excellent and the lads all respected Mark not only for what he had done as a player but also as Wales manager. During my first few weeks at the club, I hadn't thought we were fit enough but that soon changed when Mark came in along with Mark Bowen and Eddie Niedzwiecki. I worked hard and the new manager seemed to appreciate that. I like to think he saw me as reliable and someone who would always give everything on the pitch. Both were qualities we were going to need in the fight to avoid relegation. Mind, in terms of getting out of trouble, I did always think Blackburn would be all right that season – even though we remained in the bottom three almost until Christmas. My confidence was based on looking round the dressing room one day and seeing the number of strong characters we had. The vast majority were lads who had been around the block a bit and knew what was required. That had been the problem at Leeds, we'd just not had enough big characters in the season that ended in relegation. Another thing that went against Leeds was that being down the bottom of the Premier League had come as a surprise to everyone at the club and not enough of the players or staff knew how to deal with it. That wasn't the case at Blackburn. We had Craig Short, Andy Todd, Flitty and Lucas Neill, plus my two old Liverpool team-mates Brad Friedel and David Thompson. These were all lads who could be relied upon to scrap for points. Sometimes, after a defeat, that fighting spirit literally led to players coming to blows in the dressing room. David Thompson, all 5ft 5in of him, would be squaring up to Shorty and demanding to know why he didn't pull his finger out. It was great. I loved all that. I didn't get involved at first, as I was the new boy. There is nothing worse than someone coming in to a club and immediately throwing his weight around. So, initially I was just watching but I liked what I saw. It wasn't just the presence of the fighters in the squad, either, that made me believe we would be okay. There was Dwight Yorke, who was always the last to turn up for training but then put a great shift in. Some people who don't know him might think he is a bit flash. But I never did. He is just a great lad who loves life. Robbie Savage was another big character in the dressing room. Sparky had worked with him with Wales and he signed him in the January. He had the worst tattoo ever, that silly Armani thing on his arm. He was also someone who loved himself. But, to me, he was a decent lad. Sav had this thing where he would wind up the young lads about how much they earned compared to him. Unfortunately for Sav, he had to be careful who he picked on as there were a few of us who had more money than him. Sav also had ability. He may have this reputation as being a player who would chase a crisp packet around the park all day long but there were a lot of games where he made a difference. He loved rolling his sleeves up and working hard, which was exactly the sort of character we needed in Sparky's first season. Michael Gray was another. We used to call him 'gorgeous' on account of him believing he was such a good looking lad. He was also someone who could fall asleep anywhere, even on team nights out. He'd steam into the beer for two hours and then just fall asleep. Then, after an hour, he would wake up and be fresh as a daisy again. The lads all thought he had some form of sleep disorder. There was even one Christmas party in Manchester where he was so sound asleep in his chair that the first he knew about the lads picking him up and placing him on top of this huge model of a cow was when he woke up half an hour later. But, in terms of his footballing ability, Michael was exactly what we needed – someone who gave everything for the team.

The social side was good at Blackburn. We had some great nights out, which after the problems I'd had at Leeds during my final season was just what I needed. I was so relieved to discover how much the lads enjoyed a night out that I adopted the role of the team's social secretary. I would organise the nights out and then make sure we had plenty in the kitty to ensure everyone had a good time. Mind, I am sure a few bars did well out of us along the way. There was one night where our bar bill came to £25,000. We thought nothing of it and just settled the bill. But now I own a bar in Leeds, I just can't believe we got through £25,000 worth of booze in a night. It just isn't possible. But we paid up without a care in the world. They saw us coming, that's for sure. Pre-season was also a time when the Blackburn lads enjoyed a drink, even if it did leave us in danger of getting on the wrong side of the manager. One year, Michael Gray fell foul of the coaching staff on a pre-season trip after we'd all sneaked out one night for a few drinks. I was okay at hiding the effects of a session, as were most of the lads. But, as I've said before, Michael wasn't. It all came to a head during a crossing and finishing session in training and Michael sent every single cross into the bushes behind the goal. The lads were laughing but Mark Hughes and his staff weren't, so Michael ended up being sent back to the hotel.

The lads at Blackburn may have enjoyed a night out but they also gave everything in training, never mind matches. When I first joined, I was surprised about how intense training was. Shorty would fly into a tackle, as would Flitty. We hadn't had anything like that at Leeds so it was a big culture shock for me. But it also made me feel confident about the future, even during that miserable run that left us bottom of the league after 14 games with 10 points. That confidence proved to be well-placed. We beat Fulham in late November to kick-start a decent run that saw us lose just two out of the next nine games. We scrapped for every point we could and, gradually, clawed our way out of trouble. We became harder to beat and, as a result, went on to finish 15th and stay up comfortably. We also had a decent run in the FA Cup. We beat Cardiff City, Colchester United, Burnley – the big one in our fans' eyes – and Leicester City to set-up a meeting with Arsenal in the semi-finals. With Wembley being re-built, the game was played at the Millennium Stadium in Cardiff – somewhere I had never been before, so that was something to look forward to. Manchester United had been drawn against Newcastle United in the other semi-final so we couldn't really complain about getting Arsenal. The build-up was great. We went to the Millennium Stadium the night before and I really enjoyed looking around the place. I am not a big fan of the semi-finals being played at the same venue as the final but I am still glad I got the chance to visit the Millennium.

I decided to keep my record of losing every semi-final I had played in to myself. I particularly didn't want the manager to know, as I thought he might drop me. My 'secret' stayed with me, in the end, and I started at left-back, which is where Sparky had moved me just before Christmas when he wanted to shore up the defence. We went into the game feeling confident after a six game run that had seen us share goalless draws with

Manchester United and Liverpool plus beat Norwich City, Everton and Southampton. Our only defeat, though, in those half dozen games had been against Arsenal and once again they proved too good for us in Cardiff. We never really got going and ended up losing 3-0. It turned out to be a very physical game and Andy Todd was sent-off for us in the second half. By then, Robert Pires had already given Arsenal the lead and a late double for Robin van Persie meant we weren't going to the FA Cup final. To be fair to Andy, I am not too sure the red card made much difference as Arsenal were just too good on the day. Sometimes in football, you have to hold your hands up and admit the better team won. That was certainly the case in Wales. I remember sitting in the dressing room afterwards and thinking, 'What is it about semi-finals, me and 3-0 defeats?' I'd lost to Paris St Germain with Liverpool, Valencia with Leeds and now Arsenal. It was almost as if I was jinxed. Credit to Arsenal, though, as they did a good job on us that day and I was pleased when they beat Manchester United in the final a month later.

For Blackburn, missing out on a first FA Cup final appearance since 1960 came as a disappointment. The consolation, though, as the summer got under way was that anyone could see that big strides had been made under Mark Hughes. The future looked much more encouraging, a belief that was justified 12 months later when Blackburn finished sixth in the Premier League to qualify for the UEFA Cup. I had hoped to be part of that achievement but, unfortunately, injury and a breakdown in relations between myself and the coaching staff meant that, by the time Blackburn kicked off that European campaign with victory over Red Bull Salzburg, I had played my last Premier League game.

Chapter 23

A Gamble Too Far

Footballers get paid very, very well, there is no denying that. And when the money starts rolling in, the player in question usually goes down a well worn path that has been taken by generations before him. House, car, drinking and women are the four standard stop-off points for most young lads making their way in the game, me included. The fifth stage, however, is one that not everyone reaches. Gambling. It is probably the one vice that is still going strong in football. Drinking isn't as much of a problem these days, certainly not compared to when my career started. A combination of the game speeding up and the newspapers being desperate for stories on drunk footballers has seen to that. You also can't do the shagging because, as we've seen time and time again recently, the 'papers would be all over it. I often think back to those Christmas parties we had at Liverpool where some of the lads would be having it away with the strippers. Can you imagine that staying secret today? I certainly can't. The bottom line is that any married footballer who is playing away from home has a very good chance of being caught out.

Gambling, though, is different in that it is something that, thanks to the advent of the internet and telephone accounts, can be done away from prying eyes and no-one is any the wiser. In my experience, gambling is verging on becoming an epidemic in football – fuelled by the large amounts of spare time that players have and the huge wages they are being paid. To many, gambling is like a drug. I know this because I have been there. Don't get me wrong, gambling didn't grab me as badly as it has some. For me, it was a social pursuit and something to while away my spare time. But it did prove to be a costly pastime with my losses down the years probably standing at about £1m. That may be a figure that shocks some, especially as I wasn't someone who ever felt addicted to gambling or anything like that. My friends and family will have probably seen me as someone who just enjoyed going to the races, having a few drinks and then watching his horses in action. But for a couple of years when I was at Blackburn, I did gamble stupid amounts of money. Once, I put £100,000 on a horse priced at evens only for it to lose. I was gutted. But, instead of doing what any sensible human being would do and deciding to cut my losses, I put another £100,000 on the evens-priced favourite in the next race to try and get the money back. Luckily, the bet came in and I ended up level with the bookie. But it was still crazy behaviour.

Before Blackburn, gambling had never really been an issue in my life. Neither the Liverpool lads nor the Leeds lads were into it that much. Okay, we all liked the odd day out at the races but that was as far as most of our interest in gambling went. If we lost or won on the day, that was that until we next had a team day out at the races. Things probably started to change in football during my time at Leeds, when 'phone accounts and then text betting came along. Suddenly, placing a bet had become very, very easy. Where before a player would have had to physically walk into a bookies, now it could be done from the comfort of your own home. Instead of everyone in the city knowing if you had a big bet on, now no-one had a clue what you were up to. That became a big attraction to me. Another factor that led me towards gambling after I joined Blackburn was that I became a racehorse owner along with my team-mate Garry Flitcroft. I'd been part of a couple of syndicates at Liverpool but there were a lot of us involved, so my involvement was minimal. Now, however, it was just me and Flitty, and we really got into it. Soon, we were thinking nothing of finishing training and then flying off to a race meeting by helicopter in the afternoon. We'd go all over, Ascot one day and then York the next. We loved it and horses became a big part of our lives. I really took it seriously and wanted to know as much as I could. Sometimes, I used to go and watch the gallops at Alan Swinbanks's yard at Richmond, North Yorkshire, which was always something I loved doing.

The first horse me and Garry owned was called Alfie Flits, which was named after Gaz's little boy. He did very well for us and won quite a few races. The second one we bought was named Little Lu after my first child, Luisa, and we had some great days out watching both horses. That wasn't my downfall, though. In fact, if I'd just stuck to gambling on the days when me and Flitty were at the racecourse or our horses were running, then I think I'd have been okay. But, instead, I opened my first phone account with a bookie and that was when things started to get out of hand. I put that decision to open a 'phone account, which turned out to be a very bad one, down to the boredom of my drive to the training ground during my first season at Blackburn. I was still based in Yorkshire and, no matter how many routes my driver Mick tried, there simply wasn't a decent route to the training ground. So, the journey took ages. Sometimes I slept as Mick made his way along all the A-roads that seemed to go on forever. But, most of the time, I would be wide awake and bored stiff. I needed something to keep me amused, so I opened that fateful first 'phone account. Flitty was gambling with a bloke called Nigel, who offered me a free bet of £5,000 if I signed up with him. I thought, 'What's the worst that can happen?' The next thing I knew, I was spending thousands. To place a bet, all I had to do was text Nigel the words '£10g at 9-2, Alfie Flits to win'. Then, when the text came back saying, 'Bet' that was it. The bet was placed. Sometimes, Nigel would ring me up and we would then barter over the price. It became so easy that I was soon betting £10,000, £20,000, £30,000 on a race. The amount just kept going up until I placed that £100,000 bet that lost, prompting me to put another £100,000 on recoup my losses. It didn't dawn on me until later that I'd effectively had £200,000 riding on that one horse, a mad situation.

The biggest win I had was £218,000, while another bet - a £1,000 treble after I'd been given three tips – earned me about £120,000. The thing with the treble was that all three horses were decent prices so I thought, 'Why not?' The first two came in but then I had to go out to dinner before the third race had been run. I got to this restaurant in Manchester, expecting the result to pop up on my mobile phone any minute. It was only when I checked my 'phone for the umpteenth time that I realised it had no signal. The next few minutes were among the longest of my life. I desperately wanted to know the result, but didn't want to ruin the night by letting on about the bet. Eventually, I couldn't wait any longer and said I had to pop out. I ran down the road as fast as I could until my 'phone finally had a signal again. I'd got about half a mile before the first bar popped up, closely followed by a message off my mate saying, 'You jammy bastard'. I knew the bet must have come in. I then dashed back to the restaurant and tried not to let on where I'd just been. Later that night, I spoke to Nigel and he asked how I wanted my winnings paid. I said 'cash' as I was going on holiday a few days later, so one of his boys came round the following morning and handed over £60,000 and about 80,000 Euros.

Not long after that, I moved to the Lowry Hotel in Manchester as the commute from Yorkshire had become too much. Mind, I was still an hour away from Blackburn's training ground so still ended up filling the journey by reading the *Racing Post* and texting a few bets in. It had become the norm and I only really snapped out of it and cut out the stupid bets after my daughter Luisa had been born in 2006.

Everything came to a head one day after training. By now, I'd moved into a house in Manchester, and was sitting in the bedroom with the racing on television. Flitty was at his house in Bolton and we were texting which horses we fancied in the afternoon's racing. Within an hour or so, we were both £90,000 down. We weren't even at the races, just sitting in the house and yet we'd blown all that money. I thought, 'This is ridiculous and can't go on'. So, I wrote a cheque for the amount I owed to the bookie and decided, there and then, that the madness had to stop. The birth of my first daughter meant my priorities had changed. By betting stupid amounts, I was gambling with Lu's future, her inheritance. I want her to have a nice house when she is old enough. I want her to get a good education and be set up in life. Luisa was the best thing that had happened to my life so I knew the big-time gambling had to stop. And it did. I am glad as well, as there are a lot of players who are still betting despite having lost even more than I did. Some have got away with a lot of debts to bookies because they refused to pay. But others haven't. My career was also coming to an end. When you are earning fortunes, money just doesn't matter. But now, with Louisa having arrived and me having at most just a few years of my career left, changes had to be made. I was no longer just looking out for myself but her as well. She doesn't know it but my first daughter did me a big favour just by being born. I was out of control. I have an addictive personality, which basically means that anything I do has to be done to the extreme. I have always been the same, no matter what I am doing - drinking, gambling, you name it. And it usually takes something big to snap me out of it.

Working out just how much I'd lost down the years and realising it was probably a sum that ran into seven figures was sobering. I couldn't believe I'd done it. Thankfully, a good portion of the money I'd blown was offset when me and Flitty decided to sell the horses a couple of years later. Alfie Flitts had been a top horse so we made decent money, which was just as well considering the money I'd lost gambling.

Before we sold Alfie Flitts, however, I did manage to get myself into trouble one last time. This time it wasn't a big loss but a brush with the law. It came at Aintree on the Friday of the 2008 Grand National meeting. I'd moved from Blackburn to Stoke City by then and persuaded my new team-mates to come along to Ladies Day. Stoke weren't due to play Crystal Palace until Monday so the club were fine about it. We all went along and had a cracking day and night out. Eventually, by the early hours, I'd had enough and caught a taxi back to Manchester from Liverpool with my mate Bug. As fate would have it, the driver took us on a route past Aintree. Suddenly, I got the cab driver to stop and said, 'I'm off to see my horse' - Alfie Flitts was due to run on Grand National day, a couple of races before the big one. The taxi driver just looked at me as if to say, 'You what?' But I insisted and, after I'd paid him the full fare, he dropped us off near the main entrance.

Me and my mate Bug weren't exactly sure what to do next and it probably took us a couple of minutes to decide to try and bunk our way in under a fence. We got through, though Bug's jacket was a casualty as it got caught during his attempts to squeeze through the gap. Once inside, we then decided to walk up the course and were just about to jump the first, or at least try to, when the police turned up. One of them said, 'What are you doing here, lads? It's four o'clock in the morning'. I tried to explain about how my horse was running later that day and I'd wanted to check the course was okay for him. He just looked at me, as if to say, 'What planet are you on, pal?' At first, I thought he was going to nick us but, eventually, I proved who I was and the copper relaxed. Eventually, instead of arresting us, he decided the best thing to do was walk us over to the exit. He did, though, draw the line at calling me a taxi, which I suppose is fair enough. I woke up the next morning and thought, 'Did that really happen?' Seeing the state of Bug's jacket later proved to me it did and I spent the next day or so frantically worrying that the 'papers might get hold of the story. If they had, Tony Pulis would have gone mad with me and that was something I was desperate to avoid. Thankfully, nothing appeared – I'd got away with it.

Since selling the horses with Flitty, I have continued to have a bet. But now it is normal amounts and only once in a while, usually when I am down the pub with my mates. I do still enjoy a punt on a horse but I might go weeks or even months without gambling now.

Those few years when I bet big has shown me that gambling can be a dangerous business. Don't get me wrong, it was a period of my life that I enjoyed. And I wouldn't change it, even though I know the money I spent was crazy. The lifestyle was great, especially the helicopter and flying off to Ascot or wherever at the drop of a hat. It wasn't about us being flash, just wringing every last drop of fun out of the day for me and Flitty. I met some good lads through racing too, such as Flitty's mate Quigs and a few others. Also, when I moved to Bowden in Manchester, I met a local bookie called Paul who became a good friend. Then, I got to know all the lads in the bookies - Alan, Pat, Binny. They are all friends to this day and I wouldn't have met them without racing. But I also realise there is a chance that the gambling could have got out of hand if I hadn't been careful, which would not have been fair on my kids. I was fortunate in that I got out before doing something really stupid and that is why I believe gambling is a problem that football needs to urgently tackle. There are a lot of players who are still betting fortunes. There are probably even more who have horses themselves. I certainly know of plenty who you would never imagine being interested in horse racing. I maintain it is a boredom thing, particularly when a player is away with his team preparing for a match. Technology now means you can watch any race, anywhere in the world on your mobile phone. Plus, you can listen to all the commentaries. I reckon I must have wasted almost £100,000 on that over the years. In terms of what a footballer earns, that might not be much. But if you add in the £1m or so I lost in bets then it shows just how dangerous gambling can be and that is why I wish the PFA or the clubs could do more to educate today's footballers.

Chapter 24

Captain Again

For a professional footballer, and especially one in his 30s, there are few more depressing experiences than being made to train with the kids. It is the equivalent of being given a two-fingered gesture by the manager and there are not many who hang around too long after suffering such a humiliating experience. I certainly didn't. My taste of being shunned came at Blackburn Rovers under Mark Hughes and I hated every second. That is not meant to sound disrespectful to the kids who were in the youth team at the time. Some have gone on to have decent careers so clearly had the talent. But there is no doubt that youth team players are not on the same wavelength as the seniors and don't train in the same way. It means a senior player joining in is a complete waste of time. Despite that, the coaching staff at Blackburn insisted I train with them and not the rest of the first team squad. It was pathetic and something that my close mates at the club just couldn't understand. They would ask me every day what I'd done wrong. But I didn't know. I did ask the management but never got a straight answer.

Looking back, my problems probably started when I got injured just a month or so into the 2005-06 season. I actually started the first five games at left-back as we kicked off the campaign in a solid fashion with a win over Fulham and draws against Spurs and Bolton. But, once I got injured, it meant my season was more or less over as, even when I got fit again, I was nowhere near the team. In fact, I only played two more games all season – on January 2 in a 2-1 win over Portsmouth and then five days later when we beat QPR in the FA Cup. It was great to be back involved and I was hoping it could lead to a run in the side. Instead, I ended up being frozen out and it was all over an untrue rumour that I'd gone out at New Year on the lash. I hadn't done anything of the sort but that didn't stop someone telling Mark it was true. I was furious and defended myself in front of everyone on the training field. I said, 'Repeating a rumour that is not true is totally out of order'. Mark Hughes was there at the time but said nothing, which got me worried. I started to think they wanted me out. I hadn't broken any curfew but the management seemed determined to say I had. I didn't have a great relationship with the coaching staff anyway, Eddie Niedzwiecki was probably the only one I got on okay with. I didn't like the goalkeeping coach, Kevin Hitchock, and found him very childish. I got the impression the feeling was mutual, while neither Mark Hughes nor Mark Bowen, who were very close, seemed to like me much. That is not usually a problem. I've been in countless dressing rooms where players who are in the side every week don't get on with the manager or one of the coaching staff. But, at Blackburn, I felt they wanted me out – hence the repeating of this ridiculous rumour about me having gone out at New Year ahead of my first appearance in months. What I also found hard to stomach was being told a couple of months later, 'Dom, you're no longer smiling when you come in to training'. What did they expect? It was the coaching staff and their false accusation that had caused me to be upset in the first place.

I couldn't work out why it had all gone so sour, especially as I'd ended my first season at Blackburn thinking things were going well between me and the manager. The team had got out of trouble and I'd played my part. Just a few months later, however, and I didn't seem to be welcome any more. All I wanted was someone to be honest and upfront with me but, instead, there seemed to be a campaign under way to get me out without anyone having the decency to tell me why. If it hadn't been for my mates in the dressing room, I'd have left a long time before I did. I also liked the staff behind the scenes and liked Blackburn as a club. Eventually, though, I realised something had to give so I went to see the manager just before the January transfer window in 2007 was due to close. I had not been near the first-team in months so asked what was going on. He said, 'We don't think you're going to play'. That much had become apparent with me having played just twice in 15 or 16 months. But what I couldn't understand is why he hadn't been able to tell me the same thing six months earlier? Or even at the start of the transfer window. That way, I would have had time to sort myself out.

Instead, all I had was just a few days. I immediately rang my agent and asked him to see if there was any interest. I also went in to see the chairman, John Williams, to ask about the remaining six months on my contract. John, being a decent bloke, promised to honour it. He was as good as his word, too, which was something I appreciated. I liked John anyway but the fact he was the only person willing to give me a straight answer during those final few weeks at Blackburn meant he shot up even further in my estimation. It was then that Stoke City, who were on the fringe of the Championship play-offs at the time, came in for me with an offer to go to the Britannia Stadium on a six-month loan. I couldn't get out of Blackburn quick enough, especially as joining Stoke meant I could commute from my home every day and not have to move into a hotel. I also liked what Tony Pulis had to say at our first meeting. Our paths had never crossed before but I soon found out Tony is a good talker and someone who doesn't suffer fools gladly. Everyone has to be on his side, which has definitely worked in the club's way over the past few years. The final plus point was that Stoke were going for promotion.

My only reservation as I spoke with Tony was the fact it meant dropping down to the Championship, which was something I wasn't overly keen on. What I did appreciate, though, was that I was by now the wrong side of 30 and I had also suffered quite badly at Blackburn with injuries. My Achilles, knee and hamstrings had all been proving increasingly problematic, while my back had also started to hurt during my second season at Ewood Park. Getting over injury was also taking longer, with a hamstring strain that had kept me out for five days in my 20s now taking three weeks to heal. So, I appreciated why taking a step down was probably my only way of getting back to playing regularly again. Luckily, the move worked out really well.

Initially, though, I had to adapt quickly to life outside the Premier League. For instance, the standard of training on my first day at Stoke was not the best. There was a big gap in terms of quality compared to what I had been used to in keep-balls and the way things were done at Blackburn, Leeds and Liverpool. That is not meant in any way to sound disrespectful to Tony Pulis or any of the lads, it is just a fact of life that there is a big difference in standards between the Premier League and Championship. The training facilities were another thing that took a bit of getting used to. At Stoke, we got changed at the stadium before travelling to the training ground – something I'd not done since those very early days at Liverpool. There was also no indoor swimming pool at Stoke, instead we had to use a local gym. It was the same for anyone who wanted to do some weights. The only facilities at the training ground were a couple of old portable buildings, with six showers - hardly any of which worked, which I presume was why we changed at the ground. I soon found out the club's kit was a bit manky, too. My shirt was full of bobbles and had clearly been through the washing machine more than a few times. The shorts didn't do me many favours, either, as they were as tight as the ones John Barnes used to wear in the 1980s. But, I reasoned while trying to squeeze myself into the shorts, that is the harsh reality of life outside the Premier League. Clubs simply can't just go out and buy new things, whether it be kit, balls or whatever, whenever they feel like it.

It was a big culture shock for me but, in a funny way, I quite liked it. I have always been someone who doesn't mind getting their hands dirty and I went on to really enjoy my time at Stoke, even if things did end on a bit of a sour note. A big plus was that I settled in quickly. As with Blackburn, the dressing room was full of strong characters and straight away they seemed to accept me. The same went for the staff and after a few days I felt like I'd been at Stoke for years. Once out on the training pitch, it was just how I liked it - competitive and with the lads thinking nothing of kicking hell out of each other during the week. Soon, I was doing the same. My debut came in a 3-2 defeat at Preston North End, a result that left us ninth in the table. A couple of games earlier, Stoke had beaten Leeds United 3-1 and I was quite glad that the teams wouldn't meet again for the rest of the season. Leeds had been going through a difficult time and were deep in relegation trouble. I wouldn't have enjoyed adding to the problems of my old club by helping Stoke beat them.

We won my second game, against Burnley at Turf Moor, and it was only after that when I realised what sort of money a few of the lads were on. Coming from the Premier League, I was shocked. Up there, everyone, even the kids, had been on big money. Yet at Stoke, there were lads in the first-team squad who were earning hundreds of pounds a week. I am not saying they were regulars, but they had played a few games. I couldn't help but think back to that day at Leeds when one of the kids who was never going to make the grade in a million years had been shouting his mouth off at 'only' earning £6,000. I just wish that stupid kid could have come and met the Stoke lads and learned what real football is all about instead of the fantasy version that existed in his head. The best thing of all was that these lads at Stoke were not complaining, they just saw being a professional footballer as reward enough. That was a really refreshing attitude to see. Best of all, a couple of those on a few hundred pounds a week when I was at Stoke are still there today and it really pleases me that they will be getting rewarded now the club is established in the Premier League. People like Andy Wilkinson, a local lad who came through the ranks and has probably exceeded his own expectations, are the ones I am really pleased for. He has had to bide his time but is now a good Premier League player.

Along with the way things were done and the wages some of the lads were on, another part of life at Stoke I had to adapt to quickly was Tony Pulis's philosophy towards how the game should be played. At Stoke, I was mainly a holding midfielder, which a few of my mates back in Manchester would joke meant I must have a stiff neck from looking up at the ball flying over my head. It wasn't as bad as that. But I was ordered not to pass on the floor to anyone behind me. At first, I found that difficult to do and would, in the heat of battle, sometimes forget – earning myself an almighty bollocking in the process.

Stoke had plenty of talented and skilful players. Lee Hendrie was there when I signed, while I still can't believe a big club has not come in for Ricardo Fuller yet. He has fantastic ability. Liam Lawrence was also a good player, as was Daryl Russel while Andy Griffin has gone on to play a lot of Premier League games. Despite that, the gaffer had his own way of playing and we had to stick to that. Obviously, Stoke became best known for Rory Delap's throw-in once they had been promoted to the Premier League in 2008. It was the first thing the media picked up on. But we didn't use it that much when I was at the club. The pitch, for instance, was only reduced to the minimum width once we had been promoted. That was done specifically for Rory, as it meant his throw-ins would land in the six-yard box where they could hurt the opposition. Rory became Stoke's big weapon, so much so that I was at the Britannia one afternoon before we were due to play Arsenal and saw Arsene Wenger measure the width to make sure it met minimum standards.

I may have had to adapt my own game at Stoke but I don't see why their style has been the subject of so much criticism. Teams always play to their strengths, that is a rule of football. Stoke do, just as Arsenal and Manchester United do. Stoke can play if they want to but the point to remember is that if you have someone like big Mamady Sidibe up front at 6ft 5in, then it would be crazy not to use that to your advantage by playing more direct. Tony's gameplan was basically to get our diagonal balls in to Big Mama and for Ricardo to latch on to the knockdowns behind him. It was hard to play against because, the moment the ball was launched forward, we set off forward as a team. The opposition were immediately under pressure. Nine times out of ten, Big Mama would win it. The only midfielder who wasn't part of the mass push forward was me. Instead, my role was to protect the back four and pass on my experience to the younger lads. I enjoyed it, even if it wasn't quite what I'd been used to in my career, and that is why I will always defend Tony's approach when the critics start having a go.

In my first few months, the results were decent but we ended up missing out on a place in the play-offs by two points after drawing at QPR on the last day. As it turned out, results elsewhere meant we would not have finished in the top six even if we had won the game as our goal difference was three worse than Southampton who finished sixth. But we had gone into the final day really believing we would claim sixth place, which made the away dressing room at Loftus Road a very quiet place to be after that 1-1 draw. I felt gutted because I knew how hard the lads had worked. I could also see from the gaffer's face just how devastated he was. He didn't move for about an hour. It mattered to him and I had even more respect for Tony after watching him that afternoon. Looking around the dressing room at QPR, I could see a similar emotion among the lads and I knew then that this group would not allow Stoke to miss out again. At that moment, I really wanted to be part of the following season.

Whether I would get that chance was up to Tony and the club. The original agreement had been for just a six-month loan with a promise from Tony to sit down in the summer and see where we were at. He proved as good as his word and I was at the Formula One Grand Prix in Monaco when my agent Stru rang to say Stoke had offered me a 12-month deal. The money was nothing like what I'd been used to in my career but that didn't matter. I just wanted to be part of what I believed would be a special year for Stoke City. So, I got Stru to 'phone Tony straight back and accept the offer.

From the very start of pre-season a few weeks later, I sensed something had changed. I don't mean in terms of our football or anything like that. It was more our mentality. The lads and management really believed Stoke could win promotion and that gave the club a determined air. Often in the Championship, having a sense of belief is half the battle. We had also made a few signings, lads such as Richard

Cresswell, Ryan Shawcross, Jon Parkin and Leon Cort. All were big characters and big lads, meaning that when we stood next to the opposition in the tunnel before a game, I could often see a little bit of trepidation in their eyes. That was a great feeling and added to the intimidating air that was building up around Stoke. Not only did we look like extras from 'The Land of the Giants' but the Britannia Stadium being so exposed meant that, even in summer, it is not a nice place for visiting teams to play.

On a personal level, pre-season was made most memorable for me when I was made captain. Tony pulled me a couple of days into our preparations and said he wanted me to take the armband. I was delighted. To be captain of one club is an honour, but two is really special. Things might not have worked out at Leeds but I had enjoyed the responsibility of the role. Part of the gaffer's thinking was that a few of the younger lads looked up to me. Knowing that meant I was determined to make sure we had a good season. As a squad, we didn't have a target as such. By that, I mean Tony didn't sit us down and say we were going for the title or anything like that. But there was this unspoken desire to ensure that what had happened at QPR when we missed out on the play-offs would not be allowed to happen again.

Chapter 25

Through The Pain Barrier

Watching your career ebb away is one of the strangest feelings for any footballer. It certainly was for me during what turned out to be my last season in the game. Injury had caught up with me at the age of 33 and, despite being appointed captain the previous summer, my involvement in Stoke City's fight for a place in the Premier League was largely reduced to cheering the lads on from the stand. I'd been troubled by all manner of injuries for years, right back to when I was at Liverpool. But the one that eventually finished me off was when I broke two bones in my foot during the summer of 2007 and then, foolishly as it turned out, decided to play on. Looking back, it was the wrong thing to do. But, as someone who takes the position of captain very seriously, I didn't want to let anyone down – least of all Tony Pulis, who had just signed me on a permanent deal. To get through, I opted to have pain-killing injections in the sole of my left foot. With those, I was assured, there would be no problem getting through the 90 minutes.

Our first game of the season was at Cardiff City and, because it was an away game, we didn't have our own doctor with us. So, one of the Stoke coaching staff had to ask Cardiff's doctor to administer the injections. I was sitting in the treatment room when the doctor came in. He gave me a really stern look and said, 'What the hell are you doing?' He couldn't believe I was thinking of playing with two broken bones in my foot. But I insisted and he did as I asked. I'd tried out the injections a couple of times before training and the only way of describing the experience is 'weird'. Basically, I had no feeling whatsoever in my foot. Can you imagine how difficult it is to play football like that? Believe me, it is. I couldn't feel the ball at all, even if I really belted it up the field. I got used to it in the end but, at first, it was like kicking a balloon. A very, very weird sensation. I also had to wear a boot that was a size-and-a-half too big for me, because my left foot would swell up so much during a game. Once the injections wore off, I would be in total agony but, by then, the game had been over for ages. I found that out once we'd beaten Cardiff 1-0 thanks to a Ryan Shawcross goal on his debut. It quickly became clear that I wouldn't be able to train between matches and that playing twice in a week would be a problem, though I did manage to do just that on a couple of occasions when we had back-to-back Championship games on Saturday and Tuesday. I did, though, sit out our Carling Cup defeat to Darlington.

Being unable to train properly, I spent most of my time in the local swimming pool. In fact, I doubt there is anyone in Stoke who swam more miles than me that year! I can't remember training with the lads at all once the season got under way, other than going out on a Friday morning to run through a few set-piece moves.

Despite not doing much during the week, I played the first 14 games of the season but then had to sit out the next three, which all took place within eight days in early November. I still wouldn't admit defeat, though, and declared myself fit to face Burnley at Turf Moor on Saturday November 24. It turned out to be the last game of my career. We drew 0-0, which wasn't a bad result for us. Thanks to the pain-killing injections, I managed the full 90 minutes. Once back in the dressing room, however, I knew I was in trouble as the moment I took my boot off, I could see my foot had swollen up ridiculously. There had always been swelling after a game but nothing like this. A couple of the lads sitting either side of me said straight away, 'Dom, this has got to stop. You're doing yourself serious damage'.

I knew, deep down, that they were right. So, I went to the gaffer and said I needed to get the injury sorted out properly. He agreed and arranged for the physio to send me for an x-ray. It showed what we already knew, that I had a couple of breaks in my foot. It was decided, there and then, that I should go in for an operation to remove both of the broken bones. I didn't have to have my foot in a pot or anything like that but I wasn't allowed to put any weight on it, or the stitches would not heal. It was frustrating but I consoled myself by thinking I'd be back involved long before the end of the season. Unfortunately, the scar on my foot didn't heal properly and that meant I had to watch from the sidelines for the rest of the season as Stoke challenged for promotion. As captain, I decided to try and remain a big part of the dressing room so I attended almost every game. Tony Pulis was in favour of that, too, as he knew that the closer we got to the run-in the more nervy things would become. In the end, the only games I missed were a couple in midweek away from home when I had to continue my rehabilitation in Stoke. We were a very tight unit and I wanted to play my part, even if that meant just organising a night out or a meal for the boys. I even got the lads go-karting and paint-balling during the run-in, anything to try and ease the nerves.

Sitting in the stands or on the bench, I was able to watch the boys' push for promotion gradually build momentum. The Championship is a slog of a competition, where you really have to grind out the results. Being able to dig in and either win or draw games that our rivals would have lost became a feature of Stoke's season. The signings Tony had made in the summer had proved to be good ones and if I had to pick one out that made the difference it would be Ryan Shawcross. He had arrived on a six-month loan deal from Manchester United and, straight away, I could see he had come through the youth set-up at Old Trafford. The way he played and conducted himself was an example to everyone else, particularly the younger lads. Ryan went on to play in the vast majority of our games and did brilliantly. As, it has to be said, did the other lads.

They got into the play-off places around Christmas and then went top in February. We then had a bit of a wobble to win just one of eight games but then found our form just at the right time. Automatic promotion was clinched on the final day but, for me, the crucial win had come the previous weekend when Richard Cresswell had scored the only goal at Colchester United. It was the last game at Layer Road before it was due to be demolished and a bit of a party, while Teddy Sheringham was also making his last appearance before retiring so there was a really charged atmosphere ahead of kick-off. The lads just put all that out of their minds and were superb. As we headed back to Stoke afterwards, I thought that we were up - even though we still needed something from the final day game at home to Leicester City. As it happened, our nearest rivals Hull City lost at Ipswich and we were up anyway – though we did subsequently get a point from a goalless draw. West Bromwich Albion's win at QPR meant they pipped us to the title but I doubt anyone inside the Britannia cared as the celebrations got under way.

Seeing the delight in the faces of all the boys afterwards was something I'll never forget. Some had never been in the Premier League before, while others had enjoyed a brief taste but then had to drop down. But now, here they all were, Premier League players. The champagne started flowing the moment the final whistle had blown and the celebrations continued throughout the rest of Sunday and into the start of the week. It was Tuesday by the time I got home, still wearing my Stoke City tracksuit. I must have stunk! Piecing together the celebrations later took some doing, I can tell you. On the Monday night, for instance, seemingly I had done an interview on talkSport and yet when someone asked me about it a few days later I had no recollection of speaking to any radio station whatsoever. And still don't.

The one part of the celebrations I was sober enough to remember was the club asking me, as captain, where the lads wanted to go on a trip that had been promised as a reward if we won promotion. The club said we could go anywhere we wanted in the world, so I was thinking Las Vegas, Miami or New York. So, where did the boys choose? Magaluf. I couldn't believe it. The decision was unanimous as well. I was the only one with any imagination, obviously. It was 'Shagaluf', as a few of the lads called it, and that was that. The club were delighted, as you'd expect with a trip to Majorca hardly likely to break the bank. We did have a good time, though. There was plenty of drinking, bungee-jumping, drinking, eating, drinking….I didn't go to bed once in four days. I must have looked like a ghost by the end and was, in all honesty, glad to get home.

At that stage, I was still hoping to play my part for Stoke the following season. Tony Pulis said to me, 'Get yourself fit over the summer and come back to be part of things'. I took that to mean I would be able to earn a new contract as a player if I was fit. Unfortunately, it turned out what Tony had actually meant was that I would be offered a coaching role and told to forget about playing. I just wish he could have been a bit clearer. Throughout that summer, I'd set my heart on finishing my career in the Premier League at the age of 34. I also felt as fit as anyone at the club when we came back for pre-season training. Despite that, Tony's only offer was to join his coaching staff. He never really said why he didn't think I could cut it as a player any more, though I did get the impression that, once you were over 30 and in the Premier League, he felt a player would struggle. Unless they had a long throw! (Only joking, Rory).

Tony may have been right that my body wouldn't have been up to another year. I suppose we'll never know. Maybe my tendency to enjoy the social side also counted against me. During that pre-season, we had gone on a trip to Austria. The place we were staying was totally in the middle of nowhere, with not a bar for 50 miles either side. But, as usual,

I'd managed to sniff one out via a local who offered to chauffeur me, Liam Lawrence – who was Tony's favourite and able to get away with a lot more than the rest of us - Clint Hill and Jon Parkin to a bar in his American Cadillac at midnight. We had to sneak out of our patio doors and pile into this bloke's car. We drove for ages before, eventually, pulling up outside this bar that looked more like someone's house. Anyway, we piled in and found 10 locals sitting around the bar getting slowly drunk. I looked around and thought, 'If this is to be my last pre-season, at least I have come full circle from my first trip away with Liverpool'.

As for the offer of a coaching role, I wasn't particularly impressed. I'd put my body through hell the previous season and felt I deserved a chance to prove myself as a player. But, despite my misgivings, I decided to give coaching a go on a week-to-week basis. Tony asked me to look after the reserves, which I did for a short time. I quickly realised, though, that a big problem was going to be the way Tony works. Basically, there is only one person making any decisions and that is him. So, even though it was said I was in charge of the reserves, I wasn't really. I wanted the lads to see more of the ball but Tony was into his set-pieces and patterns of play, so that was what I had to work on. I stuck it out for a couple of months but, eventually, Tony making every decision persuaded me to call it a day. I walked out and never went back. That style of set-up wasn't for me. Coaching is definitely something that interests me but I would like to do it my way. I just didn't feel comfortable and thought, 'The time has come to finish'. Around that time, I'd also started to see my back specialist again and he said very bluntly, 'I didn't realise things had deteriorated so badly'. He was surprised how long I had been able to keep going.

Things may not have worked out for me at Stoke in the end but what I won't do is knock Tony Pulis. The job he has done is amazing. Reaching an FA Cup final and turning Stoke into a Premier League club says it all. His record is brilliant and shows that his methods have worked. No-one likes to go to Stoke, not even the biggest teams.

The worst part of walking out of Stoke was the realisation that my career was over. Any footballer will tell you that is a really difficult fact to handle. Some cope better than others. The worst time is when you are sitting on your own in those first few weeks and thinking, 'What am I going to do now?' In my case, I had a few months doing absolutely nothing. It probably took that long for the news to sink in. I'd heard the words of the back specialist when he said, 'You'll never play again' and felt awful. But I still don't believe the words truly sank in until a lot further down the line.

It is important to face up to retirement as quickly as possible. Those who don't can get themselves into trouble. That is why I think it is important to earn a wage. Of course, a lot of ex-footballers who played for even just a few years in the Premier League have enough money to live on for the rest of their lives. But there is something satisfying about earning money, no matter how big or small the amount is. Just sitting around, doing nothing is not healthy – even if you can afford to do so. I enjoy popping down to my favourite restaurant in Hale, which is run by two good friends Nick and Paul, but my day has to have a purpose.

One thing an old team-mate of mine once told me was that, when you retire, the days can become very long. As a result, as soon as I'd got my head around the fact my football career was over I did try to be pro-active. It was part of the reason why I decided to open a bar in Leeds. A couple of lads, Tony Hannan and Rob Carlton, approached me with the proposal. Tony is a promoter who has put famous nights on in Leeds such as Up Yer Ronson and Soak, while Rob is a local businessman. They had an idea about a bar and knew I loved drinking in The Rock Bar in Ibiza. The original aim was to link up with the Ibiza bar but they wanted to keep their own identity. So, we decided to set up on our own. I put all the money in and gave Tony and Rob shares in the business, and things are going well. The bar is situated on Call Lane, which is always an area of Leeds I have liked. It used to be a café that was painted pink, which might have put some prospective buyers off. But we went in and really liked the look of the place. I could visualise what the bar would look like and was involved in the planning throughout. I am delighted with how it has turned out. I wanted it to be a place that wasn't pretentious and where people could go for a nice chat. We have a good crowd who come in and I try to spend quite a bit of time in there, especially on a weekend when we get quite a few Leeds fans popping in. Some Saturdays, I am asked to pose for photos a hundred times or so. We even get the old Service Crew boys in from time to time. They are smashing lads and have never been a minute's trouble. Sometimes, they do like a sing-song and that is usually my cue to leave – as it is not exactly great for business to have 100 lads with scars from god knows where on their faces belting out Marching On Together at the top of their voices on a Saturday night. But the boys are smashing and it is always great to see them because they love Leeds United. Possibly the best thing about the bar is it has got me back involved with the city of Leeds and allowed me to get along to Elland Road quite often. Having a base in the city also means I see old friends all the time, including some of my old team-mates such as Gary Kelly who was back over from Ireland during the summer and popped in. Making money out of a bar, especially in a recession, is never easy but we are doing okay.

On top of my work in the bar, I write a weekly column in conjunction with the firm sportingbet.com for the *Yorkshire Evening Post* in Leeds. I enjoy having my say on Leeds and football, in general. The 'paper's football reporter Phil Hay ghosts the column for me and does a really good job of turning my thoughts into words every week. Judging by the number of people who come up to say they enjoy reading the column, it certainly seems to have gone down well with supporters. Some might not agree with what I say but that is the whole point of a column to me – to spark debate. I hope that can continue for many years. I also do bits of other media work. It is a competitive industry with a lot of ex-footballers wanting to be involved but I have been fortunate to work for BBC Radio Five Live a few times. I have been on talkSport a few times, too, and I really enjoy that side of football. There is, though, no substitute for being actively involved in the game and that is why I will go back and finish my coaching badges once I get the all-clear over my back. I still believe I have plenty to offer. I would love to work with youngsters on defending. I watch games now where a lot of players don't know even the basics of defending. I find myself at home, shouting at the television 'Stand up, don't dive in' or 'Your body shape is all wrong'. I'd love to get involved and help the kids.

Looking back on my career, I realise how fortunate I was. I may not have had much luck with semi-finals or have a cabinet full of medals. But I was lucky enough to enjoy some great, great times and I have memories that will live with me for the rest of my life. Playing in front of the Anfield Kop alongside players who just a few years earlier had been my heroes was wonderful. As was my time at Elland Road, or most of it at least. In fact, I am reminded of just how fortunate I am every time I watch Leeds play and the fans start singing my name. I'll be sitting there in the stand, minding my own business and watching the game when, suddenly, 'Oh Matteo, scored a fucking great goal…' starts. I left Leeds in 2004 and was only there four years, yet the fans choose to still remember me. It is great and something I will never take for granted, that's for sure. I'll admit to finding it a bit embarrassing at times, particularly when I think about all the legends that have played for Leeds United down the years. I would never for one second think of putting myself in the same bracket as all those great names from the past. They are true legends, whereas all I did was score a goal in an important game. I also realise that the fans singing about the San Siro is probably because it is a reminder of the last great times that Leeds supporters had. But I do still feel incredibly proud whenever it starts up. The supporters, the one remaining link from my time at the club, don't forget and neither do I. And it is because of those incredibly loyal fans that if I could have one football wish come true in the next few years then it would be Leeds United getting back to their rightful place – challenging for honours in the Premier League.

Afterword

Chris Moyles

I first met Dom ten or so years ago after we had been introduced by a mutual friend called Rossy. I would love to say, as a Leeds United fan, that it was football that brought us together but that would be a lie. It was booze, and the fact he was a Leeds player was just a bonus. We got on well straight away, which as anyone who has met Dom will tell you is not a surprise. His personality is almost addictive, in that he is the sort of bloke who everyone loves spending time with. There is no front and no arrogance about Dom. Instead, he is just an ordinary guy who loves meeting people and talking to them. And especially if they are Leeds fans. I have lost count of the number of nights out that have seen us 'lose' Dom for a good half-hour or so, and all because he has met a Leeds fan in the bar and has been nattering away about what has been happening at Elland Road.

To be honest, I have always found the 'footballer fame' thing a bit bizarre, in that I have been out with a lot of them down the years and always been amazed at just how rude some people can be. If I am spotted in the street or a bar and someone wants a word, they will usually come up and say, 'Moylesy, sorry to bother you but I really like the show and....' With footballers, however, it is totally different with the gist of how a fan will introduce himself being, 'Oi, sign this for me now'. There is no 'please' or 'thank you' and I will admit that if it was me then I would find it really wearing. But Dom never, ever did. He was - and, still is - always politeness itself and, invariably, would end up chatting away to this fan for five minutes as the rest of us were all looking at our watches and saying, 'C'mon Dom, we've got to be somewhere'. In the end, we'd have to almost drag him away, kicking and screaming. But that is Dom's personality – he is someone who just loves meeting people, even the rude ones.

Maybe it was a love of music as well as the common interest of Leeds United that brought us together as such good mates. As you would imagine, being a footballer he has distinctly dubious taste in music. But

I have always let that pass as I didn't want to offend. He has, though, had his uses when it comes to my own career in music. You might not imagine that a professional footballer would be much use in terms of career advice to someone who works in radio and television. But I did seek Dom's views in early 2004 when I started doing the Breakfast Show on BBC Radio 1. I had worked at the station for five years at that stage, but always in the afternoon. It meant I was facing a lot of changes, not least in terms of how I was going to have to live my life. So, I thought Dom would be able to give me a few pointers on how I could adapt. Not, of course, to the early mornings – what footballer ever gets up at 3.30am? In my experience, that is usually when they are getting in! But where I thought Dom might be useful was in helping me cope with finishing work at 11.30am and then having the whole day to myself. To me, that was very much 'footballer territory', as they are the only people I know who work fewer hours than me and get home earlier during the day. So, I rang Dom up one morning – yes, he was home by lunchtime! - and said, 'It's ten past 12 and I am just walking through my front door, what should I do next?' Dom laughed before, like a true professional, he started reeling off different ways that I could fill my day. He more or less went through the entire Leeds squad, and detailed how the various age groups spent their afternoons. The young lads were into X-Box, while the ones who were a bit older and had a bit more money would go into town and spend money on clothes or a posh car. After those two age groups, he said, the lads in their late 20s would often pop out for a coffee and take the dog for a walk as those with families spend their time doing the school run or whatever. I took his advice on board, and spent the next year or so playing X-Box every afternoon – even though I wasn't quite in the right age group.

Through Dom, I met quite a few of the Leeds players during the Champions League days. Great lads such as Alan Smith, Michael Bridges, Eirik Bakke and Rio Ferdinand. As someone born and raised in Leeds, I must admit I found it a real thrill to be hanging out with all these top players from my hometown club. There was a real buzz about the city and club at the time, so you can imagine how exciting it was to spend time with them all and count them as friends. I was living in London but I still went to loads of games, and a lot of that was down to hanging around with these guys who were great fun. The surprising thing I noticed was that, whenever we were all out, we rarely talked football.

I don't know why, it is probably because it was their job. To be fair, I don't go out and talk about radio shows and the like with my friends so maybe it shouldn't have been that much of a surprise. But it was still a thrill to be hanging around with these guys on such a regular basis.

As enjoyable as getting to know Dom and his team-mates was for me, what I love more than anything about Dominic Matteo's time at Leeds United is how the fans still think so highly of him. Dom might not have been the one who scored all the goals or been the hometown hero. But he is still really loved at Elland Road. I have lost count of the number of games I have been watching on television or listening to on the radio and suddenly heard the song, 'Oh Matteo, scored a fucking great goal, in the San Siro, in the San Siro…' strike up. At first, I thought he must be at the game and the fans had just spotted him. But it wasn't. The simple truth is that the fans sing it everywhere they go, and that says all you need to know about Dom and his time at Leeds.

Achieving that sort of fans' favourite status is not easy, especially as he wasn't someone born in Leeds like Smudger who every supporter took to from the moment he first played for the club. But what every fan could see about Dom was just how very proud he was to play for Leeds United. I can't imagine what it must make Dom feel like to hear his name being sung all these years after he left the club. Knowing him as I do, embarrassment is his most likely emotion – especially when he thinks about all the great players who have played for the club down the years but don't have their own songs. But, to me, he shouldn't feel like that as his name being sung every week at Elland Road is a fitting tribute to his contribution to what was a great time to be a Leeds United fan.

Chris Moyles,
October 2011

Acknowledgments

It would be remiss of me not to thank my family first for all the love and support they have given down the years. I couldn't have achieved half of what I did in my career without you all fully behind me. The same goes for my friends, who are far too many to mention here but you all know who you are. The same goes for all the great players I was fortunate enough to share a dressing room with down the years at my various clubs.

In terms of turning my story into this book, I would like to thank all at Great Northern Books for their support during the writing of this book and, in particular, Barry Cox, who gave the initial go-ahead. David Burrill is another who has played a vital role in designing the book and Matt Johnson who took the excellent photograph that is on the front cover. *Yorkshire Post* chief football writer Richard Sutcliffe, who I first met when he ghosted my 'Captain's Column' in the Leeds United programme during the club's collapse when we spent hours trying to find something positive to talk about, is the man whose job it was to commit my memories and reminisces into print. Having read several footballers' autobiographies, my only condition before we started the project was that In My Defence should capture my voice and way of thinking. I'm delighted to say Richard has done just that, so much so that when I first read the completed manuscript I got quite emotional at all the old feelings that it stirred.

Last, but most importantly, I would like to thank my two beautiful daughters, Luisa and Elin, for coming into my life and making it complete. I love you both and this book is for you.

Dominic Matteo

DOMINIC MATTEO

Born: April 28, 1974.
Birthplace: Dumfries, Scotland.

LIVERPOOL

Signed: May 27, 1992.
Debut: Manchester City 1 Liverpool 1, October 23, 1993, Premier League.
Final game: Bradford City 1 Liverpool 0, May 14, 2000, Premier League.

Season	League	*Appearances* FAC	LC	Other	Goals	Pos	*Liverpool* FAC	LC
1993-94	11	0	2	-	0	8th	R3r	R4r
1994-95	2(5)		0	0*	0	4th	QF	WON
1995-96	5	0(1)	0	-	0	3rd	R/U	R4
1996-97	22(4)	2	3	7**	0	4th	R4	R5
1997-98	24(2)	1	4	2*	0	3rd	R3	SF
1998-99	16(4)	1	0	1(1)*	1	7th	R4	R4
1999-2000	32	1(1)	0	-	1	4th	R4	R3

*(*UEFA Cup, ** European Cup Winners' Cup)*

European Competition

1995-96 – UEFA Cup

Unused substitute twice.

Did Not Play

R1L1	Sept 19	Spartak Vladikavkaz (a) W2-1 (McManaman, Redknapp)
R1L2	Sept 26	Spartak Vladikavkaz (H) D0-0
R2L1	Oct 17	Brondby (a) D0-0
R2L2	Oct 31	Brondby (H) L0-1

1996-97 – European Cup Winners' Cup

Round One

Sept 12   MyPa (a) W1-0 (Bjornebye)
James; McAteer, Matteo, Wright, Bjornebe, Babb; McManaman, Barnes, Thomas; Collymore, Fowler.

Sept 26   MyPa (H) W3-1 (Berger, Collymore, Barnes)
James; McAteer, Matteo (Ruddock), Wright (Scales), Bjornebye, Babb; McManaman, Barnes, Thomas; Berger (Redknapp), Collymore.

Round Two
Oct 17   Sion (a) W2-1 (Fowler, Barnes)
James; McAteer, Matteo, Scales, Bjornebye, Babb, McManaman, Barnes, Thomas; Berger, Fowler (Redknapp).
Oct 31   Sion (H) W6-3 (Fowler 2, McManaman, Bjornebye, Barnes, Berger)
James; McAteer, Matteo, Scales (Redknapp), Bjornebye, Babb, McManaman, Barnes, Thomas; Berger, Fowler.

Quarter-final
Mar 6   Brann (a) D1-1 (Fowler)
James; McAteer, Harkness, Ruddock, Matteo, Bjorneybe; McManaman, Barnes, Redknapp; Berger, Fowler.
Mar 20   Brann (H) W3-0 (Fowler 2, Collymore)
James; McAteer, Harkness, Matteo (Babb), Wright, Bjorneybe; McManaman, Barnes, Redknapp; Berger (Collymore), Fowler.

Semi-final
Apr 10   Paris St Germain (a) L0-3
James; McAteer, Wright, Matteo, Harkness, Bjorneybe; McManaman, Barnes, Redknapp; Collymore (Thomas), Fowler.

Did Not Play:
SFL2   Apr 24   Paris St Germain (H) W2-0 Fowler, Wright).

1997-98 - UEFA Cup
Round One
Sept 16   Celtic (a) D2-2 (Owen, McManaman)
James; Jones, Kvarme, Wright, Matteo, Bjorneybe; McManaman, Ince, Thomas; Riedle, Owen.

Round Two
Nov 4   Strasbourg (H) W2-0 (Fowler pen, Riedle)
James; Jones (Riedle), Kvarme, Matteo, Byorneybe (Berger); McManaman, Leonhardsen, Ince, Redknapp; Fowler, Owen.

Did Not Play:
R1L2   Sept 30   Celtic (H) D0-0
R2L1   Oct 21   Strasbourg (a) L0-3

1998-99 - UEFA Cup
Round One
Sept 29   Kosice (H) W5-0 (Redknapp 2, Fowler 2, Ince)
James; McAteer (Heggem), Leonhardsen, Carragher, Babb (Matteo), Bjorneybe; Redknapp, Ince (Staunton), Berger; Owen, Fowler.

Round Three
Dec 8   Celta Vigo (H) L0-1
James (Friedel); McAteer, Matteo, Babb (Murphy), Carragher, Staunton, Gerrard, Thompson (Riedle), Berger; Fowler, Owen.

Did Not Play:
RL1L1   Sept 15   Kosice (a) W3-0 (Berger, Riedle, Owen)
R2L1   Oct 20   Valencia (H) D0-0
R2L2   Nov 3   Valencia (a) D2-2 (McManaman, Berger)
R3L1   Nov 24   Celta Vigo (a) L1-3 (Owen)

SUNDERLAND (Loan)
Signed: March, 1995, for the rest of the season.
Debut: Barnsley 2 Sunderland 0; March 24, 1995, Division One.
Final game: Barnsley 2 Sunderland 0; March 24, 1995, Division One.

LEEDS UNITED

Signed: August 16, 2000.
Debut: Leeds United 1 AC Milan 0, September 19, 2000, Champions League.
Final game: Chelsea 1 Leeds United 0; May 15, 2004, Premier League.

Season	Appearances					Leeds United		
	League	FAC	LC	Other	Goals	Pos	FAC	LC
2000-01	30	1	2	15*	2	4th	R4	R3
2001-02	32	0	1	7**	0	5th	R3	R4
2002-03	20	3	0	1**	0	15th	QF	R3
2003-04	33	1	0	-	2	19th	R3	R3

(* Champions League, ** UEFA Cup)

European Competition

2000-01 - Champions League
(First group stage)
Sept 19   AC Milan (H) W1-0 (Bowyer)
Martyn; Kelly, Mills, Duberry, Harte; Bowyer, Bakke, Dacourt, Matteo; Smith, Bridges.
Sept 26   Besiktas (H) W6-0 (Bowyer 2, Viduka, Matteo, Bakke, Huckerby)
Martyn; Kelly, Mills, Radebe, Harte; Bowyer, Bakke, Dacourt (McPhail 76), Matteo; Smith (Huckerby 81), Viduka.
Oct 18   Besiktas (a) D0-0
Robinson; Kelly, Woodgate, Mills, Harte; Bowyer, Bakke, Burns, Matteo; Viduka, Bridges (Huckerby 27).
Oct 24   Barcelona (H) D1-1 (Bowyer)
Robinson; Kelly, Woodgate, Mills, Harte; Bowyer, Dacourt (Burns 75), Bakke, Matteo; Smith, Viduka.
Nov 9   AC Milan (a) D1-1 (Matteo)
Robinson; Kelly, Radebe, Mills, Harte; Bowyer, Bakke, Dacourt, Matteo; Smith, Viduka.

Group H - final table

	Pts
Milan	11
LEEDS	9
Barcelona	8
Besiktas	4

(Second group stage)

Nov 22   Real Madrid (H) L0-2
Robinson; Mills, Radebe, Woodgate, Harte; Kelly, Bowyer, Burns (Wilcox 60), Matteo; Viduka, Smith.

Dec 5   Lazio (a) W1-0 (Smith)
Robinson; Kelly, Radebe, Woodgate, Matteo; Bowyer, Dacourt, Bakke, Wilcox (Kewell 75); Smith, Viduka.

Feb 13   Anderlecht (H) W2-1 (Harte, Bowyer)
Martyn; Mills, Radebe, Ferdinand, Harte; Bowyer, Batty, Dacourt (Bakke 72), Matteo (Kewell 53); Smith, Viduka.

Feb 21   Anderlecht (a) W4-1 (Smith 2, Viduka, Harte pen)
Martyn; Mills, Ferdinand, Radebe, Harte; Bakke, Batty, Dacourt, Matteo; Smith, Viduka (Kewell 83).

Mar 6   Real Madrid (a) L2-3 (Smith, Viduka)
Martyn; Harte, Radebe (Kelly 65), Ferdinand, Matteo; Bakke (Wilcox 85), Dacourt, Batty, Kewell; Smith, Viduka.

Mar 14   Lazio (H) D3-3 (Bowyer, Wilcox, Ferdinand)
Robinson; Kelly, Mills, Matteo, Harte; Maybury (Batty 89), Bowyer, Burns, Wilcox; Kewell, Viduka (Hackworth 64).

Group D final table

	Pts
Real Madrid	13
LEEDS	10
Anderlecht	6
Lazio	5

Quarter-finals (two legs)

Apr 4   Deportivo la Coruna (H) W3-0 (Harte, Smith, Ferdinand)
Martyn; Mills, Ferdinand, Matteo, Harte; Bowyer, Batty, Dacourt, Kewell (Wilcox 84); Smith, Viduka.

Apr 17   Deportivo la Coruna (a) L0-2
Martyn; Mills, Ferdinand, Matteo, Harte; Bowyer, Batty, Dacourt, Kewell (Bakke 77); Smith, Viduka.

Semi-finals (two legs)

May 2   Valencia (H) D0-0
Martyn; Mills, Ferdinand, Matteo, Harte; Bowyer, Batty, Dacourt, Kewell; Smith, Viduka.

May 8   Valencia (a) L0-3
Martyn; Mills, Ferdinand, Matteo, Harte; Bakke, Batty, Dacourt, Kewell; Smith, Viduka.

Did not play:
Qual   Aug 9 TSV 1860 Munich (H) W2-1 (Smith, Harte pen)
Qual   Aug 23 TSV 1860 Munich (a) W1-0 (Smith)
Gp1   Sep 13 Barcelona (a) L0-4

2001-02 – UEFA Cup
Round One
Sept 20   Maritimo (a) L0-1
Martyn; Mills, Ferdinand, Matteo, Harte; Kelly, Batty, McPhail (Wilcox), Kewell; Keane, Viduka.
Sept 27   Maritimo (H) W3-0 (Keane, Kewell, Bakke)
Martyn; Mills, Ferdinand, Matteo, Harte; Bakke, Dacourt, Batty, Kewell; Keane, Viduka.

Round Two
Oct 18   Troyes (H) W4-2 (Viduka 2, Bowyer 2)
Martyn; Mills, Ferdinand, Matteo, Harte; Bowyer, Dacourt, Bakke (Batty), Kewell; Viduka, Keane (Smith).
Nov 1   Troyes (a) L2-3 (Keane, Viduka)
Martyn; Mills, Duberry, Matteo, Harte; Bakke, Dacourt, Batty, Wilcox (Kewell); Keane, Viduka.

Round Three
Nov 22   Grasshopper (a) W2-1 (Smith, Harte)
Martyn; Mills, Ferdinand, Matteo, Harte; Bakke, Dacourt, Batty, Wilcox; Keane, Smith.

Round Four
Feb 21   PSV Eindhoven (a) D0-0
Martyn; Mills, Ferdinand, Matteo, Harte; Bowyer, Dacourt, Bakke, Kewell; Viduka, Smith.
Feb 28   PSV Eindhoven (H) L0-1
Martyn; Mills, Ferdinand, Matteo, Harte; Kelly, Bowyer, Bakke, Kewell; Viduka, Smith.

Did not play
R3L2   Dec 6   Grasshopper (H) D2-2 (Kewell, Keane)

2002-03 – UEFA Cup
Round One
Oct 3   Matalurg Zaporizhia (a) D1-1 (Barmby)
Robinson; Kelly, Mills, Matteo, Harte; Bowyer, Bakke, Barmby, McPhail; Smith, Kewell.

Did not play:

R1L1	Metalurg Zaporizhia (H) W1-0 (Smith)
R2L1	Hapoel Tel Aviv (H) W1-0 (Kewell)
R2L2	Hapoel Tel Aviv (a) W4-1 (Smith 4)
R3L1	Malaga (a) D0-0
R3L2	Malaga (H) L1-2 (Bakke)

BLACKBURN ROVERS
Signed: July 7, 2004.
First game: Blackburn Rovers 1 West Bromwich Albion; August 14, 2004; Premier League.
Last game: Blackburn Rovers 3 QPR 0; January 7, 2006; FA Cup.

Season	Appearances					Blackburn		
	League	FAC	LC	Other	Goals	Pos	FAC	LC
2004-05	25(3)	4(1)	0	-	1	15th	SF	R2
2005-06	6	1	0	-	0	6th	R4	SF
2006-07	0	0	0	0*	0	10th	R3	SF

(UEFA Cup)*

STOKE CITY
Signed: January 19, 2007 (loan), permanently the following summer.
First game: Preston North End 3 Stoke City 2; January 20, 2007; Championship.
Last game: Burnley 0 Stoke City 0; November 24, 2007; Championship.

Season	Appearances					Blackburn		
	League	FAC	LC	Other	Goals	Pos	FAC	LC
2006-07	9	1	0	-	1	8th	R4	n/a
2007-08	14	0	0	-	0	2nd	R3	R1

INTERNATIONAL FOOTBALL

(1) England

Under 21s
Caps: 4. Goals: 0.

May 31, 1994 – Aubagne (Toulon Tournament)
France Under-21s L0-3
England: Nicholls (Oakes); Makin, Nethercott, Campbell, Gordon (Matteo); Sinclair, Fear (Eadie), Redknapp; Bart-Williams (Selley), Dyer, Fowler.

June 5, 1994 – Berre (Toulon Tournament semi-finals)
Belgium Under-21s W2-1 (Campbell, Dyer)
England: Oakes; Makin, Nethercott, Campbell, Gordon; Sinclair, Parlour, Redknapp, Matteo; Bart-Williams, Dyer.

June 7, 1994 – Toulon (Toulon Tournament final)
Portugal Under-21s Won 2-0 (Sinclair, Dyer)
England: Oakes; Makin, Nethercott, Campbell, Gordon; Sinclair, Parlour, Redknapp, Matteo; Bart-Williams, Dyer.

March 27, 1998 – Aarau (friendly)
Switzerland Under-21s L0-2
England: Hislop; Curtis, Redknapp (Holloway), Matteo (Hughes); Dyer, Lampard (Hendrie), Quashie (Carragher), Guppy; Barmby, Sinclair; Heskey (Williams).

B-Team
Caps: 1. Goals: 0.

Feb 10, 1998 – West Bromwich (friendly)
Chile B L1-2 (Heskey)
England: Pressman; Dyer (Guppy), Scimeca, Matteo, Hall, Wilcox (Carragher); Quashie (Lampard), Parlour (Murray), Merson; Heskey, Huckerby.

Seniors
Named in several squads but never played.

(2) Scotland
Caps: 6. Goals: 0.

Nov 15, 2000 – Glasgow (friendly)
Australia (H) L0-2
Scotland: Gould; Weir, Boyd, Dailly, O'Neil, Ferguson, Burley, Cameron, Matteo; Dodds, Hutchison.

Mar 24, 2001 – Glasgow (WCQ)
Belgium (H) D2-2 (Dodds 2)
Scotland: Sullivan; Weir, Hendry, Elliott, Boyd; Ferguson, Lambert, Burley, Matteo; Hutchison, Dodds.

Mar 28, 2001 – Glasgow (WCQ)
San Marino (H) W4-0 (Hendry 2, Dodds, Cameron)
Scotland: Sullivan; Weir, Hendry, Elliott, Johnston; Cameron, Lambert, Burley, Matteo; Hutchison, Dodds.

Sept 1, 2001 – Glasgow (WCQ)
Croatia (H) D0-0
Scotland: Sullivan; Weir, Elliott, Matteo, Naysmith; Burley, Lambert, Dailly, McCann; Booth, Hutchison.

Sept 5, 2001 – Brussels (WCQ)
Belgium (a) L0-2
Scotland: Sullivan; Weir, Elliott, Matteo, Naysmith; Burley, Dailly, Lambert, Boyd; Hutchison, Dodds.

Mar 27, 2002 – Paris (friendly)
France (a) L0-5
Scotland: Sullivan; Weir, Dailly, Caldwell, Crainey; Crawford, Matteo, Lambert, Cameron, McCann; Freedman.

LUCAS
From the Streets of Soweto to Soccer Superstar
The Authorised Biography of Lucas Radebe
by Richard Coomber

The South African international so captured the hearts of Leeds fans that they still chant his name years after he retired and the Kaiser Chiefs band took their name from his first club. In his native land he is an iconic figure, who led his country to two World Cups as they emerged from the sporting wilderness and whose reputation as a player and a man helped convince the rest of the world that the World Cup finals should go to South Africa.

This is the story of how Lucas overcame a tough childhood, survived a shooting, and refused to be diverted from his destiny by injury, homesickness, freezing English winters and terrible English food to become not only a football superstar but acknowledged as one of the nicest people in the game. Lucas Radebe's story is much more than just another biography of a footballer. It is inspiring and heart-warming, tinged with tragedy yet marked throughout by his trademark smile that has lit up two continents and touched thousands of lives.

The story of a man whom Nelson Mandela called "my hero".

★★★★★ Four Four Two Magazine

"A compelling insight into a Leeds Legend."
Henry Winter, Daily Telegraph

"This book is an absorbing and compelling account of Lucas' inspirational story."
Anthony Clavane, Sunday Mirror

www.greatnorthernbooks.co.uk

REVIE
Revered and Reviled
The Authorised Biography
by Richard Sutcliffe

Don Revie remains, more than two decades on from his untimely death at the age of just 61, one of football's most controversial and complex characters. After a playing career that brought plaudits and the prestigious Footballer of the Year award, Revie moved into management with Leeds United in 1961. By the time he left Elland Road to take charge of the England national team 13 years later, he had built one of the best teams English football had ever seen. Hailed as one of the most innovative managers of his generation, Revie was named England Manager of the Year in 1969, 70 and 72.

Yet despite winning two league titles, an FA Cup, two European trophies and a League Cup, Leeds were hated outside their own city. Later, he would be banned for 10 years by the FA for walking out on England to accept a lucrative job in the Middle East before tragically dying from motor neurone disease.

Through the eyes of those who knew him best - family, friends, teammates, players, colleagues and even a member of the Royal Family - Revie....Revered and Reviled tells how a child born in Middlesbrough in the depression-hit 1920s rose to the very top as both a player and manager.

"Superb new book [that] benefits immensely from access to Revie's family, bringing colour to a figure often depicted in black and white. The best football biography of 2010"
Henry Winter, Daily Telegraph

"A brilliant book."
Daily Mirror

www.greatnorthernbooks.co.uk

BREMNER

The Real King Billy
The Complete Biography of Billy Bremner
by Richard Sutcliffe

Billy Bremner remains one of football's most iconic figures for the huge role he played in transforming the Yorkshire club into one of the most feared in Europe. North of the Border, Bremner remains equally revered – he was one of the first to be inducted into the Scottish Football Hall of Fame.

His career was not without controversy, whether it be the lifetime ban from international football or the playing style that saw Bremner once famously described in The Sunday Times as, '10 stone of barbed wire'.

But, throughout his 18 years as a player the Scot was a figure that even his fiercest critics respected. In Bremner – The Real King Billy, Richard Sutcliffe speaks to friends, team-mates, colleagues plus a host of players managed by Bremner during more than a decade in charge of Leeds United and Doncaster Rovers. Discover the inside story on everything from just how close Maradona once came to signing for Bremner to the ups and downs that characterised a truly extraordinary career.

"Billy was a huge influence on me and his story is one that continues to inspire us all today."
from the foreword by Simon Grayson.

www.greatnorthernbooks.co.uk